Doing Money

T0382712

Traditional neoclassical economic theory should be replaced by a theory with a role for money that reflects the importance of money in our lives. What mainstream neoclassical economists call 'money illusion' is no illusion. Rather, the illusionists are those who deny the importance of money, who divide the world in two, one with 'real', the other with 'nominal' magnitudes, and maintain that rational agents can always mentally reduce the latter to the former. Unfortunately for that theory, a monetary economy is one where agents have to have money – and therefore aim for its acquisition as such – to fulfill payment obligations, fixed in dates and amounts. No 'real' good will help in face of such obligations. A better theory of money must rely on some sociological building blocks. It starts with the recognition that money is a social fact, that social facts result from interactions and that interactions imply uncertainty. Given uncertainty, one can introduce money as a means of uncertainty absorption. The use of money 'crowds out' uncertainty and replaces it by the one certainty that governs economic life: the need and desire for money.

In the context of a fully developed capitalist economy, this need turns out to be overwhelming, so that more and more participants in such an economy are busy maximizing monetary returns. For the mainstream neoclassical theorist, such behavior indicates pervasive 'money illusion' and is deemed irrational. For a historical sociologist like Max Weber, on the contrary, money use induces the continuous rationalization of economic activities. Monetary calculation, driven by the unbounded desire to acquire money, thus is a condition of rationality. In this book, Ganssmann takes the side of Weber, but adds that money use also undermines this calculative rationality by stimulating speculation, with speculative opportunities being opened wide by the evolution of credit and financial institutions. The results are bubbles, the ensuing inevitable crashes. In this way, periodic crises turn out to be the 'costs' of uncertainty absorption through money.

This book puts in place the groundwork for an alternative theory of money in a sociological perspective, proceeding by way of a critique of existing theories.

Heiner Ganssmann was professor in the Department of Sociology of the Freie Universität Berlin until 2009, specializing in economic sociology, social policy and sociological theory.

Routledge international studies in money and banking

1 **Private Banking in Europe**
Lynn Bicker

2 **Bank Deregulation and Monetary Order**
George Selgin

3 **Money in Islam**
A study in Islamic political economy
Masudul Alam Choudhury

4 **The Future of European Financial Centres**
Kirsten Bindemann

5 **Payment Systems in Global Perspective**
Maxwell J Fry, Isaak Kilato, Sandra Roger, Krzysztof Senderowicz, David Sheppard, Francisco Solis and John Trundle

6 **What is Money?**
John Smithin

7 **Finance**
A characteristics approach
Edited by David Blake

8 **Organisational Change and Retail Finance**
An ethnographic perspective
Richard Harper, Dave Randall and Mark Rouncefield

9 **The History of the Bundesbank**
Lessons for the European Central Bank
Jakob de Haan

10 **The Euro**
A challenge and opportunity for financial markets
Published on behalf of Société Universitaire Européenne de Recherches Financières (SUERF)
Edited by Michael Artis, Axel Weber and Elizabeth Hennessy

11 **Central Banking in Eastern Europe**
Edited by Nigel Healey and Barry Harrison

12 **Money, Credit and Prices Stability**
Paul Dalziel

13 **Monetary Policy, Capital Flows and Exchange Rates**
Essays in memory of Maxwell Fry
Edited by William Allen and David Dickinson

14 **Adapting to Financial Globalisation**
Published on behalf of Société Universitaire Européenne de Recherches Financières (SUERF)
Edited by Morten Balling, Eduard H. Hochreiter and Elizabeth Hennessy

15 **Monetary Macroeconomics**
A new approach
Alvaro Cencini

16 **Monetary Stability in Europe**
Stefan Collignon

17 **Technology and Finance**
Challenges for financial markets, business strategies and policy makers
Published on behalf of Société Universitaire Européenne de Recherches Financières (SUERF)
Edited by Morten Balling, Frank Lierman, and Andrew Mullineux

18 **Monetary Unions**
Theory, history, public choice
Edited by Forrest H. Capie and Geoffrey E. Wood

19 **HRM and Occupational Health and Safety**
Carol Boyd

20 **Central Banking Systems Compared**
The ECB, the pre-Euro Bundesbank and the Federal Reserve System
Emmanuel Apel

21 **A History of Monetary Unions**
John Chown

22 **Dollarization**
Lessons from Europe and the Americas
Edited by Louis-Philippe Rochon and Mario Seccareccia

23 **Islamic Economics and Finance: A Glossary, 2nd Edition**
Muhammad Akram Khan

24 **Financial Market Risk**
Measurement and analysis
Cornelis A. Los

25 **Financial Geography**
A Banker's view
Risto Laulajainen

26 **Money Doctors**
The experience of international financial advising 1850–2000
Edited by Marc Flandreau

27 **Exchange Rate Dynamics**
A new open economy macroeconomics perspective
Edited by Jean-Oliver Hairault and Thepthida Sopraseuth

28 **Fixing Financial Crises in the 21st Century**
Edited by Andrew G. Haldane

29 **Monetary Policy and Unemployment**
The U.S., Euro-area and Japan
Edited by Willi Semmler

30 **Exchange Rates, Capital Flows and Policy**
Edited by Peter Sinclair, Rebecca Driver and Christoph Thoenissen

31 **Great Architects of International Finance**
The Bretton Woods era
Anthony M. Endres

32 **The Means to Prosperity**
Fiscal policy reconsidered
Edited by Per Gunnar Berglund and Matias Vernengo

33 **Competition and Profitability in European Financial Services**
Strategic, systemic and policy issues
Edited by Morten Balling, Frank Lierman and Andy Mullineux

34 **Tax Systems and Tax Reforms in South and East Asia**
Edited by Luigi Bernardi, Angela Fraschini and Parthasarathi Shome

35 **Institutional Change in the Payments System and Monetary Policy**
Edited by Stefan W. Schmitz and Geoffrey E. Wood

36 **The Lender of Last Resort**
Edited by F.H. Capie and G.E. Wood

37 **The Structure of Financial Regulation**
Edited by David G. Mayes and Geoffrey E. Wood

38 **Monetary Policy in Central Europe**
Miroslav Beblavý

39 **Money and Payments in Theory and Practice**
Sergio Rossi

40 **Open Market Operations and Financial Markets**
Edited by David G. Mayes and Jan Toporowski

41 **Banking in Central and Eastern Europe 1980–2006**
A comprehensive analysis of banking sector transformation in the former Soviet Union, Czechoslovakia, East Germany, Yugoslavia, Belarus, Bulgaria, Croatia, the Czech Republic, Hungary, Kazakhstan, Poland, Romania, the Russian Federation, Serbia and Montenegro, Slovakia, Ukraine and Uzbekistan.
Stephan Barisitz

42 **Debt, Risk and Liquidity in Futures Markets**
Edited by Barry A. Goss

43 **The Future of Payment Systems**
Edited by Stephen Millard, Andrew G. Haldane and Victoria Saporta

44 **Credit and Collateral**
Vania Sena

45 **Tax Systems and Tax Reforms in Latin America**
Edited by Luigi Bernardi, Alberto Barreix, Anna Marenzi and Paola Profeta

46 **The Dynamics of Organizational Collapse**
The case of Barings Bank
Helga Drummond

47 **International Financial Co-operation**
Political economics of compliance with the 1988 Basel Accord
Bryce Quillin

48 **Bank Performance**
A Theoretical and empirical framework for the analysis of profitability, competition and efficiency
Jacob Bikker and Jaap W.B. Bos

49 **Monetary Growth Theory**
Money, interest, prices, capital, knowledge and economic structure over time and space
Wei-Bin Zhang

50 **Money, Uncertainty and Time**
Giuseppe Fontana

51 **Central Banking, Asset Prices and Financial Fragility**
Éric Tymoigne

52 **Financial Markets and the Macroeconomy**
Willi Semmler, Peter Flaschel, Carl Chiarella and Reiner Franke

53 **Inflation Theory in Economics**
Welfare, velocity, growth and business cycles
Max Gillman

54 **Monetary Policy Over Fifty Years**
Heinz Herrman (Deutsche Bundesbank)

55 **Designing Central Banks**
David Mayes and Geoffrey Wood

56 **Inflation Expectations**
Peter J.N. Sinclair

57 **The New International Monetary System**
Essays in honour of Alexander Swoboda
Edited by Charles Wyplosz

58 **Taxation and Gender Equity**
A comparative analysis of direct and indirect taxes in developing and developed countries
Edited by Caren Grown and Imraan Valodia

59 **Developing Alternative Frameworks for Explaining Tax Compliance**
Edited by James Alm, Jorge Martinez-Vazquez and Benno Torgler

60 **International Tax Coordination**
An Interdisciplinary Perspective on Virtues and Pitfalls
Edited by Martin Zagler

61 **The Capital Needs of Central Banks**
Edited by Sue Milton and Peter Sinclair

62 **Monetary and Banking History**
Edited by Geoffrey E. Wood, Terence Mills and Nicholas Crafts

63 **New Approaches to Monetary Economics and Theory**
Interdisciplinary perspectives
Edited by Heiner Ganssmann

64 **Social Banks and the Future of Sustainable Finance**
Edited by Olaf Weber and Sven Remer

65 **Policy Makers on Policy**
The Mais lectures
Edited by Forrest H. Capie and
Geoffrey E. Wood

66 **Prediction Markets**
Theory and applications
Edited by Leighton
Vaughan Williams

67 **Towards a Socioanalysis of**
Money, Finance and Capitalism
Beneath the surface of the
financial industry
Edited by Susan Long and
Burkard Sievers

68 **Doing Money**
Elementary money theory from a
sociological standpoint
Heiner Ganssmann

Doing Money

Elementary monetary theory from a
sociological standpoint

Heiner Ganssmann

LONDON AND NEW YORK

First published 2012
by Routledge
2 Park Square, Milton Park, Abingdon, Oxon OX14 4RN

Simultaneously published in the USA and Canada
by Routledge
711 Third Avenue, New York, NY 10017

Routledge is an imprint of the Taylor & Francis Group, an informa business

British Library Cataloguing in Publication Data
A catalogue record for this book is available from the British Library

Library of Congress Cataloging in Publication Data
Ganssmann, Heiner.
  Doing money/by Heiner Ganssmann.
  p. cm.
  1. Money. 2. Capitalism. I. Title.
  HG220.A2.G36 2011
  332.401–dc22

                                                                2011009223

ISBN: 978-0-415-75008-0 (pbk)
ISBN: 978-0-415-67738-7 (hbk)
ISBN: 978-0-203-80446-9 (ebk)

Typeset in Times
by Wearset Ltd, Boldon, Tyne and Wear

First issued in paperback in 2013

To the memory of Keith Whitehouse, MD, who taught me 50 years ago that a used dollar bill was good for polishing glasses.

Contents

Preface   xiii
Acknowledgments   xvi

Introduction   1

1 Problems and their setting   7
  1.1 Capitalism 7
  1.2 Money, a veil? 13
  1.3 Money, a symbol? 18
  1.4 Money, a language? 20

2 Clarifications   23
  2.1 Language and money 23
  2.2 Everyday use of money 34
  2.3 Prices and the metric of money 35
  2.4 Money as things vs. money as pure information 46
  2.5 Money as a social relation? 57

3 Elementary theory   62
  3.1 Contingency and interaction 62
  3.2 Origins and acceptability of money 79
  3.3 Quantitative price determination 95
  3.4 Money and uncertainty absorption 103
  3.5 Credit 110
  3.6 Money, credit and crises 129

Conclusion   133

Appendix   139
A.1 Money and inequality according to econophysics 139
A.2 Money and the state 141

Notes   143
Bibliography   159
Index   173

Preface

Writing another book on money is risky, reading it perhaps even more so. For the writer, the risk is that the inescapable pattern of person Z reading n books to produce book number $n+1$ prevents the escape from established modes of thinking among monetary theorists. For the reader, a big disappointment may be waiting. Instead of learning something about the real thing all one gets is what X, Y and now also Z have to say about money. I have tried to escape the dilemma resulting for the writer, on the one hand, by trying to remain in touch with simple everyday practices of money use and, on the other hand, by reducing discussions of what particular previous authors had to say to a minimum. Since I believe that traditional neoclassical theory is the major obstacle on the way to understanding money, I have given short shrift to the thoughts of both heterodox economists and sociologists, although I am on their side mostly. However, even given that restriction, I have not succeeded in avoiding being Z writing about X, Y ... Because what follows is a contribution to the *theory* of money, referring to other theories rather than money in the real world is unavoidable as long as a promising consensus on what an appropriate theory of money should look like has not emerged. In my case the reference is mostly to the broad body of traditional neoclassical thinking on money and is frequently critical. In contrast to other contributions from sociologists, for example, Nigel Dodd's *The Sociology of Money* (1994), I do not want to suggest that sociologists should aim for their own theory of money to compete with economic theories. Neither do I want to contribute to the ongoing sociological research on the 'social meaning' of money that is more or less complementing what economists have to say by pointing out the shortcomings of the excessive rationalism or individualism of economists. Rather, I believe that money is and should remain a subject of economics, but also that appropriate economic theories of money need sociological building blocks as foundations. My aim is to demonstrate that and to propose some such elementary building blocks.

Because thinking about social relations, their patterns and institutionalized forms is not a monopoly of sociologists, there are quite a few – mostly heterodox – economists who have been conscious of this need for sociological foundations (Lowe 1935), often without saying so or admitting that sociology could contribute anything worthwhile in their specific field of enquiry. To take an example, one of my systematic take-off points in sociology was Simmel's remark about the 'context in which the sociological character of money appears. The inter-action between individuals is the starting point of all social formations' (Simmel [1907] 2004: 174). Roughly twenty years later, institutionalist economist J.R. Commons made the same point in his *Legal Foundations of Capitalism*: 'eco-nomic theory has consistently taken the point of view of individuals on the one hand and commodities on the other hand, instead of the point of view of transac-tions between individuals' (Commons 1924: 242). However, Simmel goes on: 'The interactions between the primary elements that produce the social unit are replaced by the fact that each of these elements establishes an independent rela-tion to a higher or intermediate organ. Money belongs to this category of reified social functions' (Simmel [1907] 2004: 175). So the starting point for explana-tions of money are interactions, and the task is to show how money as a 'higher or intermediate organ' is inserted into these direct interactions so that they are replaced or mediated by relations between individuals and money.

In a nutshell, my argument in this book is: Given the starting point of interac-tions between individuals, one can show that uncertainty is an emergent property of such interactions. Given uncertainty, one can introduce money as a means of uncertainty absorption. The use of money 'crowds out' uncertainty and replaces it by the one certainty that governs economic life: the need or desire for money. In the context of a developed capitalist economy, this need turns out to be over-whelming, so that more and more participants in such a capitalist economy are busy maximizing monetary returns. For the mainstream neoclassical theorist, such behavior indicates pervasive 'money illusion' and is deemed irrational. For a historical sociologist like Max Weber, on the other hand, such behavior indi-cates that economic activities have become more and more rationalized. Mone-tary calculation driven by the unbounded desire to acquire money thus is a condition of rationality. I will side with Weber, but add that money use also undermines this calculative rationality by stimulating speculation, with specula-tive opportunities being opened widely by the evolution of credit and financial institutions. We have bubbles, the ensuing inevitable crashes and, in this way, periodic crises turn out to be the 'costs' of uncertainty absorption through money.

This argument is strictly opposed to the neoclassical mainstream, where basic assumptions rule that economic agents are both perfectly rational and extremely well informed – to the point of eliminating uncertainty in decision making. For a theory of money consistent with general equilibrium theory, the theoretical core of mainstream economics, these assumptions amount to insurmountable obsta-cles. No uncertainty, no money – except in the functions compatible with the neutrality of money, or, what is the same thing, with the absence of 'money illu-sion'. But neutral money, if it ever exists, can indeed be no more than the lubri-cant that makes the wheel of commerce turn more smoothly. It plays a kind of self-eliminating role as a means of exchange, and has no significance as a means of payment or as a store of value. As a means of accounting its acquisition cannot be a goal in itself for the maximizers of utility populating the model world of microeconomics. In such a framework, speculation can only do the beneficial work of the invisible hand and a crisis can only be the result of external shocks.

Seen from a different angle, neoclassical economics sticks to the biblical story. Maximizing monetary returns is the same thing as dancing around the golden calf. That kind of irrationality should have been exterminated when Moses had come down from the mountain. Unfortunately, however, the biblical story is a bit too simple and optimistic. Contemporary rationality, while certainly being bounded, pushes people to dance around the golden calf, although there is no gold anymore. But, as a well-known banker explained, as long as the music plays, you have to dance, and that is not – and certainly not always – irrational in the context of a monetary economy.

So it is time to replace the neoclassical tradition by a theory of the economy with a role for money that does correspond to the importance of money in our lives. What mainstream neoclassical economists call money illusion is no illusion (Marschak 1950). Rather, the illusionists are those who deny the importance of money, who divide the world in two, one with 'real', the other with 'nominal' magnitudes, and maintain that rational agents can always mentally reduce the latter to the former. Unfortunately for that theory, a monetary economy is one where agents have to *have* money – and therefore aim for its acquisition as such – to fulfill payment obligations, fixed in dates and amounts. No 'real' good will help in face of such obligations – unless it can quickly be transformed into money.

This argument might sound as if it was merely addressing an intra-economics dispute. But it is not. The contribution of sociology to the theory of money starts with the recognition that money is a social fact, that social facts result from interactions and that interactions imply uncertainty. That may sound trivial, but the implications are interesting and will, so I hope, stimulate fresh thinking about money.

Acknowledgments

To finish this book, as far as a book on money can ever be finished, took much longer than expected. I started work on it in 2006/2007 when I received the John G. Diefenbaker Award from the Canada Council of Arts. The grant allowed me to spend a year at the University of British Columbia in Vancouver as a guest scholar in the Institute for European Studies. I owe special thanks to its former and present directors, Sima Godfrey and Kurt Hübner, for their hospitality.

During that year I presented work in progress in lectures and seminars at the UBC Department of Sociology, at a workshop organized by Brenda Spotton-Visano at York University, at the Centre canadien d'études allemandes et européennes, Université de Montréal, in Harrison White's seminar at Columbia University, in the Economics Department faculty seminar at the New School for Social Research, and in a session organized by John Smithin at the Canadian Economics Association meeting in Halifax.

Back in Berlin, work on the book was slowed down by oversize teaching obligations and the turbulences accompanying retirement, but I had opportunities to present pieces of my argument in 2008 at the 38th World Congress of the International Institute of Sociology in Budapest, Hungary, at the 2008 interim conference of the Research Network of Economic Sociology of the European Sociological Association in Krakow, Poland, at a meeting of contributors to a special issue on economic sociology at the Max Planck Institute Cologne, at a NSF-DFG joint conference on 'Contextualizing Economic Behavior' in New York, and in 2009 at a workshop: 'Money – interdisciplinary perspectives', that I organized at the Freie Universität Berlin, and at the workshop 'On either side of the economic science of money' organized by Jean Cartelier in Paris; I also presented an appraisal of search theory models at the economics faculty seminar of the University of Kassel.

I am grateful for discussions and comments at all these events and additional comments and recommendations by anonymous reviewers, by Jens Beckert, Christoph Deutschmann and Riccardo Bellofiore. Linda Josefowicz and Hannah Zagel helped with the diagrams. Special thanks are due to Jean Cartelier and Ernst Michael Lange for a prolonged, most helpful mixture of criticism and encouragement from their respective viewpoints as economist and philosopher. Last but not least, friends and family have provided extremely patient moral support, most of all, my wife Uschi.

Introduction

> Few writers seem able to avoid references to 'money' that are metaphorical: com-
> ments that seem on the surface to refer to money 'objects' but refer in truth to an
> unspecified complex of institutions associated with monetary economies.
>
> (Clower 1995: 525)

It is said about sculpture that you take a slab of marble, you chip away everything that is not the Venus of Milo and you end up with the Venus of Milo.
Unfortunately, the theory of money cannot be built like that. There is endless
controversy and confusion about money. Money has left bumps on many heads
trying to understand it. But even if we could succeed in taking away all wrong-
headed, inconsistent and fuzzy ideas, there would not be much left and we would
still be far from an adequate theory of money.

Nonetheless I hope to contribute to such a theory. My argument differs from
most existing contributions to monetary theory by combining four features: (1)
The use of material and arguments from all relevant social sciences, but in a perspective shaped by the sociological tradition inspired by Marx, Weber, Simmel
and Polanyi; (2) the focus on interaction, uncertainty and institution building in
analyzing the social construction of money; (3) conceptual clarity and consistency; (4) the avoidance of inappropriate simplification.

First, I do not respect established disciplinary boundaries. While it is obvious
that money should be primarily a concern for economics,[1] it is well known that
mainstream economics has extreme difficulties to incorporate money into its
core theory in a consistent way. I think that the reason behind these difficulties is
the enduring refusal to fully acknowledge that uncertainty is a normal condition
of social life. Therefore, it is promising to look beyond the boundaries of economics in proposing that the basic problem from which a theory of money
should start is one that all social sciences share: How can we understand action
coordination in social settings characterized by contingency[2] and therefore
uncertainty?[3]

Second, as the title 'Doing money' is to suggest, money is not something that
happens to us but something that we continuously produce and reproduce in specific social settings. The neoclassical mainstream has traditionally neglected

interactions by focusing on the individual as a decision maker in a quasi non-social world. As money is a social fact, constituted in interaction, it is no wonder that traditional economic theory lacks an adequate concept of money. In contrast, game theory is all about strategic interaction, but game theorists seem to remain too attached to the economists' preoccupation with quantitative determination and, therefore, equilibrium.

Third, I will take more than usual care in working out and using a clear and consistent vocabulary. When we say 'money', do we mean money objects, like bills and coins, or these tangible things plus one of the other ingredients of money supply estimates, or are we referring to a system of institutions, or a kind of game people play? Unfortunately, all these and more meanings are permanently confounded not only in everyday language but also in many texts on money in the social sciences. It is both possible and important to avoid such confusions.

Fourth, to observe and analyze money use in the context of action coordination under uncertainty requires extreme care with respect to the standard model building strategy of 'dividing up the difficulties'. As we will see, 'dividing up the difficulties' in mainstream theories of money has mostly amounted to assuming away uncertainty in one way or another. As an alternative, along with strong undercurrents of heterodox economic theory (for the program, see Keynes (1931a) and as a complementary version of economic sociology, see Lowe (1935)), I suggest considering the use of money as a social response to uncertainty. If that turns out to be plausible, it is obviously not promising to assume away uncertainty as a starting point for understanding money.

Without uncertainty, what is left to explain is the use of money as a more or less convenient social tool that facilitates exchange. This has been the attitude towards money in traditional economic thought even before the rise of neoclassical theory. Typically, John Stuart Mill argued

> that the mere introduction of a particular mode of exchanging things for one another, by first exchanging a thing for money, and then exchanging the money for something else, makes no difference in the essential character of transactions.
>
> (Mill 1900: 10)

In contrast, if uncertainty is inherent in all exchange and if – and this is a big 'if' – the use of money makes it possible to reduce uncertainty, money *will* make a difference in 'the essential character of transactions'. It significantly increases the probability of successful action coordination. But at the same time, 'first exchanging a thing for money, and then exchanging the money for something else' implies what Marx ([1867] 1975: 114) called 'the possibility of crisis'. In contexts of uncertainty, things are likely to go wrong sooner or later. While the use of money offers the means to protect oneself individually against economic mishaps, it also increases the probability that the individual pursuits of maximizing gain while minimizing risks lead to collective damage. The basic reason is simple: Successful sellers do not immediately have to become buyers. They can bridge uncertain situations by holding on to money. If enough of them do that, the macro-effect of many individuals seeking security or waiting for more profitable opportunities will be a crisis. If everybody wants or needs cash, the level of economic activity can decline quickly and drastically. So money use is a two-faced affair: It increases the chances of welfare enhancing action coordination as well as the possibilities of crisis.

In line with the thrust of some recent contributions to economic sociology[4] my argument is based on the premise that social action requires coordination and coordination requires coping with the contingencies inherent in interaction. These contingencies – agents cannot know for certain what other agents are going to do while the outcomes of their own actions depend on the actions of others – imply a background of general uncertainty in *all* social contexts. In the specific economic context of markets and money, this uncertainty associated with interaction in general is both drastically *increased* – due to the coexistence of a complex social division of labor, the *ex post* coordination of private economic activities and the difficulties of maintaining a stable monetary system – and *reduced* – due to the simultaneous functioning of money as a medium of communication, a metric allowing for rational calculation and an instrument of peaceful appropriation. Or, to put it more shortly: Money use largely replaces the many uncertainties of economic life by one certainty, namely, that everybody needs money to survive.

To work out the theoretical implications of this proposition requires a re-examination of existing theories of money. While my main argument consists of constructing a kind of implicit dialogue with economists, the introductory Chapter 1 is more interdisciplinary. After an introductory section sketching the capitalist economy as the setting I take for granted as the background of monetary analysis, I start with questioning three widely accepted propositions about money: Money as a veil in economics (Section 1.2), money as a symbol in anthropology (Section 1.2) and money as a language in sociology (Section 1.4). The issue here is to identify typical but insufficient reasoning on money so that we have a catalogue of the problems to be tackled in the rest of the book.

In Chapter 2, more elaborate and constructive arguments about the nature and foundations of monetary systems are presented and discussed: first of all, the necessity of explicitly understanding money as a social fact (Section 2.1). Second, I rely on observations of everyday use of money to introduce a sort of Wittgensteinian perspective into the project of rebuilding monetary theory. Such a perspective should lead us away from such trivia as 'money is what money does' to observing the properties of money and its significance by focusing on its use in interaction – albeit at the risk of neglecting the systemic aspects and effects of money use (Section 2.2). Third, the notion of money as an instrument of measurement is discussed. Traditionally, 'value' is supposed to be measured with money, whatever 'value' is taken to be. There is a lot of vagueness in the use of the term. In any case, measuring value with money would presuppose a monetary invariant. But can that be more than a 'working fiction' (Mirowski

1991: 581)'? (Section 2.3). Fourth, older practices of sustaining such a working fiction relied on money objects that were supposed to have 'intrinsic value', like quantities of gold or silver. In contrast, modern monetary systems seem to have lost all significant connections with the physical world of tangible objects. How can monetary systems operate in which money more and more seems to take the form of pure information? This question opens the opportunity for examining the ideas behind recent search-theoretical approaches in monetary economics (Section 2.4). Given this background, what insights do we gain, fifth, from the sociological proposition that money is a social relation (Section 2.5)?

In Chapter 3, the emphasis changes from critical examination of existing theories to presenting the building blocks of an elementary theory of money based on the idea that money is, above all, a social device for coping with uncertainty. First, I show how contingency is inherent in interaction in general (Section 3.1). To bring this idea into the theory of money and construct a systematic argument, I start from micro-foundations and reexamine action coordination in what Edgeworth (1881: 31n) called the 'catallactic atom'. My main argument here is that standard economic analysis of bilateral exchange (or barter) ignores the possibility for human agents to assume the perspective of the other. In social settings we choose our own actions not only in the knowledge that their outcomes are dependent on the actions of others, but also in mutual anticipation and observation of these actions. To understand money, it is furthermore necessary to move beyond the 'catallactic atom', first in the sense of extending the time horizon of interaction, second in the sense of introducing an expanded material environment and third by introducing more players. Fourth, an economy with a division of labor and private independent producers (henceforth referred to as the DoL-PiP economy) is explicitly introduced as the background of exchange analysis. When production is for exchange, agents regularly have to anticipate the needs and demands of others if they want to sell their products in an economy with a more than rudimentary division of labor. The transformation of these products into money can, depending on the price realized, be understood as the confirmation of the producer's anticipations. In any case, contrasting the use of money to a fictive barter setting raises two explanatory problems: How can we understand the 'origins' of money? While research on the beginnings of money use is a task for historians (see Seaford 2004 as an excellent example), what is at issue here is an account of the social 'conditions of possibility' of money. How can a social innovation that must be the result of coordinated collective action be accomplished by individuals with conflicting interests? Under which conditions will such individuals agree to perform their transactions with the help of money? And, a related but more implicit problem: How do individuals regularly overcome the risk of accepting something as money that may not be seen as such and therefore not be accepted by others (Section 3.2)? Before such problems are tackled, it does not make much sense to busy oneself with issues of quantitative price determination that appear to be of primary concern for traditionally minded economic theorists (Section 3.3). The tools they developed for this led away from taking seriously the fundamental uncertainty prevalent in economic life. In general, uncertainty in interactions generates indeterminacy of interaction results (Hardin 2003). With respect to the economic problem of the 'provision of material means' (Lowe 1965: 8) in social contexts that require action coordination and cooperation, we cannot simply assume an absence of this general uncertainty. Rather, it is more plausible to assume that conflicts of interest will actually increase uncertainty. As prices are the results of interactions among agents equipped with money, quantitatively determined prices can only result if agents' choices among actions are extremely constrained. The Walrasian idea of perfect competition is the result of driving such an assumption of constraints to the point where prices are no longer the result of interaction in markets, but rather the result of the interference of a fictitious mega-agent, the auctioneer. A more adequate approach to quantitative price determination would require a concept of the competitive process that is closer to Austrian or game theoretic ideas than to the Walrasian tradition. But neither of these alternatives has included a concept of competition in which money is essential. Following Max Weber, I suggest (Section 3.4) to see money as the social tool that allows agents to participate in the competitive struggle. The prices resulting from this struggle provide tentative solutions for coordination problems in an environment of uncertainty. But money, at least in its simpler forms, in turn is a rather constraining tool: The possibilities of active participation in markets are limited by the requirement of disposition over money. Some of these constraints are removed or loosened by credit relations (Section 3.5) that allow agents to bridge uncertainties with mutual promises, but at the cost of an increased probability of periodic crises that occur when too many promises cannot be kept.

Highlighting the double-faced nature of monetary economies in terms of both uncertainty absorption and uncertainty generation brings me to concluding observations on how and why we live with money.

My procedure is to simply examine and discuss the literature on money in economics, sociology, and some anthropology, philosophy and history in the light of questions and puzzles that I will outline in the first part, moving from basic issues to more complex ones. Evidently, this literature on money is far too much to read and comprehend for a single person – and I apologize for omissions right up front. My claim is nonetheless to discuss the major approaches to the *theory* of money. To emphasize *theory* allows me to leave aside a big share of the literature on money, not only historical accounts but also much of the policy-oriented work of economists. I am tempted to add that much of what goes for monetary theory in economics is actually spoiled as *theory* by the urge of its authors to be advisors in matters of monetary or general economic policy. The urge can perhaps explain why so many economists remain attached to such simplistic stuff as some version of quantity theory and the concomitant emphasis on somehow controlling and regulating the 'money supply'. This kind of 'consultant'-theory is, I think, no longer a matter for serious theoretical debate but rather a problem for the sociology of knowledge.

So what follows is theoretical analysis, mostly based on a critical examination of the existing literature. Since I reject the traditional architecture of economic theory according to which money seriously enters as a problem only on the macro-level, most conveniently in a combination of the quantity theory with some agency determining the money supply, this critical examination takes up basic arguments concerning the micro-level. This perspective is sociological in the emphasis on interaction, in the effort to always identify the agents, their intentions and their capacities to observe each other. They 'do' money in the sense of being the moving force of monetary processes, in the simplest cases the pair-wise transactions of buying and selling or borrowing and lending. Although a complete theory of money should move on from this micro-level all the way to the analysis of macroeconomic circular flow processes, this is beyond the reach of this book. But it should be clear that the micro-level analysis is not meant to be exclusive. Rather, the point is to see how macro-effects, including the formation of institutions, can be explained as both intended and unintended outcomes of interactions on the micro-level. Since traditional microeconomics has a sort of barren quality due to assumptions that seem to owe more to the dual desire to prove the beneficial nature of free markets and to explain prices in a deterministic manner than to the desire to explain what is actually going on, I have also relied on simple observations of everyday experience with money. In drawing on everyday experience I do not use the standard tools of empirical social science to observe in a controlled and representative way what people do when they use money. That has been the concern of much of the recent empirical sociological research on money and finance (for example, Zelizer 1997; Knorr-Cetina and Preda 2005). Rather, I rely on common knowledge and experience to show, sometimes *via* thought experiments, how improbable our everyday use of money is, especially in the light of established standards for rational action. The discrepancy between what we actually do when we use money and what we should be doing as *prima facie* rational agents generates many of my questions. Once one takes into account all the difficulties and obstacles rational agents have to overcome or ignore when using money, monetary practices appear highly improbable. That calls for explanation. By generating this pressure to explain, the common assumption in economics that agents are rational is a useful heuristic device. But that should not be taken to imply that this assumption should be as far-reaching as it is in traditional microeconomics. One major point of my argument is, instead, that money use is understandable only if uncertainty limits the possibilities for rational action.

My undertaking has clear limitations. Only fundamentals of money are discussed, neither fancy new financial instruments nor the ups and downs of global financial markets. What Hegel noted for philosophy – that insight is always late, that Minerva's owl flies only at dusk, after all the important things have happened – certainly holds for the theory of money. Or, to put it more prosaically, 'the subtlety of the monetary facts has gone on increasing, and theory has had a hard job to keep up' (Hicks 1967: 59). In fact, theory has *not* kept up, but as we will see, we can at least identify some reasons for this laggardness. That must be enough for a start.

1 Problems and their setting

Money should be looked upon not merely as one type of reward among others, but as a symbol of the fact that goods (means of subsistence) can be had only by work.

(Mannheim 1951: 262)

1.1 Capitalism

The main argument that I want to develop and defend in this book is simple: In a monetary economy, a large and decisive part of the uncertainties of economic life is replaced by one certainty, namely, that you need money in order to survive, if not in the literal, than at least in the economic sense of having regular access to commodities. In that sense, money absorbs uncertainty.[1] Insofar as it does, however, participants in a monetary system trade multi-facetted uncertainties for one certainty, the need for money.

The corresponding general attitude of agents in a thoroughly monetized society is well expressed in the popular 1960s song 'Money – that's what I want':

the best things in life are free,
but you can give them to the birds and bees,
I want money, a lot of money ...

If the writers of this song observed correctly, what economists call 'money illusion'[2] is a general, inescapable predicament in a capitalist economy. People want money not only because it takes money to articulate their needs for 'real' goods and services, but also because they have obligations not in terms of 'real' goods and services, but in terms of money. In addition, the acquisition of money evolves into a goal in itself. The overwhelming question in economic life then is: How can you get money? For most people, the answer is: Work for money! Or, in Marxian terms: Sell your labor power! In capitalism, money has turned not only into a symbol for the obligation to work, but also the work in question is work for and under the control of others. Work for others who will pay you, that is the core activity constituting capitalism.[3]

Thus, the big project waiting behind the efforts to build a theory of money is to improve our understanding of capitalism. But why bother extensively with the theory of money if the decisive force in contemporary society is capitalism? How does the theory of money fit into this larger project? In systematic terms, it serves as a sort of prologue to the theory of capitalism, as the use of money evidently is a necessary, but not a sufficient condition for a capitalist economy. How are money use and capitalism connected, then? There are several answers to this question.

One suggestion to explain the beginnings of capitalism, labeled 'primitive accumulation', was that would-be capitalists have to accumulate a money stock sufficiently large to turn into capitalist entrepreneurs. So the virtue of thrift would have made possible the take-off of the capitalist mode of production. In contrast, Marx ([1867] 1975, part viii), skeptical about any virtue at the roots of capitalism, proposed that the 'so-called primitive accumulation' consisted mostly of driving large shares of the population off the land, thus separating them from the possibility to produce their own means of subsistence. While Marx had a point, considering the long history of enclosures and their effects on rural populations in Britain, his argument against the requirement of some kind of primitive accumulation as a condition for the take-off of capitalism does not much help us to understand the historical connection between this take-off and money use. Be that as it may, the crucial issue is to understand the central role of money in the fully developed capitalist economy, not in its beginnings. To approach such an understanding, it will be useful to roughly indicate the notion of capitalism that forms the background for the theory of money to be developed in this book.

Capitalism is a mode of organizing economic life that is dominated by the profit-oriented use of wealth. Its precondition is a monetary economy, since only money as abstract wealth drives the desire for continuous and unlimited gain typical of capitalism. However, the use of money is only a necessary, not a sufficient condition for capitalism. As Marx pointed out, typical transaction chains in a simple monetary economy can be described as C–M–C circuits, exchanging a commodity C for money M in order to obtain another, more useful commodity. In such a context, money is simply a means in the general effort to increase available utility. By contrast, the typical capitalist transaction chain is M–C–M' (with M'=M+ΔM), using money to buy commodities in order to sell them for more money, thus making a profit. But again, the drive for maximizing profits is only a necessary, not a sufficient condition for modern capitalism and its revolution of economic life since the seventeenth century. Capitalist traders and adventure capitalists maximizing profits already existed in antiquity. In contrast, occidental capitalism, as Max Weber called it, started only once the M–C–M' transaction pattern was broadly applied not just to trade and credit, but to production. Industrial capitalists spend money to buy means of production and hire workers. Production then results in products intended to be sold for a profit. An owner of M turns into an (industrial) capitalist as soon as he repeatedly buys means of production and labor power, organizes a production process and succeeds in selling the resulting products for a profit. This way of organizing production became dominant with the Industrial Revolution. Its major precondition in terms of social structure was the availability of labor power as a commodity, in other words, the creation of a labor market. For this to happen, on one hand, workers must *not* be able to produce their means of subsistence on their own, a condition that, according to Marx, basically came about by separating them from the land. On the other hand, workers – in contrast to slaves or serfs – had to be able to enter contracts as legally fully recognized persons, even though their only property was their ability to work. Whereas Marx emphasized this social structural condition of workers being 'free in a double sense' for transforming money into capital, Weber emphasized the gains in rationality achieved by capitalist organization and made possible by precise monetary calculation. The capacity to abstract from concrete products and needs that underlies the evaluation of goods and services in terms of money is the major cultural precondition of capitalism and its specific 'formal rationality'. An amount of money defines the starting point of the capitalist enterprise. Its success is measured periodically by comparing returns in terms of the money gained in sales to the initial outlay. Such calculation is possible as a sustained and rational operation only under the condition – external to the individual enterprise – that trade on markets and the use of money are widespread and effective prices are generated for the most important goods and services. The formation of effective prices presupposes a competitive struggle that moves traders away from purely subjective, more or less arbitrary evaluations to socially objective evaluations. This condition of rationality – external to the individual enterprise – is complemented by an internal condition, namely that work in the factory is subject to the discipline required to make wage costs calculable. In both Marx's and Weber's views, this discipline is achieved, on one hand, by the threat of dismissal, of non-renewal of the labor contract which leaves workers without money to buy their means of subsistence, and on the other hand, by domination, that is hierarchical organization and top-down control of work performance (however, see Tilly and Tilly (1998) for an analysis of more refined modern varieties of organizing work).

Competition is not only important because it endows the prices formed with social objectivity so that they are the foundations of bookkeeping, calculations of returns and corporate or individual planning. Capitalist firms also produce for exchange, so they compete to attract buyers, people who hold money that they can spend when and for what they choose. This competition operates in two basic ways: To attract buyers one can offer at prices lower than those for similar products, or one can offer better or newer products. In both ways, the capitalist system puts a premium on innovation, either in terms of process or product innovations. This monetary premium results in the uniquely dynamic properties of capitalist economies. Striving for maximum profits induces a constant search for new ways to produce things, be it new means of production or new forms of organizing production, plus a constant search for new things to produce. The competitive pressure on the capitalist to keep costs low is translated into pressures on workers to work as much as possible for as little pay as possible. In early capitalism, this constellation resulted – and still results in underdeveloped economies – in widespread immiseration. Workers organize to be able to better resist the pressures on wages and adverse working conditions. Both the organization of labor unions and the introduction of universal suffrage helped to secure better legal and bargaining positions of workers. Nonetheless, it remains a characteristic feature of the capitalist mode of production to generate conflicts both over working conditions and the distribution of the net product, or *surplus*, that is the proceeds of the production process minus the outlays for means of production. Typically, these conflicts are softened during periods of strong growth and become harsher during periods of recession. Their strength thus varies with economic cycles typical of capitalist development.

Classical political economists distinguished the three classes of agents composing a capitalist economy: landowners, capitalists and workers. They all receive money incomes, namely rents, profits and wages, in return for providing land, capital and work as 'factors of production'. These incomes enable them to buy a share of the surplus. The resulting circular flow between firms and households depicts the capitalist economy as a self-reproducing system to the extent that it produces its own inputs as outputs. Self-reproduction implies that means of production used up are at least replaced and that the revenues of the three classes can induce their members to reappear continuously in sufficient numbers on the respective markets. These conditions mean that both real and monetary magnitudes, products and prices have to fulfill complex requirements of proportionality. To determine these conditions of reproduction was one of the major problems of classical political economy since Quesnay, culminating in Sraffa's (1960) demonstration that the prices supporting reproduction cannot be determined independently of distribution. Growth, that is expanded reproduction, comes about insofar as part of the surplus is not consumed but used to expand the productive apparatus. In monetary terms, those individuals or households able to save part of their current income face competing attractions: Either spend on consumption now or increase future income by saving and accumulating wealth. In the early phases of capitalism, the drive to accumulate at the cost of current consumption was supported by the religious beliefs emerging during the Reformation, as Weber ([1905] 1970) has shown (see also Tawney 1954). But Weber as well as Marx observed that, once the capitalist system comes to stand on its own feet, maximizing money income (maxM) turns into a general action pattern, replacing the habit of seeing money income merely as a means of access to consumption. MaxM, the subjective response to money as the 'absolute means' (Simmel 1907: 206), corresponds to a systemic property of a capitalist economy, insofar as capitalist firms maximizing profit continuously strive to improve their market position. To accomplish this, they normally have to invest. Investment is financed either internally out of accumulated returns or externally out of savings, stemming dominantly from the incomes of the wealthy, or through credit creation, that is the granting of loans to investors by banks in excess of the deposits they administer. In either case, the trade-off between profits and wages as shares of the surplus turns out to be, in a dynamic perspective, a trade-off between current and future consumption: If wages are too high, investments will be depressed so that current high wages translate into lower growth, thus into lower future income for all. However, depressed investments imply declining employment. Since workers' bargaining power is inversely related to unemployment, the wage share of the surplus will decline. The resulting increases in profits will feed higher investments that, in turn, imply increasing employment. The bargaining position of workers improves again – and the whole cycle may start anew (Goodwin 1967). Goodwin's simple model, in which aggregate demand as well as finance and interest payments are ignored,[4] demonstrates that the processes of capitalist reproduction and growth involve complicated balancing conditions which, in a self-regulating system with decentralized decision making, will be fulfilled only at the cost of periodically returning crises, where crises are feedback mechanisms that wipe out disproportions.

Major change in the development from early industrial to contemporary capitalism came about by two related institutional innovations: the evolution of the banking and credit system and the establishment of the modern corporation. Together, they not only involved a change in the nature and use of money – as we will see in more detail in Section 3.5 – but also led to industrial capital being pushed from center stage by finance capital. On one hand, practically all savings are now channeled into the banking system by offering savers interest; on the other hand, anybody can turn to the banking system for financing additional consumption or investment. Most importantly, the capitalist entrepreneur no longer has to rely on owning financial resources but can, in theory, be as property-less as the worker. The entrepreneur merely has to convince a money-holder or a financial intermediary, most likely a bank, to lend the money required to build or extend an enterprise (Schumpeter 1939: 110ff.). In turn, banks have learned that they can, by leveraging, lend money they do not have, thus creating money to equip entrepreneurs. The possibility of financing investments by borrowing implies a crucial role of the rate of interest: It serves as the benchmark defining the minimum returns on any investment. Profits come to be defined as the excess of such returns over the interest due on the capital borrowed. Since the nation state competes with private investors for funds, and lending to the state, with its power to tax, is considered the lowest risk investment, the rate of interest on the public debt serves as a parameter for money-holders deciding what assets to hold. Financial markets thus offer choice in a range of assets such that perceived risks and expected returns come to be proportional. At the same time, the volatility of financial markets due to the speculative element involved in calculating risks implies a recurrent premium on liquidity: The more an asset is money-like, the quicker the possibility to adjust to perceived market changes, the lower the chance of being locked in with an asset shrinking in value or of missing the opportunity to reap windfall profits.

The second major innovation, the modern corporation, emerged in the context of financial markets in which claims to future income streams are traded as ownership papers. Instead of borrowing, an enterprise raises (additional) capital by selling shares or stocks. By buying them any money-holder can become a part-owner of an enterprise. With dispersed ownership, the entrepreneurial function is taken over by managers who – in principle – are employees like anybody else, selling their specific labor power and supposedly being paid according to their performance.

While firms can satisfy their needs for funding by offering shares, money-holders can invest in such shares with low risks insofar as their liabilities are limited. In case of bankruptcy, the value of their shares can be annihilated, but no further obligations result. Expected returns on capital in relation to the rate of interest drive the price of shares. Such expectations are speculative since they have to be formed in an environment with limited and asymmetric information. Despite this speculative component, share prices are held to be the major indicator of the performance of firms, implying that management is more and more preoccupied with the way the firm is observed by financial markets. However, such observations are not necessarily tightly coupled to the firm's actual performance. In financial markets an additional layer of speculation is created by professional traders who seek gains by observing and predicting the behavior of each other, not the so-called fundamentals (Keynes 1936: 154f.; Iwai 2011). As Schumpeter (1954), Keynes (1936) and Kalecki (1954) have argued, this constellation implies a hierarchy of markets different from industrial capitalism where product markets took center stage. Now, financial markets governed by the interests of wealth owners, speculators and banks dominate, as firms operating in product markets have to compete for their funds. The rate(s) of interest generated in these markets determine(s) the lower limit of returns on investments in production. Such investments in turn are linked to the demand on product markets in a self-referential manner so that, as Kalecki put it, 'capitalists earn what they spend while workers spend what they earn'. Thus, the employment generated by a modern capitalist economy turns out to be a residual. Financial markets dominate product markets that dominate labor markets.

This dominant role of financial markets has been further enhanced in the last three decades by globalization and the associated public emphasis on so-called shareholder values. The withering away of socialist economic systems was accompanied by a worldwide opening of markets, clearly increasing the mobility chances of capital, and above all, of financial capital. The ease of investing wherever one wants, supported by new information and communication technologies, in turn increased the credibility of the exit threat used by firms in their bargaining both with employees and with states. As a consequence, the capitalist process has reaffirmed its decisive role not only in economic matters, but also in the sense of stronger selective effects on culture and politics. Globalization has been interpreted as driving the convergence of historically quite different, nation state based capitalist economies towards a uniform system governed more and more by market relations only. However, research on 'varieties of capitalism' demonstrates that, to a considerable degree, capitalist firms have remained embedded in institutional frameworks shaped by the political and cultural traditions bundled in nation states. This embeddedness is continuously reproduced because, in their business strategies, firms based in nation states attempt to use available 'comparative institutional advantages' (Hall and Soskice 2001), thus at least partially strengthening rather than abolishing the distinct institutional settings in which they operate. Since nation states, cultures and most of the people populating them remain rather locality bound and immobile compared to the supranational coordinating capacities of markets and the mobility of capital, the tensions between capitalist economies and their social environment remain as relevant as ever, as do attempts to rein in capitalist forces, with their innovative, disciplining but also destructive capacities, by countervailing political powers. Polanyi's 'double movement'[5] continues …

This sketch of the capitalist economy and its development should do to indicate the broader framework in which the theory of money should be positioned. On the one hand, a functioning monetary system is a necessary condition for a capitalist economy. On the other hand, the development of the capitalist economy induces changes of the monetary system and its role in the organization of production, distribution, exchange and consumption. For a start, however, we will only consider the monetary system as a necessary condition for the capitalist economy. The question is: How can the capitalist economy and a compatible social order be built on the use of money?

1.2 Money, a veil?

> No ordinary consumer today has even proximate knowledge about the production techniques of the goods he uses daily: most do not even know of which materials and by what industry these goods are produced. The consumer is interested only in those expectations of practical importance for him regarding the performance of these articles. The same applies to social institutions such as the monetary system. The money user does not know how money actually acquires its remarkable singular qualities, for even the specialists argue strenuously about that.
>
> (Weber [1908] 1981: 117f.)

Obviously, economics is the scientific discipline responsible for working out the theory of money. However, what Weber observed a century ago is still true today: Economic experts have very different and in many ways incompatible views on money. One reason for this confusion is the neglect of money in the main body of economic theory. Where things went wrong is well described – affirmatively – by Mises. Although he was one of the most influential monetary theorists of the early twentieth century, Mises celebrated the abstraction both from money and from social interaction as a sort of founding act of economic theory:

> The historical starting point of the reasoning that led to the formation of economic theory consisted of enquiries into the money prices of goods and services. The first step that opened the way to success for these enquiries was accomplished with the insight that money 'only' plays the role of a

mediator, that through its mediation, in the last instance, commodities and services are exchanged against commodities and services, and that, logically, the theory of direct exchange, operating with the fiction that all exchange transactions are conducted without the intervention of an exchange mediator, had to be placed before the theory of exchange mediated by money (the theory of indirect exchange, or the theory of money and circulating media). Still further possibilities of gaining knowledge were opened when it was understood that exchange transactions between economic agents were not different in essence from what the individual – without reaching out into the social sphere – changes within his household, meaning that each disposition over goods – including that in processes of production – is a form of exchange, so that the basic law of economic action could be deduced from the operations of an isolated economic agent.

(Mises 1931: 75, transl. HG)

Despite numerous assertions to the contrary, this dual abstraction has remained typical for mainstream economic theory until today.

The belief in the, at most, secondary significance of money was concomitant with the belief that the 'relations of commodities to one another remain unaltered by money' (Mill 1900, vol. 2: 11). Money is neutral. In fact, the whole architecture of economic theory since the marginal revolution of the late nineteenth century only makes sense *if* money is neutral. In general equilibrium theory, the core paradigm of modern economics, a moneyless but competitive market for goods and services is the unquestioned starting point of an axiomatic construction that includes money at best as an afterthought (Debreu ([1959] 1976).[6] Unfortunately for monetary theory, this starting point frequently coincides with the conviction that money is a mere veil underneath which the 'real', that is, the really important transactions take place. According to that conviction, whatever there is to say of importance about the economy can be said without referring to money.[7] At most, money may help to facilitate exchange and reduce transaction costs. Its minor importance for the theory is expressed well with the analogy that equates 'the productivity of money with the "shoe leather" saved by avoiding trips to the bank or the market place' (Brunner and Meltzer 1971: 800).

The conviction that money is a mere means to facilitate transactions that can just as well take place in the absence of money implies that the use of money can only seriously modify the allocation of resources if something goes wrong. In other words, most economists think about money in an asymmetric way: If all goes well, money is not important. But money will become important because it can be and frequently is abused. Since perfect markets do not leave room for such abuse, it must be the fault of monetary authorities or the state in general if serious disorder emerges. For political reasons, authorities may be tempted to fool those market participants who suffer from 'money illusion'. This is assumed to be a cognitive disorder that induces agents to confound 'real' and 'nominal' magnitudes, reacting not to 'relative', but to 'absolute' prices. This disorder can be magnified into a mass phenomenon by irresponsible governments – for example, when they attempt to fight unemployment by pushing up aggregate demand using traditional Keynesian recipes. However, according to the – somewhat perversely named – 'monetarist' school of thought such policies are ultimately self-defeating. Any 'money illusion' should be overcome after short period turbulences because the market puts a premium on rationality and rationality dictates that agents maximize utility, not money income. As the allocation achieved if agents adjust only to 'real' magnitudes is Pareto superior compared to the allocation achievable by trying to maximize monetary returns (which is what those suffering from 'money illusion' tend to do), the market itself provides the incentives for the rational behavior that will *make* money neutral. Thus, at the end of the day, the traditional economist will always be justified to see money as the mere lubricant of exchange.[8] It can only have serious consequences for the performance of the economy if abused by misguided authority.[9] This is a neatly constructed argument, a sort of monetization of the Smithian invisible hand: The natural harmony of a self-regulating market is supported by the monetary system as long as the latter is not manipulated, for example, in futile attempts to escape such equilibrating devices like the 'natural rate of unemployment' (Friedman 1968).

The underlying view that markets – in any version beyond local small markets operating on the basis of a combination of barter and trust between people who know each other – could function without money is quite contrary to historical knowledge. That would not matter much in the realms of theory, but it is also hardly compatible with any notion of normal economic agents that have to operate without being the information super-processors assumed in general equilibrium theory. Why does maximizing utility on competitive markets require superhuman information processing capacities as a prerequisite of rationality?[10] The plausibility of the economists' program of constrained maximization rests on the 'parametric function of prices': Individual agents maximize utility by engaging in quantity adjustments in face of *given* relative prices. For relative prices to remain parameters in that sense, no individual can be endowed with the power to change a price. To ensure such powerlessness the number of agents operating on competitive markets has to be so large that it leaves any individual agent unimportant. However, with the increase in the number of agents the number of transactions will increase as well. In order to maximize in such an environment and arrive at an efficient equilibrium in which all individuals have used all chances of improvement, these individuals have to know what all other individuals are doing. Either it is assumed explicitly that all agents have perfect knowledge and foresight or some functionally equivalent assumption is made. Prices may be assumed to be equilibrium prices to start with, agents may be assumed to be instant learners capable of forming rational expectations, or it may be assumed that they are able to presently use the available markets to trade in all future 'contingent' commodities. Evidently, these kinds of assumptions do not add up to anything like a realistic concept of *homo oeconomicus*. However, just as the critical reference to historical experience is regularly and – in a sense – justifiably rejected by mainstream theorists, so is the plea for a more realistic concept of *homo oeconomicus*. Realism is not the ultimate virtue in theory building. The only argument that would pull weight in terms of established theory has to be theoretical itself, meaning that it has to show how the architecture of the theory is inconsistent or inappropriate for dealing with the basic problems that the theory is to address.

I believe that such an argument can be constructed starting from the problem of uncertainty inherent in interaction. In such a framework money will play a much more important role than in what one can call 'thin' theories of money. As far as economics is concerned, such thin theories result if one tries to construct a concept of money compatible with the ideal world of the moneyless market generating equilibrium.

The conviction that the market can do its beneficial work without any serious role for money implies seeing money as a neutral instrument that has its purposes beyond itself. It merely functions as a mode of representation of 'real' commodities, simplifying the task of expressing and calculating exchange ratios by converting them into money prices (Niehans 1978), or as a means to overcome obstacles to barter like the absence of the 'double coincidence' of wants (Jevons 1876: 3), or as a means to reduce information costs (Brunner and Meltzer 1971; Alchian 1977), or as a store of value in overlapping generation models (Samuelson 1958), or, more generally, as a social instrument reducing transaction costs (Hicks 1967) and facilitating exchange (Tobin 1992). I call these 'thin' theories because they leave little for money to accomplish and basically convey the idea that money is a harmless 'social contrivance' (Samuelson 1958). A strongly expressed counter-position to these views of money can be found in Max Weber's economic sociology:

> 'Money' is not a harmless 'voucher for unspecified utilities' that could be arbitrarily transformed without fundamentally abolishing the nature of prices that are shaped by the struggle of man against man. Money is, rather, primarily a means of struggle and prize of struggle, but a means of calculation only in the form of the quantitative estimate expressing chances in the *struggle* of interests.
> (Weber [1922] 1964: 211 (ch.2, §13, translation slightly corrected, HG))

Following Weber, what would be the role of money in a 'thick' theory? A first step would be to emphasize that conflicts of economic interests – what Weber somewhat emphatically calls the 'struggle of man against man' – are pursued in terms of money. Money allows you to overbid and undersell, grant or refuse credit, withdraw your resources from a project, speculate, place your bets on an innovation, punish, and so on. Many of these moves create or react to unforeseen circumstances and have unintended consequences. That implies giving up the idea that money can be 'neutral', that it does not affect the play of 'real' activities underneath the 'veil' of money. By contrast, the bottom line of the neutrality assumption is that players in a monetary economy have to actively abstract from money to achieve optimal results.

The most important aspect of monetary neutrality, and the one that represents a genuinely deep principle of economic theory, is the proposition that
decisions about the supply and demand of goods and services should (if
decisionmakers are rational) depend only on the *relative prices* of different
goods, and not on the *absolute* price (price in terms of money) of anything.

(Woodford 2007: 11)[11]

But given that rational people do use money, can they both use it and abstract
from it? I will argue that penetrating the 'veil' of money in the way suggested by
the 'money is neutral' argument is not possible. The reason is that the world is
fundamentally different from the one depicted in traditional economic theory in
which the goal state of general equilibrium functions as a sort of certainty equivalent. Knowing that they will attain equilibrium – with its implication of efficient
use of available resources by all – agents will not need to shield against uncertainty. By contrast, in a world of uncertainty, everybody has to make decisions
under more or less ignorance. There is a double need, to decide and to be protected against unforeseen events generated by the interplay of these very
decisions.

The sources of uncertainty to be recognized in a 'thick' theory of money
include: Social interaction in general and, more specifically, the institutional
infrastructure of a DoL-PiP economy with producers who have to anticipate
what others want. The primary rationale for the use of money then is: Money
does 'absorb' uncertainty. Commodities are brought to markets with tentative
prices attached. Their sale generates 'effective prices',[12] created in the interactions of buyers and sellers. In turn, such prices can be used as primary information about the state of markets, information used when agents decide on what to
do next. In other words, money prices function as a sort of anchor in an otherwise turbulent and non-transparent environment. They allow us to make
decisions in contexts of contingency. To return to the neutrality issue: While we
may attempt to base such decisions on relative, not absolute prices, we can
perform the required abstraction from money only *post festum*, when evaluating
the outcomes of past decisions. By contrast, in anticipating what is going to
happen when we bring commodities to markets or in searching for ways to meet
payment obligations, referring to money prices is the required simplifying move
that does not eliminate, but does 'absorb' uncertainty in the sense of enabling us
to decide and act despite our considerable ignorance (whether the latter is admit-
ted or repressed).[13]

The major positive accomplishment of a monetary system is to create and sta-
bilize *mutual* expectations about the courses and goals of actions and to establish
a shared system of evaluation in a context of uncertainty. But using money does
not effectively eliminate uncertainty. On the contrary, using money will be a
source of additional uncertainty whenever the speculative drive for monetary
gain as such becomes dominant in a market, generating bubbles and their implo-
sions. In short, instead of treating money as a 'veil', a 'thick' theory of money
should relate money to socially generated uncertainty and show how it is used to

cope with such uncertainty – while not neglecting the opportunity costs of money use, most prominently those periodically emerging as monetary crises.[14]

1.3 Money, a symbol?

To produce 'thin' theories of money is not a privilege of the practitioners of the 'dismal science' of economics alone. Sociologists and anthropologists contributed their share of 'thin' theories, mainly by glossing over the explanatory problems that economists were at least struggling with. Rather than bother with the economists' concern to explain price formation in quantitative terms, sociologists and anthropologists were satisfied with the idea that money is a symbol.[15] Thus, Talcott Parsons proposed that money 'is symbolic in that, though measuring and thus 'standing for' economic value or utility, it does not itself possess utility in the primary consumption sense' (Parsons 1963: 236). To stress that money is a symbol seemed to get rid of some self-inflicted problems of economics in matters of money, most clearly the problem of explaining the long-term transition from coins, as – in some sense – intrinsically valuable objects, to the modern forms of fiat paper money or to the electronically processed numbers in accounts – a transition Michel Aglietta (2002: 36) refers to as the 'hyperbole of monetary abstraction'. If money is a symbol, functioning as a sign for something else, 'its particular physical character is arbitrary within certain practical limitations' (Codere 1968: 559). It follows that old ideas about money objects having to be valuable or anchored in something valuable, as in the gold standard regime, belong to the age of monetary superstition. Instead, money objects conform to the true nature of money only when they are valueless.[16]

But granted that money objects are symbols, what do they symbolize. Usually, they are held to symbolize something called 'value', or, more directly, 'utility', or, even more directly, 'goods'. However, to think of symbols, along with a long tradition, as something 'standing for' or representing something else, explains neither why the symbol is used – why not directly use the objects symbolized instead? – nor how symbolization works. And if any money object is a symbol, would it not be necessary to introduce the idea of a symbol of a symbol, and so on, to understand modern forms of money that seem to work without a physical counterpart?

For sociologists, one way to deal with such questions has been the construction of an analogy between money and language. Language clearly is a system of symbols, so why not understand money as a 'special language'? This analogy will be discussed in the next section. The issue here is whether the traditional notion of a symbol as a representation, a sign, something 'standing for' something else, is adequate for understanding money. Certainly, after centuries of argument about the importance of the money 'stuff', like gold, silver, paper, etc., it is a step forward to learn – in line with historical practice – that the physical characteristics of money objects may not matter for much of their functioning. But unless we take a step like Codere (1968) and see money directly as a sign for goods, the idea of money 'standing for' something else leads straight to the old issues of value theory. If money is a 'symbol of value', the question of money turns into the question: What is value?

In view of centuries of discussions about value – in the economic sense, to be sure – it is likely that assuming some inherent property named 'value' to explain the movements of goods and services and money objects in market transactions is a dead-end. This holds especially since the theory of value in economics has mostly been a device to keep money *out* of the picture (for the canonical form see Debreu 1959). Nonetheless, most writers on money use the term 'value', while hardly anyone ever bothers to tell us what the term is supposed to mean. To avoid getting entangled in these old discussions again, I have tried to drop the term 'value' from the vocabulary in what follows. The point is to leave behind the notion that money objects as 'symbols' are in some way 'representing' value, where value is taken to be some hidden intrinsic property of commodities.[17]

Luhmann (1988, ch.7) suggested a move in the right direction. He firmly rejected the notion of symbols as signs while he did follow Parsons (1963) in suggesting that money is one of several 'symbolically generalized media of communication'. To clarify the meaning of the term 'symbol', Luhmann referred to the origin of the word in the Greek '*symbolon*' (something that puts matters together) and its opposite '*diabolon*' (something that separates matters in two). But then Luhmann's play with the distinction between the symbolic and the diabolic functions of money did not make his version of the idea that money is a symbol easier to understand. When money is used in exchange, he holds, differing interests

> must be brought to convergence in the assumption of an equivalence of values. This is the ad hoc functioning symbol, the intention to exchange brought to convergence. Money, seen in its exchange function, is a generalization of this symbol, a condensation of this value equivalence for re-use in other exchange contexts.
>
> (Luhmann 1988: 257f. my transl. HG)

Luhmann does not tell us why buyers and sellers have to agree not only on a price but also on 'value equivalence' (whatever such a pleonasm is supposed to mean). He also does not explain how such value equivalence can be 'condensated'. Equally, his notion of money as the generalization of a symbol expressing convergence on the intention to exchange remains obscure.[18] Nonetheless, Luhmann's rejection of the traditional idea that symbols are signs standing for other objects such that money as a symbol is a sign of 'value' points in the right direction.

For the argument pursued in what follows, I found the starting point for developing a useful concept of symbol in Wittgenstein. Discussing the role of signs in mathematics, Wittgenstein appears to follow Frege in his argument against the formalist view that arithmetic is a mere play with signs. However, Wittgenstein has one reservation:

For Frege, there is the alternative: Either a sign has meaning, that is, it represents an object … or it is only the shape drawn on paper with ink. But this
alternative is not correct. There is, as the game of chess shows, a third possibility: The pawn in chess neither has meaning in the sense of representing
something, of being a sign of something, nor is it just the piece carved out
of wood. What the pawn is, is determined by the rules of chess.

(Wittgenstein 1984a: 150)

Can we transfer Wittgenstein's idea into the theory of money? For example, by
saying: The €10 banknote does not have meaning in the sense of representing
goods or their utility, nor in the sense of a sign of 'value', nor is it a mere piece
of paper elaborately imprinted. What the banknote is, is determined by its use in
the money game. The question then is: What are the rules of this game? How is
it played?

The money game in its simplest form is about buying and selling. Buying and
selling are interactions taking place in markets. If we follow Wittgenstein's
advice, we need to observe the uses of money in markets, rather than abstracting
from money in order to analyze markets, as most economic theorists did and do.
So to understand the functioning of money objects as symbols, I will proceed
from the proposition: There is no money without markets and there are no
markets without money.[19] Both are the results of a co-evolution, or:

Markets as economic institutions are no more than the joint product of the
bootstrap mechanism which has produced money as a social entity.

(Iwai 1996: 28)

1.4 Money, a language?

Working as a newcomer in New York in the late 1970s, on my walks during
lunch hour, I was puzzled by a sign in a shop window at the lower end of Fifth
Avenue. The sign said: 'Money talks'. Maybe that was an ironic comment on the
signs in other shop windows that said: 'Nous parlons français' or 'Wir sprechen
deutsch' and so on? Instead, I decided that it most likely meant: If you want anything we are offering, come in, even if you do not speak the language. But do
not come in without money. If you don't have the money, go away. As I learned
much later, the rhyme on 'money talks' is 'bullshit walks'.

Thus, the sign signals that money is a starter for transactions in a context
where, possibly, no common 'natural' language is available. In such contexts,
we can use money as the means to communicate our interest in buying or selling
something. Money is language-like in allowing for such communication, communication understood as an interactive process uniting information, message
and understanding. The information is a price expression – a quantity of money
associated with a quantity of a good. The message is the wish to buy or sell.
Understanding the message is simple for practiced users of money: The buyer is
asked to pay that much to get the commodity; the seller is asked to hand it over

for that much money. Thus, to use money as a means of communication involves expressing bids and offers in the form of prices with the aim of arriving at an agreement. Prices specify conditions of transfer of goods or of the performance of services. Before any such transfer or performance effectively takes place, buyer and seller have to agree on a price. The simplest of monetary transactions, the buying of a good, then moves beyond the realm of commitments. It is completed when the good is handed over from the seller to the buyer and money is handed over from the buyer to the seller: 'When money talks it says good-by.'

So the sign 'money talks' signals: Come and make an offer. We will negotiate. Given a good in a given quantity, negotiations are simplified to the form of adding to or subtracting from the quantity of money offered or demanded. Once we agree on a price, you hand over the money and we will give you the good. This basic mode of operation does not change, regardless of the form of the money objects used: cash, credit card payment, checks, etc.

'Money talks' implies: Money is a means of communication. It can be used to express intentions to buy or sell in ways that everybody will understand – given a currency area and basic arithmetic skills. In such a loose sense, money indeed works like language, like a 'special language' (Habermas 1980: 74) that is appropriate for communication in the bounded context of commercial activities, but most likely inappropriate and leading to misunderstanding in other contexts. Insofar as money works like language, we should therefore be able to improve our understanding of money by learning how language works. Then, we can examine the ways in which communication with language differs from communication with money. As we will see, there is indeed a sense in which money can be understood as a special language, but it is crucial to move beyond this sociological conception to see in what sense money does both *more* and *less* than language. Monetary transactions frequently reach beyond the realm of communication.

In sum, in this preparatory discussion we have examined three problematic propositions about money. The first, prominent in traditional economic thought, states that money is a veil, to be ignored if one wants to understand 'real' economic problems. There might be short-run effects of money, but in the long run, when – along with Keynes – we are all dead, money is neutral. The second, quite frequently encountered in sociological and anthropological, but also in more heterodox economic texts, states that money is a symbol, with very different and inconsistent answers given to the questions of what is being symbolized and how symbolization works. The third, exclusively sociological, suggests that money should be understood as a linguistic phenomenon, as a medium of communication in analogy to language. What is ignored here are the properties and effects of money that reach beyond communication. However, the notion of money as a medium of communication has one definite advantage over traditional economic views of money: Money is placed squarely into a social context. That may not sound like much. After all, what could money be if not a 'social contrivance' (Samuelson 1958)? However, while there may be lip service to the proposition that money is a social fact, the implications of that proposition are not recognized in most – including some of the most advanced – models of a monetary economy. A good part of economic theorizing about money operates on the assumption that an economy – with or without money – is something that can be usefully described in physical terms.[20]

Against this, the first step to take towards an adequate theory of money is to clarify what it means that money is a social fact, an institution and a constitutive part of a social system.

2   Clarifications

2.1 Language and money

In *The Construction of Social Reality*, John Searle (1995) proposes an ontology of social facts, and, more narrowly, analyzes the role of language in the formation of institutions. For our purposes, it is useful that he frequently refers to money as an example of a social fact and institution. Social facts are generated by coordinated actions. Institutions are a subset of social facts that involve a 'deontic' dimension, meaning that institutions are systems of rights and obligations. As we will see, they cannot work without language.

Though Searle emphasizes that societies are extremely complex, he maintains that the building elements, as it were, of social reality are limited in number and simple in principle. Basically, he proposes four such building elements: collective intentions, the assignment of functions, the distinction between regulative and constitutive rules and the background.[1] In this section, I will recapitulate Searle's argument as far as it is necessary to understand its implications for the theory of money.

What distinguishes social facts from other facts? The first element is *collective intentionality*: According to Searle, social facts are based on what he calls 'collective intentionality'. For social facts to come about, there must be a collective, a multitude of agents that have something to do with each other. These agents must share an intention, as when they pursue the same objective or play the same game. In collective action, individuals do not cease to act as individuals,[2] but what each individual is doing is doing it as a part of what the collective is doing, such as playing a cello in an orchestra or being the goalkeeper in a soccer team. The capacity for collective intentionality is not restricted to humans. Many animals choose to live together with mates, raise their young together or hunt as a group and in so doing they create social facts. There is an extensive debate about collective intentionality, especially about Searle's claim that we-intentions are not further analyzable into I-intentions (Searle 2002; for a discussion, see Turner 1999). Pettit (2001) demonstrates that for us to recognize something as a 'center of intentions' requires a minimum of consistency in the selection and pursuit of objectives. Collective intentions therefore presuppose a minimum of organization that allows the collective in question to pursue intentions despite occasionally deviating preferences of individual members. Thus, the threshold where specifically human forms of collective intentions become effective is likely to be a degree of organization that requires elaborate communication.

The second element is the *assignment of function*: Human agents (but some animals, too) distinguish objects in their environment that they can use for their own purposes. In such use they assign functions to these objects. Functions are not properties of objects as physical facts – described as a physical object, this chair consists of pieces of wood. Functions are assigned – we use a properly shaped set of pieces of wood to sit on. That the physical object has this function is 'observer-relative' (Searle 2005: 8). The physical components of a hammer, a piece of wood and a piece of iron stuck together, do not tell us anything about its function. We can know about functions only by observing the use agents make of objects. Functions involve a normative dimension. Whatever the function in question, it can be performed in better or worse fashion. Or, to use an economic example: A good is only a good relative to an agent with needs and desires, not as part of the physical world. Specific physical properties will normally be required to fulfill a function – something needs to be liquid to quench your thirst – but the function exists only in relations between an object and an agent.

The assignment of function can be described with Searle's formula: 'X counts as Y in context C'. Who is counting? It can be an individual, like Köhler's chimpanzee using a stick to get at the banana, but it can also be a group. Thus, collective intentionality and assignment of function can be combined. A group can assign functions. Just as I can sit on a piece of wood and it functions as a chair, so we can sit on a piece of wood and it functions as a bench. A noise we make with our vocal cords is a physical fact (X), but it may be a word (Y) in a language (C) for one collective, and just noise in another language.

A special case of the assignment of function is the *assignment of status function*: Status functions *have* to be assigned collectively and the function cannot be performed simply because the object has certain physical features (like a hammer …). Rather, people 'are prepared to regard things or treat them as having a certain status and with that status a function'. Status functions are the building blocks of institutions. 'The creation of institutional facts requires that people be able to *count something* as something more than its physical structure indicates' (Searle 2003: 301).

To illustrate the difference between a function assigned due to physical properties and a status function, Searle uses the example of a wall enclosing a territory. Its physical properties keep out intruders. Now, let the wall decay into a line of stones. This line may lead people to respect the boundaries of the territory just as the physical wall did, not because the line of stones as a physical obstacle could keep them out, but rather because they have collectively assigned the status of boundary markers to the line of stones and they have learned to respect such boundaries. Again, Searle uses the formula 'X counts as Y in C' to depict the logical form of the assignment of status functions. They can only be performed by a collective. 'X counts as Y' only if *we*, the collective, assign the status Y to the object X. If the collective ceases to exist or if its members ignore the status, Y deteriorates into X. If we all ignore the police uniform, its bearer reverts to being a civilian. If we react to the uniform as we have learned, the uniform is a status indicator. Wearing the uniform signals the status of an organ of the state, authorized to exercise the monopoly in the use of legitimate force attributed to the state, and so on. Status depends on collective recognition and collective recognition depends on collective representation.

This is where, according to Searle, language must come in. Because the association of physical fact and status function is not determined by the physical fact, it can only be brought about by collective intentions. As the association cannot be established in a collectively binding way by an individual, these intentions have to be shared. To share intentions they must be communicated. Communication that reaches beyond pointing to a physical fact requires representation. The representation has to be performed and recognized as such by the members of the collective in question. This means that a firm association of the physical fact and the social status can only be established in communication. Language is the primary means for such collective representation. In its reliance on language, the circular structure that seems to support the status function is de-tautologized, as it were. For a collective to 'count X as Y' as a collective when the physical properties of X alone do not suggest its function, the members have to *say* to each other that they are counting X as Y. '*A status function must be represented as existing in order to exist at all, and language or symbolism of some kind provides the means of representation*' (Searle 2005: 14f.). In other words, status functions are social constructions that work only because they can be and insofar as they are represented in language and are recognizable for everybody who understands the language.

The irritating aspect suggesting circularity is that language is an institution and, at the same time, the foundation of all other institutions. The components of language are physical facts like noises, sequences of sounds or ink spots on paper. They are distinguished from other physical facts in that we use them – they 'count' for us – as signs or symbols in communication. In that sense, we 'do' language. That language as an institution can serve as the foundation of all other institutions is due to what Searle calls the *iteration* of the 'X counts as Y' formula. Status assignments may be built on each other through iteration, so that 'X_1 counts as Y_1', and '$Y_1 = X_2$ counts as Y_2', and '$Y_2 = X_3$ counts as Y_3', and so on. A sound you make may count as a word, a word can be part of a sentence, a sentence may count as a promise, a promise may be a promise to pay, and a sentence written on a piece of paper may count as a promise to pay to anybody who presents the paper, and so on. As the example indicates, we can modify and extend the iterative use of the 'X counts as Y in C' formula as applied to language until we arrive at something money-like.

The use of language rests on our capability to represent the outside world – not just insofar as it exists as physical facts, but including processes, dynamic relations among objects and persons, etc. – in our minds. We use language to communicate about these representations with each other. When I say the word 'dog' you are – if you speak English – able to understand that I am referring to these furry four-legged creatures that occasionally produce sounds like 'wough, wough'. When we speak, the objects we refer to do not need to be present, to be pointed at, in order for listeners to know what we are talking about. By communicating representations we can bring our intentions into contact with each other and thus accomplish understanding in the medium of language. Moreover, as the word 'dog' does not simply refer to a singular dog, words involve generalization, a potential reference to a whole class of particular objects. But we can also refer to individuals by using singular names.

This ability to communicate with and about representations (in the form of symbols which may simply 'stand for' real objects, but may also represent more complicated matters like social relations) supports and enhances our capacity to form expectations about each others' behavior and thus, via communicating our intentions, the capacity to influence one another, to coordinate actions, to cooperate. Such mutual expectations can solidify into rules, norms and institutions.

This then is the third of Searle's building elements. To respect a status is a case of following a rule. Rules serve to coordinate actions, but not only that. Searle distinguishes between *regulatory* and *constitutive rules*, the former regulating behavior that exists without the rule, the latter being conditions for the social fact in question to emerge. The rule 'always drive on the right side of the road' regulates a behavior, driving, that could be happening without the rule, but would be less safe. By contrast, the rule that a pawn in chess can only move forward is part of the set of rules constitutive for the game of chess.

How is a constitutive rule related to status assignment? We cannot play chess without both knowing the rules and agreeing on status. If you think that this piece of wood is the king and I think it is the queen, we are not able to play although we move the pieces according to the rules. To play, players have to agree on status and they have to follow the rules of the game. In this way, 'acting in accordance with a sufficient number of the rules is constitutive for the behavior in question' (Searle 2005: 11). The outcomes of such behavior are the institutions that are – in Searle's framework – the larger building blocks of society.

> An institution is any collectively accepted system of rules (procedures, practices) that enable us to create institutional facts. These rules typically have the form of *X counts as Y in C* where an object, person, or state of affairs and lower and lower X is assigned a special status, the Y status, such that the new status enables the person or object to perform functions that it could not perform solely in virtue of its physical structure but requires as a necessary condition the assignment of the status. The creation of an institutional fact is, thus, the collective assignment of a status function.
>
> (Searle 2005: 26f.)

Whereas simple social facts are the outcome of behavior guided by collective intentions, institutions as social facts rest on the assignment of status functions. Status functions in turn are essential for structuring social relations because they 'carry recognized and accepted deontic powers' (Searle 2005: 24). Recognition of the status implies rights, obligations, responsibilities, duties. In this way, the range of permissible actions is reduced for all those accepting the status. This not only makes actions mutually predictable, but the rules followed gain normative force as a result of such mutual expectations. For such deontic power to persist, 'they have to be represented in some linguistic or symbolic form' (Searle 2005: 17).

A difficulty about the 'X counts as Y in C' formula is that it first describes institution building as a shared mental activity of explicit status assignment, whereas such collective assignment does not seem to be required as an explicit act every time a status function is played out. Perhaps this is the point where Searle's concept of the 'background' could be fruitfully introduced. Once institutions are established, all players operate according to the 'X counts as Y in C' formula because this has become part of their habitual, routine behavior. They do not 'count' anymore but act 'as if' they counted. One implication of rule following sinking into the 'background' of non-intentionality is that the physical underpinning of status assignments may become redundant. Searle goes as far as saying that – for established institutions – the X term can simply disappear:

> The whole point of institutional facts is that once created they continue to exist as long as they are recognized. You do not need the X term once you have created the Y status function.
>
> (Searle 2003: 305)

This is a point for debate especially when we return to money (see Section 2.4). Do we actually need physical money objects to 'carry' the status functions of money? Or is money a case of a 'free-standing Y term' (Searle 2005: 19) where a physical X term is no longer needed? For the time being, we can leave that issue open and conclude with Searle that we operate on two levels in the institutional world:

> We have to think from the brute level up to the institutional level, and the capacity to think at different levels enters into the actual cognitive processes of our perception. I literally see a twenty dollar bill, I do not just see paper. But the cognitive capacity to see these things requires a linguistic or symbolic capacity.
>
> (Searle 2005: 15f.)

We can now try to draw on Searle's framework to better understand some issues raised in Chapter 1. First, in what sense is money a symbol? Is Searle's formula 'X counts as Y in C' equivalent to saying 'X is a symbol of Y in C'? This piece of wood, carved in that way, is a pawn in the game of chess. X is the piece of wood, C is the game of chess, Y is the assigned status of 'pawn', where the importance of physical objects serving as pawns lies in the possibility of distinguishing them from the other pieces used in the game, thus of using them according to the rules (pawns can only be moved in a specific way) and in the limited number of pieces available. Regardless of the concrete material and its form, the status 'pawn' can only be understood by somebody knowing the rules of chess. The players have to agree on assigning this status to specific objects.

Can we apply this to the idea that money is a symbol? One immediate difficulty is: What does the term 'money' in the sentence 'money is a symbol' refer to? If somebody holds up a $10 bill, we can say: This green piece of paper imprinted with numbers, odd pictures, and so on, counts as ten units of the currency of the United States. We have to distinguish between *money objects*, like dollar bills, and a *monetary system* – the game played in the United States with these money objects. In Searle's terms, we can say that the green pieces of paper with numbers on them serve as status indicators.[3] The holder of the bill has the status of owning so and so many units of the currency of the United States. If somebody presents one of those pieces of paper, this signals what game is being played. To play, we have to know the rules of the game. We buy and sell, offer and demand, borrow and lend, and so on. We play according to rules when we respect property rights, fulfill payment obligations, etc. The money object *symbolizes* these possibilities and capabilities of playing the money game in the sense of functioning as a placeholder for potential actions.

So how do we now understand the sentence: 'Money is a symbol'? It does not make sense when referring to the monetary system or the money game. We can understand it as meaning: Money objects are status indicators. As such, they can be used in the money game. They function because *we* assign that function to the physical objects used.[4] Such a 'symbol' is not an object in a relation of representation in the sense of 'standing for' another object (or some property of another object like its 'value'). The 'X counts as Y in C' formula characterizes the status of an object or event with respect to the rules in a game. The symbol signals potential use in that context. To say that 'money is a symbol' is only a vague and imprecise way of saying that the physical object/artifact in question, the green piece of paper, has its status, being a dollar bill, as the result of an underlying collective assignment that has significance only in the context of the game played.

Second, what is the relation between money and language? Searle makes it very clear that an institution like money is dependent on language. In a monetary system, objects have status functions and status functions can only be collectively assigned by way of representation and the representation must be communicated in language as the medium of representation. 'We must have some means of representing the fact that this stuff is money … in order that the stuff can acquire the status of money. No representation, no status function'. In short, 'no language, no status functions' (Searle 2005: 15f.).

Interestingly, this does not mean that players of the money game have to speak the *same* language. All that is required is a shared understanding among players according to the 'X counts as Y in C' formula: They must (implicitly) agree, more or less worldwide, that these green pieces of paper with numbers and pictures imprinted on them count as money. They know from their respective backgrounds in their native societies and languages what the rules of the money game are. In that sense their playing the money game across the barriers of different languages still presupposes their command of language in general. But no common natural language is required. Everybody can participate in a soccer game, wherever it is played, if the rules of the game are the same and common knowledge and players are able to follow the rules. Although these rules need to be expressed in language, the players do not have to speak the same language.

The sociological analogy between language and money discussed above in Section 1.3 (and in Section 2.1.1 below), the suggestion to regard money as a 'special language', does not arise in Searle's framework, in which 'language is the fundamental social institution' (Searle 2005: 14). Monetary facts can only exist relative to language, so money cannot replace language. This does not prevent, as we all know from everyday experience, the possibility of communicating by using money.

So, to sum up, what have we learned about money from reading Searle? First, money is a social fact rooted in collective intentions. A description of money objects in physical terms cannot contribute anything to understanding money. That is because, second, only the collective assignment of status function turns physical objects like pieces of metal or paper into money objects. As money objects, they function in a game, signifying action potentials. Third, this status assignment requires representations and therefore language. Thus, it is possible only given an institutional background. Fourth, money is itself an institution, based on agents acting according to constitutive rules, implying rights and obligations.[5] Fifth, money as a higher order institution is constructed by means of iterations of status assignments. Sixth – as we may add beyond the summary – once the institution is established, new players learn the money game as an ongoing practice, without the need to again and again repeat the 'founding acts' of declaring that 'X counts as Y in C'.[6] We grow into a world of institutional facts and learn them by doing, without normally questioning their character as facts. Such questioning can occur as a result of ruptures or crises, once we recognize that institutional facts are dependent on our confirming them as facts in everyday practices. But as long as we respect the constitutive rules to which they owe their existence they remain objective – institutional – facts.

To put it in terms of Searle's questions, we can now understand what transforms a piece of paper into a dollar bill, or rather, how we combine the physical fact with the institutional fact. We are creating money by 'counting X as Y' and by following the rules of the money game. In this way, Searle's social ontology allows us to specify the conditions of possibility of a monetary system, how it has to be installed and maintained by collective intentions. However, this is where the ontology ends. When the question is: *What* are we doing with money?, the social sciences have to come in. To what uses we put the institution of money is a question beyond philosophy. We can approach answers by taking a look at everyday experience. Before we do that, the background of Searle's framework provides the occasion for a brief intermezzo on the analogy between language and money in some sociological theories.

2.1.1 *Money as a special language?*

Social theorists who see *money as a special language* normally have other functions of language in mind than language as a means to represent the collectively
assigned status function according to the 'X counts as Y in C' formula. The sociological analogy tends to be quite direct: Like language, money functions to coordinate actions. We can influence what others are doing by offering or demanding
money. For example, I give up control over/or ownership of my bicycle once you
have paid me $100, or you paint my fence if I pay you $50. So the basic structure
of interactions with money appears to be similar to language-mediated interaction.
In a speech act, *ego* puts forward a claim (for truth, authenticity, goodness, fairness, etc.) that *alter ego* can accept or reject. We may even see language communication as consisting of exchanges, as a game of offer (claims) and demand
(acceptance) between two or more actors. In that perspective, the difference
between using money to 'talk' and using language proper first of all seems to be
that using money is so much simpler: It has both a built-in convincing power and a
built-in metric,[7] so that, given sufficient quantities, it is said to buy everything –
without so many words being used. Once again: 'Money talks'.

   Money as a 'special language' is thus conceived as a sort of shorthand that
can be used in the realm of economic transactions. It facilitates action
coordination among instrumentally oriented players. As Adam Smith taught us,
we do not have to appeal to love, friendship, solidarity, truth, the law, or what
have you, to convince the baker, the butcher and the brewer to share their products with us. We appeal to their self-interest and we do that – not, as Smith
seemed to hold – by offering goods or services in 'truck, barter and exchange',
but by offering them money. As almost everybody involved knows how to play
the money game, action coordination becomes very simple. This is why anthropologist Bohannan concluded his account of the impact of money on a traditional tribal society with the famous observation: 'Money is one of the
shatteringly simplifying ideas of all time' (Bohannan 1959: 503).

   But its simplicity must have disadvantages. The 'money code' is restricted.
Compared to language, it only transports limited information in the form of
prices and their changes. It can be misleading because of this simplicity. At the
same time money cannot be used universally. Not only, as with the limits of language, because there are different monies just as there are different languages,
but also because only a subset of social interactions is accessible to coordination
via money. As an old pop song has it: 'Money can't buy me love'. As an
example of improper use, think of the sale of indulgences during the later Middle
Ages by pardoners: That the pope granted remission of punishment in purgatory
in exchange for money was an abuse that offered Luther big leverage against the
Roman Catholic church. This possibility of applying money in wrong contexts
points to differences between money and language:

   First and formally, language cannot only be used more generally but it can be
used reflexively: We can think and communicate about the nature and uses of
language using language, something impossible with money.

Second, the 'money language' relies parasitically on language proper. While it is frequently maintained that the 'language of prices', given a currency, is sort of self-contained, operating in terms of quantitative variations only, we only need to examine what a price as a 'sentence' in that language refers to in order to notice that it is not self-contained. When we express a price, such as: One barrel of Brent crude oil costs $100 (or the price p_i of 1 unit of good i, $p_i = \$100$), more is involved than a simple reference to money: A price always includes two terms to make sense. It couples the reference to a quantity of money with the reference to a quantity of a specified good or service – or whatever else may have a price, for example, an ownership title. For a complete price expression, the objects to be traded have to be described in a language capable of referring to possible use, unique qualities, etc., and referring to a system of measures. The descriptions become simpler and communication easier the more the objects to be traded are standardized (Carruthers and Stinchcombe 1999).

Third, prices are formed by using the *metric* of money. This implies another difference between communication through language and money use. The mapping of a manifold of goods, each with a manifold of qualities, into quantities of more or less money replicates the logic of exchange and involves an abstraction from all these qualitative differences and their translation into simple quantitative differences in price. To accomplish this reduction, players need to be able to use the metric of money and they need to develop some skills in translating qualitative differences into price differences. Why is a used car with a dent worth $150 less than a similar car without a dent? Why not $100, or $500? For some of these translations there may exist well-known conventions on developed markets, others may involve discussion and arriving at some compromise before a trade can be completed.

In addition, the metric implies that price expressions may be combined and aggregated, as in accounting, so that summary descriptions of economic processes in terms of money stocks and flows can be composed. In a balance sheet, the bottom line sums up and juxtaposes assets and liabilities. The reference to particular goods or resources has disappeared. The interest here is to calculate the total wealth of an individual, a public or private household, or a firm. Whatever the individual price expressions used as entries refer to, it disappears in such an aggregate. What would be an analogue to that in language? Language does not involve a metric, so forming aggregates by summing up is not possible. An analogy can at most be seen in terms of the generalizations and abstractions involved in language use, where a manifold of individual elements can be subsumed under one concept.[8]

Finally, if money were a special language, it should – analogous to language proper – be a 'public good'. Language is undoubtedly useful most of the time, so it is a good. It is a 'public good' because nobody can be excluded from its use and there is no rivalry in use – unless one thinks of the noise produced by everybody talking at the same time. Table 2.1 shows the standard typology of goods.

Table 2.1 The classification of goods

Rivalry Excludability	Yes	No
Yes	Private good	Club good (e.g. toll road)
No	Commons	Public good

Language is a 'public good'. Once learned, everybody can use it. The fact that I use it does not prevent you from using it or diminish your capacity to speak or write. If we each had a private, individual language, we could exclude all others from what we say or think or write in that language, but its usefulness would be very limited. Communication works only insofar as there is no exclusion. Seen in such a perspective, a monetary *system* may also be considered a public good, but certainly the access to money *objects* like coins, bills, bank accounts is restricted and there is rivalry in use. Since we use money to regulate the access to private goods, the access to money as a tool of appropriation has to be restricted as well. Therefore, a big part of the semantics of money is about exclusion or limited access. 'I work all day and get no pay.' Like words, money objects are not consumed when used, but unlike words, you can use a money object only once in most functions,[9] because using it means giving it away. Money objects circulate, but in order to have them circulate towards you, you have to fulfill conditions that you must negotiate with the current holder of the money objects. There is rivalry in use: The piece of money in the possession of A cannot be used by B – unless B has borrowed it with the consent of A.

In contrast to money objects, an established *monetary system* has positive general effects, for example, allowing for an extensive division of labor or lowering transaction costs. Therefore, it may be considered a public good (Tobin 1992). Even when people do not actually use money themselves, for example, because they have spent it all, they cannot be excluded from the benefits of the established general level and intensity of action coordination made possible by the use of money. Nonetheless, it is misleading to simply call money a public good. One of its major effects is precisely to exclude agents from transactions. If you do not own (or have other access to) the required amount of money, you cannot compete with other buyers, you cannot buy and you are thus excluded from the use of the goods in question. This cannot happen with language. Once you have learned a language, you can participate in communication. In contrast, you may have learned how to use money, but if you don't dispose over money objects, you cannot participate in the money game. We will have to find out exactly which properties of money are responsible for such exclusion.

We may think about words in the classic Augustinian way, as names for things: Here is the word and there is the object the word refers to. We may also construct a parallel to money: 'The money, and the cow that you can buy with it' (Wittgenstein PI 120[10]). Or, here is the good and there is the money that lets you buy it. The price can be tagged onto the cow like a name. However, to think that words are only names for things is quite a simplistic notion of language, as Jonathan Swift had Gulliver learn in the Academy of Lagado:

> The other project was a scheme for entirely abolishing all words whatsoever; and this was urged as a great advantage in point of health, as well as brevity. For it is plain, that every word we speak is, in some degree, a diminution of our lunge by corrosion, and, consequently, contributes to the shortening of our lives. An expedient was therefore offered, that since words are only names for *things*, it would be more convenient for all men to carry about them such *things* as were necessary to express a particular business they are to discourse on. And this invention would certainly have taken place, to the great ease as well as health of the subject, if the women, in conjunction with the vulgar and illiterate, had not threatened to raise a rebellion unless they might be allowed the liberty to speak with their tongues, after the manner of their forefathers; such constant irreconcilable enemies to science are the common people. However, many of the most learned and wise adhere to the new scheme of expressing themselves by *things*; which has only this inconvenience attending it, that if a man's business be very great, and of various kinds, he must be obliged, in proportion, to carry a greater bundle of *things* upon his back, unless he can afford one or two strong servants to attend him.
>
> (Swift [1726] 1973: 230)

For these wise men, extra-verbal reference to the things they were carrying was a sufficient way to communicate. Should we think of prices analogously? As if a price were a name? (Dyer 1989) Representing the cow in terms of money means stating a price for it. The price can be understood as a summary expression of all properties of the cow for the sake of representing it as an object for sale or as an asset in the balance sheet. But although a price, like a name, can be used to mentally represent an object, a price is not just a name. It states a condition for the transfer of ownership. Language is not used like that. We can mentally represent this animal and communicate about it by associating the word 'cow' with it, but we do not exchange the cow for the word 'cow'. In that sense, a price is more than a name and money is more than language. Money objects can be used as social tools for the appropriation of goods and services, not only for communicating about them.

In sum, referring to money as a 'special language' (Habermas 1980) is somewhat misleading. If anything, it seems clearer to refer to the 'language of prices' (Luhmann 1983: 165). Prices in the form of bids and offers signal trading possibilities or, as effective prices, describe completed transactions in which economic objects changed proprietors. In any case, the language analogy neglects one important property of money. Money is not only used for forming prices, as mental associations of goods with money, and for communicating about prices,[11] but it is a social tool (Simmel 1907: 205), a lever in transactions, the *quid pro quo* that allows us to accomplish a desired change of ownership: You get the money, I get the goods – or vice versa. Nothing like that is happening when we use language proper.

To deepen our understanding of this decisive difference between communicating with language and using money, let us look more closely at how we use money in everyday life.

2.2 Everyday use of money

We can observe the typical everyday use of money by following somebody who is shopping in a supermarket, for example. People take carts, go along the shelves packed with goods, occasionally take a look at items or prices and collect goods. Then they all make their way to the cash register. What happens? Goods are taken out of carts, placed onto a little conveyor belt. The cashier slides them past a bar code reader or types in numbers on a keyboard, names of articles and prices appear on a screen, a computer does the sum, shopper pays, with cash or a credit or debit card or a check. The shopper gets a receipt, goods are put in bags and can be taken out of the shop. Mostly, there is no need to talk. Everyone present knows what the transaction is about and how to accomplish it. You as a consumer take goods and give money. The shop gives you the goods and takes the money. Money can have different forms and the ways of transferring it from buyer to seller differ accordingly, but whatever the form, the buyer loses some amount of money and the seller gains that amount. (For now, ignore complications that would result from referring to all the hidden third participants in such a transaction, like the tax state, the central bank, the credit card organizations, the banks). There is no need to talk because 'money talks'.

Almost everybody uses money almost every day. As children, we were sent to the corner store, counted coins in hand, to buy bread or milk, perhaps we were allowed to add some candy. We learned the ritual of buying: You ask for the good, it is put on the counter. The price is named. You hand over the coins. You can take home the good. Much later, perhaps we learn the ritual of selling. You display what you want to sell and look for a customer. You may already have put a label on your goods, stating your asking price. A customer comes, there may or may not be a bit of negotiating, there may be an agreement. If both parties agree, money and good change hands.

Whatever we do in the economy, we base our actions on prices, expressed as multiples of units of money. As we have seen, prices seem to be attached to goods or services like names to people or words to things. However, prices differ from names not only because money is a tool of appropriation, but also because prices involve a metric: Prices would be like names only if all commodities were named Fritz and would be distinguished only according to more or less Fritzness.[12] To apply the money metric means: An object with a label '$10' in a shop is positioned in the world of commodities – the set of all objects for sale. Seen purely in the dimension of money, the distance to other commodities with labels '$9.99' or '$20,000' is observable for everyone who can do basic arithmetic. On the other hand, seen from the side of goods, we need to hold constant the goods' side to make sense of prices. If an apple costs thirty cents, but one is red, the other small, the third slightly rotten, the thirty cents price does not mean the same thing. To be correctly informed and able to perform the calculations involved in buying and selling, we need unit prices, expressions in which both the goods and the money side refer to the same units and standards, respectively (Carruthers and Stinchcombe 1999). For some reason, we mostly take the measurability of goods and services – that is economic objects like two cups of tea or five tons of bricks or one haircut – for granted, although for a significant subset of trades there are problems in establishing commodity identities insofar as they are not standardized. The problem of measuring quantities of goods – kilograms of flour, numbers of 1957 Studebakers – is not trivial, in part because it is difficult to standardize them – unlike pork bellies in Chicago. But at least measurement seems to have some grounding in physical or other conventionally measurable properties of the objects in question. Measuring services and labor is a more complicated issue: Do we measure the effects or the labor inputs, the efforts? On the current level of generality, we can ignore the goods/services distinction and simply use the term commodities: all objects offered for sale.

In any case, in everyday economic life we seem to rely on money as a measurement device when we form or read prices by associating quantities of commodities and quantities of money. But does such association really mean that we 'measure' commodities with the help of money? A price expression, $p_i = xM$ (in words: the price of a unit of commodity i is x units of money) certainly looks like a measuring statement (for example, it has the same form as saying that the length l of object i is two meters: $l_i = 2m$). But how can we measure something with money if we do not know what money is and what we are measuring?[13]

2.3 Prices and the metric of money

> Money is the instrument of measuring the quantity of pain or pleasure.
>
> (Bentham 1952: 117)

> (F)or purposes of quantification and the attribution of causal efficacy, something must be treated as conserved. This is the role of the monetary unit in a market system…
>
> (Mirowski 1990: 711)

As we have seen, one of the reasons why money is not simply like language or simply a 'special language' is that money comes with a metric. Alfred Marshall started his *Principles* by highlighting the crucial role of the money metric for economic life and, thus, for economics as a science.

> Economics is a study of men as they live and move and think in the ordinary business of life … the steadiest motive to ordinary business work is the desire for the pay which is the material reward of work… the motive is

supplied by a definite amount of money: and it is this definite and exact money measurement of the steadiest motives in business life, which has enabled economics far to outrun every other branch of the study of men.

(Marshall [1890] 1966: 12)

The reasoning seems to be: If we can measure motives, we can explain the actions driven by those motives. Marshall believed that economics has an advantage over the other social sciences because it can rely on measurement of motives, not as performed by the observing scientist, but as taking place within the object of inquiry itself, 'in the ordinary business of life' that has somehow turned into 'business life'. The money metric can be taken as given.[14] Most of us work for money. Monetary returns for work efforts come in definite amounts. What Marshall seems to say is: The efforts we make to acquire a given amount of money are 'measured' by that amount of money, while the efforts in turn correspond to our motives, the intensity of our desires. So, indirectly, the intensity of our desires is measured by the amounts of money we are willing to spend to satisfy them.[15] It would be an interesting question for the history of economic thought why – if money is so important for the distinctive character of economics – it has nonetheless practically disappeared from the main body of economic theory. But this is not our concern here. The problem at hand is to describe more precisely the functioning of the money metric and to explain how spontaneous measurement – if this is what is actually happening – is possible in social life.

To at least get some idea of the social conditions for such a metric to develop, let us first take note of the embeddedness of monetary systems in other social practices that are conditions for the use of money. Second, the question is how a monetary metric can function given that the validity of money measures cannot be borrowed, as it were, from the validity of physical measurement. Third, we will see that monetary operations rest on assumptions of invariance that are precariously grounded.

2.3.1 *The embeddedness of monetary systems*

In an evolutionary perspective, anthropologist Helen Codere has described the interdependence of monetary systems and systems of counting, measuring and writing. She starts by discarding the idea that the physical properties of money objects have more than a supportive significance by pointing out that money is a symbol, a 'symbol of both past and future exchangeable goods' (Codere 1968: 559). This, as we have already seen, is a rather inappropriate notion of symbols, but we can let that be for the moment. The important argument she makes is that

money as a symbol can be integrated with other symbolic systems which are in logical developmental order – a number or counting system, an amounts, or weights and measures, system, and a system of writing and recording.

(Codere 1968: 561)

Before such integration only 'crude ratios and convertibilities are possible'. By contrast, a monetary system relies on a developed 'amounts system that makes ratios, calculations and convertibilities generally possible' (Codere 1968: 564f.). According to Codere, once a developed amounts system is complemented by a monetary system 'various multiples ... of the money stuff *symbolize* various multiples ... of all the goods' (ibid.). But money in definite amounts does not simply symbolize goods in definite amounts. That is a rather crude idea, as we have seen. However, someone who is mentally associating money units and amounts of goods is forming a price, albeit in a purely individual, subjective manner. Formally, prices result from a mapping of amounts of goods in amounts of money. Such a mapping can be performed by any individual. Substantially, price formation that leads to prices that can inform agents about market conditions and promising strategies presupposes market interaction: A multiple of agents with conflicting interests negotiate, find compromises, complete transactions in terms of effective prices. Given established markets, agents form prices by referring not only to the monetary unit – as a common, shared reference construct – in combination with a numeral system and an amounts system. They also observe the prices generated in transactions of buying and selling completed by others. As a result,

> we have an over-all money symbol system of such symbolic powers that its realisation or utilisation to even a limited degree taxes the capacities of the human mind beyond the holding powers of its memory and its computational powers.
>
> (Codere 1968: 564f.)

Therefore, the full use of the potential of an emerging monetary system requires writing. The more widespread the ability to keep records of inputs, of inventories, of past transactions in terms of money prices, the more markets are taken to a new level of importance. They become the foundation for economic rationalization. Transactions can be recorded and evaluated in forms of accounting. Using such recorded information, transactions can be integrated into strategies, so that agents can move beyond decisions according to customs or rule of thumb.

Codere's important general point is that money use and accounting evolve together once the required cognitive/intellectual capacities have formed. Only this co-evolution makes possible the rationalization effects attributed to modern market economies,[16] most prominently by Georg Simmel and Max Weber. As Codere sums up:

> It seems to make sense to regard money as an intellectual system, comparable to mathematics in its range of development from the most rudimentary calculations and systems to the most elegant and diversified refinements, and to see it as then necessarily related to every major aspect of the lives of the people who hold and apply their version of the concept. One would not

expect the people in a society in which householding was the unit of both production and distribution to have or to require any but the crudest symbology and calculus of exchangeable goods, while our contemporary mixed social, economic and political system exists through the continuous exchange of every imaginable kind of good and service and requires the technological and intellectual means of both adjusting and keeping its accounts and making economic decisions.

(Codere 1968: 574)

Codere's main point is clear: The significance and shape of monetary systems differ historically in line with the evolving cognitive capabilities of market participants. One implication of this observation is that it does not exactly further our understanding of money if, by using the same term, we lump together transactions that require highly sophisticated cognitive capacities and institutional back-up with transactions that hardly involve quantitative calculation and take place in the face-to-face relationships of small communities. Such lumping occurs, to take an important usage in the literature (Innes 1913, see Section 3.5), when the term 'credit' is applied to all transactions involving deferred delivery of a quid pro quo, whether we are talking about reciprocal relations between neighbors in a rural community or bills of exchange circulating as promises to pay among overseas traders or contemporary central bank money.

2.3.2 Measuring with money?

According to traditional economic thought, one of the functions of money is to serve as a measure of 'value'. Evidently, the idea is that money is – among other things – an instrument of measurement of a property of goods or services called 'value'. Naturally, the next question is: What is 'value'? As I pointed out above I have become convinced that the reference to 'value' in economic theory is mostly misleading or redundant. Instead of getting involved in disputes about 'value', there should be a twofold question with respect to money, not only the traditional question of value theory: What do we measure? But also the complementary question: What do we measure with? An old suspicion, derived from observing measurement in everyday life and in the natural sciences, has it that the two questions are connected: With respect to the physical world, theories of measurement (Pfanzagl 1971; Ruben 1979) clearly postulate that the object to be measured and the object with which we measure have to share the property to be measured (mass, length, energy …).[17] *Why* we measure seems to be self-evident: In order to represent, communicate about, and handle defined objects in a coordinated way we need to establish a way of precisely comparing them. Measuring is a form of comparing and establishing identities. It starts from defining an underlying unit and thus a criterion for equivalence:[18] Say, the meter is the unit, then all objects that are x meters long are equivalent in terms of length. If I want to build a table, I want to make sure that its legs have the same length. If I collaborate with somebody else, we want standardization of the means of measurement in order to communicate effectively about quantities. So behind all this is (also) a social need: Robinson can measure length with his own left foot, but as soon as he communicates about length with Friday, they need to agree whether Friday's or Robinson's foot should serve as the standard. Standardization means that participants in communication refer to the same reference object when measuring, so they have to agree on such a common reference object. Usually, a standard is sooner or later established under the auspices of an authority. It can produce a prototype of the basic unit and proceed to distribute copies of it to users or certify the validity of the copies in use in its domain.

To return to money: Assume that money is a means of measurement. What is measured? If we extend the argument from measuring physical objects to measuring with money, that question means: What is the property that money shares with the objects whose prices are expressed as the results of measurement?

Traditional answers refer to forms of commodity money, where money objects share the property of having 'value' with the commodities whose value is to be measured. So, given a quantity of gold defined as the monetary unit – or representing the unit in coined form –, a money price measures the 'value' of a commodity by relating it to a quantity of gold. If we leave out the reference to 'value' we can simply say: The price of a commodity states the numbers of units of money demanded or offered to gain ownership of the commodity. The numbers of units of money can be translated into a quantity of gold, if a nation state, as was historically the case under the gold standard, officially defines the respective monetary unit in terms of a quantity of gold. Thus, prices expressed in such a monetary unit implicitly relate quantities of commodities to quantities of gold – and via gold to each other. The meaning of the relation seems to be: Whether you have so much of the commodity or so much money, given the price and given the official definition of the monetary unit, the two quantities are equivalent. They should be exchangeable backwards and forwards *al gusto* in the market[19] – at least as long as transaction costs are negligible.

Much of this story is of course merely part of the ideological superstructure of monetary systems. That there is an official definition of the monetary unit in terms of gold or silver does not necessarily mean that the circulating currency corresponds to that definition or is convertible into the respective amounts of gold or silver on demand. The practical links between circulating money objects and the definition of the monetary unit in precious metal quantities differ. They have attenuated over time. According to one version of the history of money, we have moved from – presumably – gold or silver quantities defined as the monetary unit and used in the form of coins to more devious links between money and precious metals, first on the level of nation states, then, internationally, for example, in the Bretton Woods[20] currency system. Since that system was abolished, currency units seem to have lost any tangible anchor in the world of 'crude facts', be they precious metals or Louisiana land or cows. What Schumpeter called the 'golden brake on the credit machine' has disappeared. We have to see later on whether or how it was replaced by some functional equivalent.

In any case, once that last link of central bank monies to gold had been severed, as happened in the early 1970s, the answers to the question of what money is measuring had to be modified. If the monetary unit is no longer defined by relating it to something other than other monetary units or to commodities in general according to a price index expressing something like general purchasing power, what is the property that money shares with the objects 'measured' in terms of prices? It would be in vain to look for such a common property in physical terms. Rather, such a property can only be a result of our doings, of a social assignment of function, to use Searle's term.

Of course, one common property is that both commodities and money are there *for* exchange. If money is a tool for extracting commodities from the ownership of others, commodities in turn are tools for extracting money from the ownership of others. But such symmetry seems to be precarious and it rather deepens the mystery of money. Why do we trade commodities that can be used *outside* of exchange, in consumption or production, for money that can only be used as a tool *in* exchange?[21] At least part of the answer must be: because money is the universal entrance key to the whole world of commodities, whereas any particular commodity is just that: a particular commodity. It may or may not be transformable into money according to an expected price. To be sure, a particular commodity will have a more general significance whenever it is placed and ranked in the collection of things available for consumption by any participant in an economy. But such a classification remains an individual affair whose social significance is not self-evident, whereas exchange is all about social relations.

Return to the measurement issue. When we form prices in terms of contemporary central bank money, do we *measure* some property of commodities in any sense?[22] Or, if we are not exactly 'measuring', what are we doing when we form prices? We have already seen that prices, to start with, are mental associations of quantities of commodities with quantities of money. Mathematically speaking, we 'map' elements of the set of commodities, the objects populating the n-dimensional commodity space, into the one dimension of money. The metric of money allows us to create a world of pairs, so and so much of each of the heterogeneous commodities (in terms of their units and multiples thereof) are associated with so and so much money. The operation lets us treat heterogeneous economic objects as 'commensurable',[23] so we can, at least, act 'as if' they had a common measure. More money for this, less money for that. Add what you paid for this to what you paid for that and compare the sum to your budget, and so on. But if all that is to make sense, prices as the associations between money and commodities have to be formed according to rules. There has to be some order in price formation. What are the rules we are following when we do such 'mapping'?

To understand these rules, we have to go back to objectives. What do we, as players of the money game, want when we form prices? To stay with the simplest case: First of all, we want to communicate our intentions to buy or sell. In buying and selling, we do not just want the change of form: You get the money, I get the commodity, or *vice versa*. Rather, we want to maximize the returns from the intended transaction or, at least, we want a fair deal. If I am the buyer and you are the seller and we are in serious business, I will offer the lowest price that still promises a positive response from you and you will ask the highest price that still promises a positive response from me. In addition, we both know that the other is following this rule. Thus, the price proposals we start with cannot have anything to do with measurement. Each agent expresses intentions in quantitative terms, as more or less money to be paid. These first price proposals are merely introductions to open the way for further communication. Although our proposals as buyer and seller are likely to differ, we are both talking the same 'language' – as long we are referring to the same currency. With the help of that language, we can negotiate. I may offer more, you may demand less. We may eventually arrive at an agreement by bringing our initially divergent price proposals into line. If we close a deal and money objects and commodities change hands, we create an effective price. If we consider, as we are doing here, price formation as a form of measurement, the difference between prices as offers and bids and an effective price is that the former may be the result of individual spontaneity or subject to strategic distortion, whereas the latter, the effective price, involves an inter-subjective agreement between at least two agents with opposing interests. There is 'unanimity without conformity', as Milton Friedman put it. That is not much, but since we are talking about a mode of 'measuring' social facts in the social world, it is a beginning. The only way to increase the validity of such measurements is to get more and more agents – with opposing interests as buyers and sellers – to agree on such a price and to accept it as a premise of their own activities.[24] We can imagine unrealistic perfection in that sense: If the 'law of one price' were to rule, we would have valid measurement in the sense of a complete inter-subjective agreement on the 'weight' of a given kind of commodity in monetary exchange. What does all this contribute to understanding money?

First, again, does it make sense to view the use of money as involving *measurement*? The traditional semantics of money simply assumes that it does.[25] Economic texts are full of references to money as a measure of value, or, outwardly more modest, as a means of accounting, or unit of account. Intuitively, it seems that we can accept the semantics of measurement to describe the uses of money – but with the proviso that we may have no idea of what is being measured when we form prices.[26] Staying in touch with everyday experience suggests, for a start: We measure the salability of economic objects, thereby classifying and ranking them according to quantity in the world of buying and selling or in other more complicated transactions of property transfer. Measurement results in price expressions of the form: one pound of flour costs, or can be sold for, seventy cents. Insofar as prices are effective and stable, this would mean that one pound of flour is in the same equivalence class with all other things costing seventy cents. But even if we insist on reading prices as measurements, we should also admit that they are not just given and uniform. They cannot be objective facts resulting from objective measurement procedures as in the physical realm. Rather, prices are *made* by different players in different circumstances and will vary accordingly. They may be announced as uninformed conjectures, as results of momentary individual whims.

Or they may be prices determined by political fiat, or prices fixed in organized markets, functioning as benchmarks for trades on a given trading day. In short, if we want to consider prices as statements of measurement, we have to concede that the quality of such measurements can vary. They have greatly differing social validity or significance. But before we therefore discard the whole notion of measuring with money, we have to examine whether practical procedures for forming prices reduce arbitrariness and exclude subjective whims to an extent that establishes a modicum of inter-subjective agreement.

One possibility is that, in price formation, we follow rules just as we follow rules when we measure weight. However, given that price formation takes place in settings of opposed interests, where normally buyers want to pay as little as possible and sellers want to earn as much as possible, it is unlikely that a rule analogous to those guaranteeing the objectivity of measurement of physical properties, like weight or speed, will be voluntarily observed.

According to economic theory, the more important possibility to achieve order in price formation is not primarily due to agents following rules – whether internalized or imposed by authority – but due to their being subjected to the constraints generated by competition. Once more assuming imaginary Walrasian perfection, perfect competition would stick everybody into the cage of a 'single-exit situation' (Latsis 1972). The exit opens only when all agents accept prices as given and adapt to them by variations in the commodity quantities offered and demanded until market-clearing prices are found. They signal a new social quality: equilibrium. However, if everybody just adapts, nobody is left to observe excess demands and change prices accordingly, resulting in the paradox that 'competitive equilibrium involves no interplay between the competitors' (Shapley and Shubik 1963). 'Situational determinism' (Latsis 1972) does not work, as the need to introduce the Walrasian auctioneer as a fictitious super-agent indicates. Moving away from such imagined perfection, we can nonetheless observe markets where prices mostly do have a parametric function and changes are slow and incremental. The observable inter-subjective agreement, the outcome of 'measuring' with money, is implicit. Most of us as buyers of everyday consumption goods simply accept observed prices in most transactions. We look for the best offer. We not only refer to these prices in immediate decisions to buy and sell, but also as the foundation on which we build our records, calculations and market strategies. In other words, we frequently plan all sorts of transactions starting from prices that we passively 'read' in our economic environment. Normally, we do not bother to find out how these prices were formed. We react to these prices as if they transported some socially valid information. This is reasonable under two conditions. First, we need to assume that prices are proposed by sellers observing each other and competing for buyers. Second, we need to assume, as the background of price formation, that the 'measuring rod of money' is stable.[27] Given how much of our economic fate does depend on correct price estimates or information this dual foundation for making our economic decisions and forming our strategies as buyers appears to be precariously fragile. We are skating on thin ice here.[28]

2.3.3 A monetary invariant?

The foundation looks even more fragile if we do not just consider price formation using a *given* monetary unit but also take into account variations in the purchasing power of the monetary unit. Wittgenstein once noted: 'The procedure of putting a lump of cheese on a balance and fixing the price according by the turn of the scale would lose its point if it frequently happened for such lumps to suddenly grow or shrink for no obvious reason' (PI 142). We can adapt and repeat this observation with regard to the balance: If the same piece of cheese arbitrarily weighed more or less now and then, the balance would not be a useful instrument of measurement. Can something analogous happen with money? Or are we able to construct something like a monetary invariant,[29] so that at least our means of measurement is reliable?

The long run historical record suggests no such reliability. When we observe price changes, we cannot immediately see whether the changes are due to the commodity or the money side of price expressions. But in the history of money, frequent debasements of coins or other 'currency reforms' are clear cases of authorities manipulating monetary systems, mostly for some exploitative, redistributive purposes, but with the collateral damage of destroying the fragile measuring function of money. Typically, the name of the monetary unit is kept, but its former association with a defined physical object, an amount of precious metal, is loosened, whether by authority or by forgers. The effect is that the same (nominal) price expression: $p_i = aM$, means something different as M, the monetary unit, has been redefined. It is as if, by decree, what we call 1 meter was changed to a length of 98 cm. After that, if we re-measure using the new standard, all mountains or buildings will be a little higher. To analyze such experience, economists have introduced the distinction between 'real' and 'nominal' magnitudes (Arrow 1981). Starting with early versions of the quantity theory (Hume 1752), it was proposed that, after a transition period, the effects of manipulating the monetary unit on the price level would be analogous to those of changing other measuring units: Debasing the circulating currency pushes up the general price level, but the change is merely 'nominal', just as the 'real' height of mountains does not change, whether we measure them in feet or meters or other units. Rational agents will take account of the difference between the nominal and the real magnitudes in their calculations, thus freeing themselves from 'money illusion'. However, from early on, there have been complaints about what is happening in the transition period:

> Once again, it is a great nuisance and … despicable for the prince to never hold the money of the domain at the same level, but to change it from day to day: more in this place than in that at the same time. So one does not know during these shifting times and changes, how much this or that coin is worth and whether one should buy commodities or sell or spend money or change the price, which is against its nature. Thus, there is no certainty

with respect to the one thing about which one should be entirely certain, but rather greater and most general confusion, to the bad repute of the prince.

(Oresme [1356] 1999: 47f., my transl, HG))

Money loses its measuring function and, consequently, prices lose their orientation function.

Now, if we turn to modern monetary systems, can the analogy between physical measuring units and monetary units still hold? Monetary units are no longer defined in terms of quantities of gold or silver. A dollar is a dollar is a dollar. Beyond the green piece of paper, there is no tangible, specified reference object signifying the meaning of a dollar anymore. To be sure, dollars themselves have a price. They can be bought and sold on foreign exchange markets. Or, I can 'buy' the use of your dollar: You lend it to me and I pay it back with interest. Also, we can measure its purchasing power in terms of index numbers based on the price changes of bundles of commodities. But we do not have a simple way of observing changes of the meaning of a dollar as a measuring device, as the unit of account. There is no longer a legally fixed, much less a practically realized[30] relation of the monetary unit to an external object, like 1/x ounces of gold; a relation that – when in doubt – can be practically tested by trying to convert the paper into gold. Now, variations on the monetary side of transactions can be monitored only by constructing price indices. These are mostly taken at face value. The statistical exercises required for their construction are normally not known by market participants. As such, we rely on information transmitted through price variations and estimate their significance for our own economic activities by relating them to changes in our income and wealth. Purchasing power estimates arrived in this way may differ quite substantially from official data on changes in the general price level or rates of inflation.

In sum, how does 'measurement' with money differ from measuring elements of the physical world? With money, both the objects measured and the means of measurement belong to the social world.[31] There is no inherent physical quality (or bundle of such) in commodities whose variation would automatically lead to higher or lower prices. *A fortiori*, a parallel proposition holds for modern money. 'Measuring' with money is an activity relying on a more or less precarious social construction. The qualities measured are observer relative, not only in the sense captured by marginal utility theory. A price can be translated into a statement like 'X counts as aM in C', where 'counts as' means: 'is exchangeable for' when things get serious. A price, $p_i = aM$, looks like a measurement statement, but can be proposed by an individual, can be disputed by another, can be consensual after bargaining, can be observed as the result of a completed transaction once X has changed ownership from A_i to A_j, while aM has gone the opposite way. A price can be declared fixed on a market as the result of many such transactions. A price change may be a reaction to all sorts of events, both on the side of money and on the side of goods.

Ultimately, only effective prices, in which potential changes on both the commodity and the money side of transactions are 'frozen' for the moment, can serve as guidelines for actions. When trading in a given market stops, say in the market for securitized subprime mortgages, the result is uncertainty.

Money 'measurement' in the sense of forming such effective prices is crucial not just because it imposes an observable social order on the commodity world. It also generates reasons for action. Everybody can read a price: the observed 'weight' of a commodity in exchange is comparable to that of all other commodities insofar as they also have effective prices. The same price for different amounts of different commodities signals: In the social context of the market, these things are currently equivalent, indistinguishable in terms of exchangeability. Each player can relate this equivalence in exchange signaled by prices to her individual objectives. For example, if I prefer good A to good X and I observe that p_A is equal to p_x, I have a reason to sell X and buy A, and so on.

To conclude, first, there is no way in which we can understand these – somewhat inaptly named – acts of measurement and the ensuing transactions by moving outside the social world, by searching for reductions to physical or, for that matter, psychological dimensions of what is going on. Natural or individual psychological factors will play a role as variations of context C (a glass of water in the desert …) or in qualities of X (gold of fineness …) and as such they may influence prices. To speak of measurement with money makes sense at best for completed[32] transactions, most commonly transactions involving effective changes of ownership. Both the transactions and the measurement are social processes. Because social processes are inevitably[33] associated with uncertainty, they may include attempts to somehow anchor them in the physical world, as the role of precious metals in monetary history and monetary crises demonstrates. Such anchoring seemed to promise stability – but what about fluctuating gold or silver prices? – as a reward for moving money as a measurement device outside the realm of manipulability.

Second, there are different degrees of validity of price measurements in terms of who and how many agree where on what. For example, despite the way in which fixed prices are quoted in the media, has there been a universal consensus that an ounce of gold of quality z could be bought for $1 on 5 January, 2007? No. The law of one price does not rule; nonetheless there may be asymptotic movements towards uniform world market prices. There are myriads of relatively independent one-on-one transactions generating effective prices, but they become more observable in more organized, more tightly linked, even global markets. The farther the informational reach of markets the more the prices generated will be interdependent and the more they may have a binding effect for observing traders.

Third, as to the reliability of measurement, despite the repeated attempts to anchor money as a means of measurement in the physical world, there is no such thing as a monetary invariant, so measuring with money is an 'as if'-exercise. Variations in the purchasing power of money do occur all the time. We use statistical artifacts to express such variations in a summary way. They occur in myriads of transactions, but are reported in such single numbers like the rate of inflation. We use such numbers to make decisions. That can only be a pragmatically tolerable way to act as long as changes in the purchasing power of money tend to happen in a somewhat orderly, expectable fashion, as they do most of the time. Otherwise monetary systems could not function, as Nicolas d'Oresme already pointed out in the fourteenth century. When the prince manipulates money, the effect is a general loss of 'certainty with respect to the one thing about which one should be entirely certain …'. Although Oresme was a bishop, that 'one thing about which one should be entirely certain' was not God, but money.

2.4 Money as things vs. money as pure information

As can be observed in any supermarket, contemporary money comes in many forms: cash, 'plastic', checks are used as means of payment and the differences between them do not seem to matter. That more and more payments are accomplished without the use of cash, of tangible money objects like coins or central bank bills, has led to the belief that cash – if not money as such – is about to disappear. There are people who will tell you with a certain pride that they are not touching the stuff anymore. As we all know: *pecunia non olet*, money does not stink. So what are the reasons for such pride? Is it really more convenient to pay a taxi with a credit card than with cash? More secure? More reliable? More up to date?

More seriously, there is a growing conviction that 'money is independent of the means whereby it is represented, taking the form of pure information' (Giddens 1990: 25). Searle has recently pointed to a difficulty in his earlier frequent use of money as an example of a physical fact, the green piece of paper, being the carrier of an institutional fact, the dollar bill, according to his 'X counts as Y in C' formula. Searle explains that he was 'operating on the assumption that currency was somehow or other essential to the existence of money', but he no longer thinks so:

> You can easily imagine a society that has money without having any currency at all. And indeed, we seem to be evolving in something like this direction with the use of debit cards. All you need to have (as) money is a system of recorded numerical values whereby each person (or corporation, organization, etc.) has assigned to him or her or it a numerical figure which shows at any given point the amount of money they have. They can then use this money to buy things by altering their numerical value in favor of the seller, whereby they lower their numerical value, and the seller acquires a higher numerical value. [In short,] currency is not essential to the existence or functioning of money.
>
> (Searle 2005: 19f.)

Even hard-core monetary theorists who start by describing the economy in physical terms alone arrive at propositions like: 'Money is memory' (Kocherlakota

1998). More exactly, Kocherlakota tries to show that money, in the form of tangible money objects, is functionally equivalent to a sort of public record-keeping institution. There, as in Searle's cashless world,

> an imaginary balance sheet is kept for each agent. When an individual gives consumption to someone else, his balance rises, and his capacity for receiving future transfers goes up. When he gets consumption from someone else, his balance falls, and his capacity for receiving future transfers declines.
>
> (Kocherlakota 1998: 233)

The conclusion is that in the world we actually live in, 'money is merely a physical way of maintaining this balance sheet' (Kocherlakota 1998: 233).

More empirically bent writers have examined the experiences with innovations like 'electronic cash' or EFTPOS ('electronic fund transfers at the point of sale'). But the story is the same:

> Indeed, it is possible to imagine a world in which there is no need for any specific medium of exchange, but the means of payment is provided by bookkeeping entries that track changes in ownership of financial assets arising from economic trades. If, for example, agent A purchases an item from agent B, this transaction can be settled by a cheque or EFTPOS instruction subtracting the item's price from A's bank balance and crediting it to B's account, without the need for any medium of exchange.
>
> (Dalziel 2000: 381)

All three writers ask us to 'imagine' a world slightly different from the one we experience in our daily use of money in order to argue that cash is not a necessary ingredient of a monetary economy. To use a bit of imagination is a welcome theoretical device, but is money in the form of tangible cash really just a functional equivalent for 'a (typically imperfect) form of memory' (Kocherlakota 1998: 233)? Isn't the role of money somewhat broader? What are the conditions for replacing these old-fashioned, circulating, tangible money objects by social bookkeeping arrangements?

2.4.1 *Money and budget constraints*

A link between the 'money as pure information' argument and the proposition that money no longer has to take the form of tangible money objects is suggested in Niehans' theory of money:

> Exchange is a way to make sure that nobody can escape his budget constraint(s). If one could be perfectly certain that everybody always stays within his budget constraint, everybody could be allowed to obtain goods without a specific *quid pro quo*.
>
> (Niehans 1978: 62f.)

In other words, monetary exchange using cash, along with barter, solves a problem that any economy beyond the household of an isolated Crusoe has to solve: People have to be prevented to spend more than they earn or own as wealth. One way to describe the problem is to imagine the set of all commodities as a common pool of resources. As a general rule, based on norms of justice, nobody should take out more than he or she contributes without the consent of the others. To solve the problem, the first thing needed is an accounting system that defines equivalence relations over the set of all commodities. Otherwise, if we want to be sure about everybody respecting budget constraints, a player who delivered corn to the pool could only take out corn, since all we know is that 1 lb of corn is equal to 1 lb of corn.[34] In order for the corn producer to take out meat, there has to be a commonly accepted corn/meat transformation ratio. If there are n different commodities, we need to define $1/2n(n-1)$ such transformation ratios.

The question then is: Who is to define these ratios? Can a consensus be reached on all of them? Instead of bothering with determining a set of consistent and universally accepted exchange ratios, for example, by installing a planning authority à la Lange or by applying linear programming to the overall reproduction problem of the economy, a market system provides a decentralized solution: Ownership rights are distributed over the set of all commodities. If they are respected – and, ultimately, we need the state to ensure that – access to any commodity one does *not* own is subject to the consent of the owner. The owner can refuse access by others, demand a *quid pro quo*, or whatever. With each access through barter, a single, more or less arbitrary transformation ratio is defined as a by-product. We can leave open here whether it has any significance beyond the individual transaction in which it was generated. However it is defined, as long as all transactions are spot transactions, all players must stay within their budget constraints, as Niehans stressed. All transactions are subject to a local constant sum condition: if x_a, x_b are the commodity bundles owned by A and B before exchange and x_a', x_b' are the respective commodity bundles after exchange, $\{x_a, x_b\} = \{x_a', x_b'\}$.

Does having to pay cash do the same job? Evidently, to guarantee the respect for budget constraints, the access to money objects has to be governed by the same restrictive ownership rules as the access to commodities. Given that, each transaction now generates a price instead of barter ratios. Money becomes not only the *tertium comparationis* in all transactions, but also the tool that allows a buyer to remove something from the ownership of the seller. Observations and comparisons of transactions and communication about them are enormously simplified.[35]

Thus, apart from such simplification, the reason why tangible money objects have been used in most everyday transactions until the recent spreading of credit and debit cards and electronic account keeping could indeed have been: Cash on the spot ensures that buyers stay within their budget constraints. However, there is a question we have to ask Niehans: While an economic system would be easily ruined if nobody had to worry about budget constraints and everybody could shop on credit all the time, this is not a worry for individual agents. All they have to worry about is to get something worthwhile in return for what they trade away. So with money, they have to check whether the money objects they accept are valid, not whether the buyer has not respected his budget constraint, has borrowed, stolen, found money on the street or whatever.

But there is no reason why there should not be other means to accomplish budget discipline. The problem of preventing people spending more than they have can be solved without the use of money objects as tangible things. In an appropriate institutional setting pure 'book money' is sufficient. If a device can link buyers and sellers to an information system so that monetary income and expenditure streams between them are recorded by a neutral third party, everybody can pay with a debit card,[36] for example. Access to accounts is controlled and spending is possible only as long as one has a positive balance. Payment promises by the buyer can be fulfilled on the spot. Thus, modern information and communication technologies provide functional equivalents for using tangible money objects: Both ensure the imposition of budget constraints.

In contrast to the huge techno-institutional back-up required for modern payment systems, using tangible objects as money is a very simple or even primitive functional equivalent. With cash, the worry whether others are respecting budget constraints cannot even arise. Incidentally, such a worry can only plague ordinary private traders if they are asked to accept a promise to pay instead of a spot payment. When receiving cash, there is no reason why the seller of a commodity should worry about the future payment capability of the buyer. Once the commodity and the money have changed hands, the relationship between seller and buyer is finished. The social relation involved in the transaction is an ephemeral (as Max Weber put it) two-player affair. Although the use of money always implies the intrusion of a larger social context into such a two-player setting, this intrusion is rather limited when cash is used. The money object must be recognized as such by the respective currency 'community' and it must have come from someone else – it is unlikely to be recognized as money if it is home-made – and it will be moving on to third players in the future. But circulating money objects used in spot transactions connect players only in a loose, short-term way. What happened in the *past*, how the buyer got his money, does not matter for the seller: *pecunia non olet*. Once a transaction is completed, rationality dictates to 'let bygones be bygones'. What the seller will do in the *future* with the newly acquired money, does not matter to the buyer, either. With respect to a potentially intrusive social environment, the terms of a cash transaction are not controlled or controllable from the outside and they cannot be so controlled retrospectively: 'cash leaves no paper trail' (Shubik 1999, I: 236).

Such a loose social network – established by money as cash circulating from a buyer to a seller who turns into a buyer and meets the next seller, and so on – is insufficient to support the use of credit instruments. By contrast, cashless monetary transactions are possible only if they leave a paper trail. There has to be some background agency keeping the accounts and assuming controlling and mediating functions. In addition, as soon as credit is involved, there has to be a second order institutional background generating and regulating reactions to defaults, bankruptcies, broken promises to pay. To compensate for the loosening of budget constraints through credit, the communication network of the 'cashless credit' economy has to be much tighter than the cash network. Or, to put it into the language of search models: If there is a range between no monitoring and perfect monitoring, credit relations are located closer to the perfect monitoring end, whereas cash transactions are close to the no monitoring end.

2.4.2 Limits to money becoming pure information

To see why the trend toward money as 'pure information' rests on the evolution of an adequate institutional back-up, compare the money game to chess: Before the age of the personal computer, one normally learned to play chess by using a board and tangible chess pieces – and a tutor. More accomplished players then learn to read the diagrams depicting a situation in a game and the notation used to keep records of games: d2–d4, d7–d5, and so on. Reiterating such abstraction from chess pieces as tangible objects, some advanced players develop the ability to play whole games by simply announcing their moves and keeping track of the game in their memory. Except for the minimal reliance on physical facts – using brain-cells to memorize previous moves and voices to produce sounds, etc. – two such players can indeed reduce the game to the 'form of pure information' (Giddens 1990).

Is this a learning sequence similar to the development of monetary systems? You start playing with board and tangible pieces, you move on to using paper and keeping records and you may end up announcing moves and using memory – without any 'embodiment' except some traces in the mysterious brain? Interestingly, in chess that last stage not only demands considerable mental skills, but two people can play in that way only as long as there is no dispute. If White says 'check' to the Black King on f7 and Black says: 'But my king is on f6', it is difficult to imagine how these two players can continue the game. They might do so if they can reconstruct every move and agree on where the virtual black king 'really' is, but it is more likely that they stop playing and start swearing. It is difficult for them to distinguish between error and fraud by the other player. Written records would help, but only if each move is recorded at the time it is made and the record cannot be manipulated afterwards. Only records written by a third, neutral person to whom the players announce their moves are a sure means to avoid all such difficulties. In other words, blind chess is a sustainable activity only if, or as long as, players trust each other or if a third party records the moves made.

Now, imagine two traders[37] frequently buying from and selling to each other. Like the chess players, they could rely on their memories and perhaps meet once a week to check whether they both arrive at the same balance. Then, they could again trade in the next week, starting from that balance. This can go on and on as long as their claims for delivery and payment roughly cancel each other out over time. Not only is there no need for cash to change hands, there is not even a need for written records. As in playing 'blind' chess, this can work as long as there is no dispute. A slight difference may be noted: If both traders do not announce the balance simultaneously, some additional trust is required. Let A_1 announce the balance first. A_2 has calculated a different one, but A_1's balance is more favorable for A_2. Then A_2 may correct A_1's error or may exploit the opportunity and make a gain by simply announcing the same balance as A_1. There are several ways to avoid such a risk and to settle disputes in general. First, you can select your trading partners according to their reputation for honesty.[38] Second, in case of a discrepancy, the traders can go through their transactions together step by step, identify the one on which they disagree and try to settle their dispute and find the correct balance. Third, if they cannot trust each other, they can use written records of transactions that cannot be altered but can be examined *post factum* by both. Fourth, they can use a third neutral agent to record their transactions as they take place and to keep the accounts.

What does this analogy between chess and trade tell us about the need for cash, for tangible money objects? As long as there is no dispute, memory can do the work of cash flows. But one has to keep in mind that memory is something distributed among players with divergent, opposing interests. Disputes are likely. To avoid or resolve them, a third agent is required, either the 'public' or a trusted neutral third agent who can keep records and do accounts. Then, memory as record keeping can do the work of cash flows. Money is still required for price formation and accounting, but only on the level of mental representations that can be communicated in the language of prices and recorded in writing. No tangible money objects have to be present or change hands. There may be a point where cash may still enter the game: If there is a prolonged, sizeable imbalance in transactions, one of the traders looks more and more like a pure debtor and the other like a pure creditor. The latter may demand at some point that the imbalance be corrected: Pay up. Settlement will also be demanded if one of the traders wants to discontinue the relationship.[39]

In sum, cash can be replaced by records of transactions, preferably written by a neutral third party. Cash will still be needed if balances have to be settled.

One effect of replacing cash by monitoring and keeping accounts is a considerable, if unacknowledged tightening of the social network of money users. The implication of the 'money is memory' argument is extreme in that respect: If all actions were perfectly monitored by Big Brother and the records were publicly accessible so that everybody could know on demand what everybody else had ever done, there would be no need for circulating money as a means for enforcing budget constraints. But there would be a steeply increased interdependence of transactions. Instead of acting on vague notions of the state of the world and hunches of where it is going, it is assumed that players could and would act on the tremendous amount of information collected. By contrast, tangible money objects are needed only in contexts of 'imperfect monitoring'.[40] By showing cash, a buyer can demonstrate on demand that the claim he makes on resources is valid: Excluding force, fraud and forgery, holding money is proof that he has done something that was worthwhile to be paid for by at least one holder of money. So if a buyer has earned enough cash earlier to pay the price agreed upon in the transaction now, business can go on with very limited knowledge.[41] The seller does not have to know or trust the buyer, all he needs to know or trust is the buyer's money.

2.4.3 Money, common knowledge and conflicts of interest as foundations of price formation

Neil Wallace has plausibly argued that an adequate theory of money has to demonstrate that money is 'essential'. To see whether money is essential in a given model, he suggests to construct a parallel model that includes 'an intangible state variable' as a functional equivalent for money. If such a functional equivalent exists, then money is not essential. This led Wallace to the proposition that money is essential in a context of 'imperfect monitoring'.

> To emphasize the role played ... by perfect monitoring, consider its polar opposite: no monitoring in the sense that each person's previous actions are private information to the person. If so, then a person could misrepresent to any extent his or her assigned value of any intangible state variable. In other words, if there is no monitoring, then to have an intangible state variable play the role of money would require that any possible misrepresentation of the intangible state variable is also possible for holdings of money. However, misrepresentation of holdings of a tangible object is limited by the possibility that others can at least say 'show me'.
>
> (Wallace 2001: 850)

Thus, the use of money in the form of tangible objects suggests that not all actions are perfectly monitored and everybody does not know what everybody else had ever done, because in a perfectly monitored economy there would be no need for money. The argument is analogous to Kocherlakota's proposition that money is memory. According to both arguments money in the form of tangible objects is needed to show that the claim one makes on resources held by others is legitimate because one has provided a corresponding service or produced a good for somebody else before. One can hold money as part of the initial endowment, but beyond that my holding money is proof that I already have done something worthwhile for some member of the community of money users. I have contributed to the basket of goods or the stream of services, therefore I can now legitimately demand a corresponding share of the total available resources. It seems that perfect memory and perfect monitoring lead to the same result: common knowledge. So the Wallace–Kocherlakota hypothesis is: If it were common knowledge – knowledge shared by all the players involved – that a player has done something worthwhile in the past, that player would not have to rely on money now.

However, this argument ignores the essential function of money as a means of decentralized price-setting. The general knowledge that I have performed a haircut for agent *B* does not imply that everybody agrees on how relevant my contribution was. I will be able to forward my claim to a share of the available resources corresponding to my service only if agent *B* rewarded me either with a generally accepted means of exchange or if agent *B* registered such willingness to pay a definite amount with a bank that adjusted our accounts accordingly. The alternative could be a board supervising all transactions and acknowledging the size of my contribution in terms of a generally applicable unit of account. But how can the board arrive at generally acceptable evaluations? By contrast, in a decentralized monetary economy, the fact that agent *B* pays me a definite amount of money signals simply that I have found *one* person willing to make a quantitatively determinate sacrifice for my service. Note that nobody else will have to agree that the price agent *B* paid for my service was appropriate. Once I have received the money, I can turn around and buy something else, selecting from the set of sellers in the market. My *individual*, particular contribution to the presumed well-being of another agent has been transformed into *general* purchasing power. The price I pay with it in turn is subject to a separate agreement to be reached *now* between myself and agent *C*, the seller of the commodity I want to buy. So there are two transactions, one past, one present.[42] I form a link between them as the holder of a definite amount of money, but the former transaction does not determine, it only constrains the latter. Both transactions result in prices, but the determination of those prices is, in principle, taking place on the spot, one in the past, one now. The 'perfect monitoring' or 'money is memory' argument cannot say explicitly why perfect information about past transactions should be relevant for current or future price formation except as a constraint on the ability to pay of a potential buyer. But prices are frequently assumed to be fixed, given and stable – they are equilibrium prices holding for sequences in the whole period considered. Thus, underlying the 'money-is-memory' argument is an assumption of equilibrium. This rules out a theory of money in which money is used to *form* prices in decentralized transactions. Why? Because if agents move in a world of equilibrium prices over time, they know exactly what they can buy at t_1 with the money (held and) received at t_0. By contrast, the story should be merely one of transmitting budget constraints, not one of quantity adjustments in view of given prices. If I receive money in an arbitrary transaction at t_0, the amount received limits my potential to buy at t_1. But within these limits (abstracting from credit at this point), I can buy and I can bargain about the price to pay.

To illustrate, think of Neil Wallace's story of Ellen and the hairdresser. Ellen wants a haircut and has a lecture in economics to offer in exchange. Ellen runs into the standard difficulty of barter, the absence of a double coincidence of wants. As we know, it can be overcome by using money, by splitting the transaction and expanding the game to include more players: Ellen sells her lecture to the university for money. Ellen uses money to buy a haircut. The hairdresser can use the money in turn to buy whatever is in the attainable price range. Wallace argues that such a use of tangible money would be redundant if there was perfect monitoring:

If everyone knows whether or not the hairdresser provides a service to Ellen, then the hairdresser can be rewarded or punished in the future depending on whether or not the service was provided. The role of tangible money is to provide this evidence. Hence, with perfect monitoring, tangible money is not needed. The result fits well with the somewhat commonplace notion that strangers use money, but that people who know each other well often accomplish trades without using money.

(Wallace 2000: 851)

What Wallace appears to overlook: The hairdresser has provided a service to Ellen, but third persons do not have to agree on the value of that service. So the hairdresser – simply by providing the service to agent A – cannot make a quantitatively determined claim on rewards by agents C, D .... In a self-regulating market economy, price formation can take place in each transaction. Whatever the deal between Ellen and the hairdresser, it is their private affair. Without money, they can generate a haircut-for-economics-lecture barter ratio, if the hairdresser is willing to be lectured. With money, they can agree on the price Ellen will have to pay for the service. The hairdresser as a money-holder can then go on to buy other goods and services, searching agreements with sellers and purchasing within the limits of his budget constraint. But he could make definite claims on resources held by others only if there was a fixed, known, accepted and therefore stable set of exchange ratios of haircuts vs. everything else or a corresponding set of fixed prices in money terms. In other words, by assuming that the mere common knowledge of a service performed is a functional equivalent of money, Wallace ignores the role of money in splitting up transactions and allowing for independent, decentralized price formation among pairs of buyers and sellers.

To put it a little differently: Given the likelihood of a divergence between particular and general evaluations and the standard conflict of interest between buyers and sellers, namely, to buy cheaply and to sell dearly, only the hairdresser himself can accept Ellen's economics lecture as a direct quid pro quo for his service. Neither he nor Ellen can create an obligation for third persons to accept the lecture as a quid pro quo, for example by Ellen writing an IOU for the hairdresser to use. Whether he can use it to buy depends on the willingness of a third agent. Even if she had been paid for the lecture by the university and would use the money received for the hairdresser that would not create a binding obligation for any third agent to accept money from the hairdresser. The terms of a transaction in which the hairdresser is the buyer will have to be negotiated with the respective seller. As soon as the impossibility of barter is overcome with money, we have two transactions which are only loosely coupled.

The argument against the Wallace–Kocherlakota proposition can be summed up very simply: In a world of conflicting interests, common knowledge, perfect memory or perfect monitoring do not imply common evaluation.

To conclude: Wallace, Kocherlakota and others ignore an essential feature of monetary economies, namely, that prices are formed in pair-wise, decentralized, only loosely coupled transactions. However, this objection does not damage the general proposition that tangible money objects are replaceable and effectively replaced by money more and more taking the 'form of pure information'.[43] Given an appropriate institutional back-up, there seems to be no reason why those pair-wise, decentralized, loosely coupled transactions cannot be performed without tangible money objects.

2.4.4 Money as reification?

Interestingly, one prominent nineteenth century author already had a problem with this de-materialization of money because he had heavily invested in seeing money as a case of the 'reification' of social relations. Karl Marx, following Hegel, used a theorem according to which actions and their results are externalizations of subjective potential.[44] Regarding the economy, the subjective potential is the capacity to work. Activated and externalized, this potential will be embodied in things, objects, in artifacts as its products. Although they belong to the agent as subject, as producer, their existence as external things makes them prone to alienation: In a social context, others can appropriate what truly belongs to the agent as the subject of production. If appropriation by others takes place with the consent of the producer, it is legitimate, if not, it amounts to robbery or exploitation. The agent then is in a state of alienation, having lost control of the product. Under such conditions, the agent can become a true subject again, free and sovereign, only by re-appropriating what is properly hers or his.

Marx saw money as a prominent instance of such reification *plus* alienation. For him, the fact that money is used and has the form of tangible things indicates that the economy is not rationally organized. Commodities are produced for exchange. Operating in a spontaneously developing division of labor, each private individual producer tries to anticipate what can be sold in the market. Since the fates of all producers are interdependent, they have to coordinate their activities. But in commodity production, they do not coordinate *ex ante* by communicating about what and how much to produce for whom before they produce. As formally independent producers and holders of private property, they rely on *ex post* coordination through the market. The market operates as a feedback mechanism and money is the tangible means to express market feedback as sanctions and rewards in terms of the ups and downs of prices. A favorable price is the reward that tells producers to go on with what they have been doing, a bad price tells them that they have to change their product or their ways of producing. Money can have this crucial function of generating feed-back messages if and insofar as all commodities must be 'transformed' into money. As Marx put it, the sale for money is the '*salto mortale*' that all commodities have to perform.

Part of this story is familiar[45] and can be found in praises of the miracle of self-regulation that the market performs. How does a fierce critic like Marx turn this praise against markets and capitalism? His general premise is that the necessity of labor is part of the human condition, required for the reproduction of the species. Each individual person is in harmony with the nature of the species if he or she contributes to general human well-being through labor. But the conditions under which labor is performed in commodity producing societies are alienating: Although there is a division of labor implying that any individual act of labor has to fit into a supra-individual macro-social process, labor is performed as private labor. It takes place within the institutional context of private property rights. Therefore, the fit of the individual contribution to the social whole needs to be tested and confirmed. Such recognition of private efforts, for private goals, as valid contributions to aggregate social wealth will normally[46] happen only *post festum*. Private efforts are guided by anticipations of the wishes and desires of others, but anticipations may be wrong. Commodity production is production of 'use value for others', but these others come to the sales room only after production. Evidently, there is no centrally installed instance for the recognition of the results of private efforts as contributions to the 'common wealth'. Who could be the judge acting for the social whole, as it were? Such a privileged position cannot exist. So social recognition, if it happens at all, has to happen implicitly. It takes place as the unintended consequence of all pair-wise encounters in markets.

This is where money plays its crucial role. Any particular individual contribution has to pass the test of being sold for money. The successful[47] transformation of a commodity into money indicates that the private, individual effort is recognized as a valid contribution to aggregate social reproduction. By transforming the seller's commodity into money, individual buyers act as inadequate and inadvertent proxies for the social whole. Both sellers and buyers can be wrong. If too many are wrong, there will be a crisis.

For Marx, such a crisis indicates that, as far as the economy is concerned, we do not fully use our inner potential as humans, as subjects endowed with reason. As such, we would coordinate our activities *ex ante* and could thus directly and consciously contribute to the 'common wealth'. By contrast, in the alienated state of the capitalist economy, we can use our potential only in a severely limited, if not perverted way. We stick to our private goals, seek individual success in the form of monetary returns in the market and care about the functioning of the whole only as far as our individual success requires. But we cannot escape being part of the social reproduction process. This message is brought home to us from time to time by the drastically adverse fate of our products in the market. They have to perform their *salto mortale* and that test may result in the finding that our private efforts were wasted or misdirected. Prices signal such mistakes but, again, they may do so only in a distorted way.[48] They are the results of more or less random market encounters between buyers and sellers, all pursuing their private goals and using money to express them.

That we allow our economic fate depend on the fate of the commodities we produce is a symptom of 'fetishism' for Marx. A price states a relation between things, money on one side, commodities on the other. The realized price as such a relation between things decides whether we are winners or losers. 'Commodity fetishism' means that we let our relations with one another be mediated by and hidden beneath relations between things, commodities and money. Like a fetish, they are objects of our making, but the market teaches us that they have power over us.

Marx holds a social formation characterized by such 'fetishism' to be inferior, beneath the potential level of enlightened practices that human reason can sustain. He opts for replacing relations between things by relations between persons, for *ex ante* coordination through deliberation, collective decision making and the distribution of tasks in the light of common ends.

Whether this radical rejection of mediation in favor of deliberation among equals can lead to a feasible way of organizing socio-economic reproduction is not our concern here. Certainly, one can have doubts. The more narrow issue here is the role Marx attributes to money. What happens to his fetishism-diagnosis if money no longer comes in the form of things? Has reification ended even though alienation continues? I think that in terms of Marx' framework, the fact that money has new, more abstract forms does not really matter that much. A social division of labor and private, independent production are the crucial characteristics of the system that generates the need for money as a medium for *ex-post* coordination. Whether money objects are tangible things, or whether money merely exists as the means of price formation, of representing and record-ing transactions in accounts, does not change the basic mode of action coordination. Money is indispensable for the market to generate prices as a feed-back mechanism regardless of its form. Commodities have to be sold. That means that they have to be transformed into more or less money, not only mapped in the money dimension as in accounting. Only in this way are com-modities validated as private individual contributions to the aggregate social reproduction process.

In Marx's terms, it would be premature to conclude that commodity fetishism is a thing of the past just because most of us no longer hold the barbarian belief that gold or silver are money by nature. If one wants to extrapolate Marx's thought in view of contemporary forms of money, it seems to be more adequate to con-ceive them as iterations in Searle's 'X counts as Y in C' formula. Fetishism, as it were, is not reduced because we have forgotten that the original 'X' the ancient Greek counted as 'Y' consisted of little round pieces of yellow metal imprinted with a picture of a lion and a bull. That we now use green pieces of paper or accounts recorded and processed in the computers of banks has not changed the basic mechanism of *ex post* coordination of economic activities. Our economic fates still depend largely on the fates of the commodities we bring to the market in the hope of finding others who will give us some money for what we have to offer.

2.5 Money as a social relation?

> Money is a social relation.
>
> (Foley 1989: 248)

On his own terms, Marx would still be justified to speak of fetishism even if money took the 'form of pure information'. Therefore, if the Marxian description of social relations in a commodity producing economy, as relations between agents but mediated by things, is correct at all – and I think that it is correct regardless of what further arguments Marx put forward on money or value – it is descriptively misleading to simply propose that 'money is a social relation'. The mere observation of the slow historical shift away from using tangible money objects does not support such a description. To stick to the simple case, money – regardless of its form – *mediates* social relations between agents who communicate on one side as sellers using commodities and on the other side as buyers using money, whether tangible or not. This mediation gives the social relations the impersonal and abstract quality that Simmel, Weber[49] and – as we will shortly see – Knight underlined. Mediation is brought about by persons playing the roles of buyers and sellers. They use quantitites of commodities and quantities of money to generate price expressions and perform transactions according to them.

To be sure, any potential contribution of sociology to the understanding of money rests on firmly placing monetary phenomena into a context of social action or interaction. This sounds innocuous, but we have already seen that much of traditional economic theory is about strictly avoiding the analysis of economic phenomena in terms of interaction. Inspired by some sociological theory, one can, unfortunately, also make the opposite mistake and attempt to see the world solely as a system of pure social relations.[50] In the terms I introduced in an older paper on money in sociological theory (Ganssmann 1988), the issue is still whether there can be a fruitful division of labor between economics and sociology if economics is exclusively focusing on subject–object – and sociology is exclusively focusing on subject–subject relations. Following Ingham (2004: 16f.) I now would lighten up the vocabulary and speak of agent–object vs. agent–agent relations. But instead of postulating that 'money *is* a social relation', I suggest that money should be understood in a conceptual framework that is open for something we can call *agent–object–agent* relations. In other words, and one could make this a general claim: Agent–agent relations are normally mediated by (physical) objects. One could build a scale. On the one end, we place 'pure', unmediated agent–agent relations, speechless Platonic love perhaps being a case. On the other end we have phenomena like 'commodity fetishism', in which social relations disappear, as Marx maintained, 'behind' relations between things, but are nonetheless constitutive for such object–object relations.

Now, if we want to place the use of money on that scale, where should we place it? In one of the best sociological contributions to the theory of money, Geoffrey Ingham argues that 'money *is* a social relation' (Ingham 1999), placing money right at the pure agent–agent relation end of the scale. By contrast, I think that money is better understood if placed close to the other end. To repeat the obvious: Monetary relations are social relations mediated by money objects. As such peculiarly reified social relations they are the elementary building blocks of the modern monetary economy. Agents achieve coordination among themselves by buying and selling, exchanging money for commodities. So in that sense, agents still 'disappear' behind the relations between the things they are dealing with. It is not just a mistake when theory depicts exchange relations as non-social, as Frank Knight observed:

The »economic man« is not a »social animal«, and economic individualism excludes society in the proper human sense. Economic relations are *impersonal*. The social organization dealt with in economic theory is best pictured as a number of Crusoes interacting through the markets exclusively. To the economic individual, exchange is… a mode of using private resources to realize private ends. The »second party« has a shadowy existence, as a detail in the individual's use of his own resources to satisfy his own wants… The relation is neither one of cooperation nor one of mutual exploitation, but is completely non-moral, non-human. The relation is theoretically like the »silent trade« of some barbarian peoples.

(Knight 1951: 182f.)

The point is that as far as social relations are monetized, as in buying and selling, the important component for each participant is *not* the other person but the other person's money or the other person's commodity. Even if money becomes something ever more intangible, it does not dissolve into a pure social relation, and, certainly, neither do commodities disappear from the social relations mediated by money.[51]

By contrast, Ingham refers to the distinction between agent–object and agent–agent relations to argue that theories of commodity money *in toto* adhere to a misguided naturalism focused on agent–object relations. Rejecting notions of commodity money, Ingham maintains:

Money is a social relation of credit and debt denominated in a money of account.

(Ingham 2004: 12)

As a general statement, this looks much like a case of reading history not – as is inevitable – by looking backwards, but by looking backwards through a rearview mirror that came into being only with the modern automobile. When – as we are told – the kings of Lydia used the innovation of electron[52] coins to reimburse soldiers for their services – or to settle their debts with them – their obligation to pay was fulfilled. Coins were used to accomplish exactly that. Why should the fact that a service was paid turn money into a social relation? And why should that social relation be one of credit and debt? Ingham ignores the agent–*object*–agent character of monetary relations and suggests properties of money in general that, in the emphasis on credit, at best hold for modern money. By asserting that money *is* a social relation he overlooks or misunderstands Marx's point, namely, that money fetishism is merely an extension of commodity fetishism, where the latter means that relations between things (commodities in exchange) have usurped the place of relations between human agents. Agents tie their fate to the fate of their commodities in markets instead of coordinating their actions directly among each other. Such 'fetishism' is not just an ideological ornament attached to an otherwise transparent and rational mode of action coordination, but – if we follow Marx – a necessary implication of the *ex-post* coordination of economic activities.

Of course, nobody has to follow Marx in his specific argument on commodity money and commodity fetishism. But at least, one insight by Marx should be preserved: Money *mediates* social relations. Due to this mediation, social relations have a specific form, with agents playing specific, complementary roles: buyers and sellers, lenders and debtors and so on. For most of the history of money, this mediation was performed by tangible money objects. We have already seen why. By contrast, Ingham runs the risk of overlooking all those aspects of money use that *cannot* be subsumed under the simplifying heading: 'Money is a social relation'. Even though monetary relations tend to be less and less mediated by tangible money objects, this does not eliminate the role of commodities in these money mediated social relations. The principal mode of economic action coordination remains that of coordination *ex post*, after production, so that agents disappear behind their products or their money, as in the price form. Private producers anticipate demand by unknown others and expect to transform the commodities they bring to markets into money.

In short, buyer–seller relations are social relations, but social relations mediated by objects. So they are better described as agent–*object*–agent relations. That label also seems appropriate for describing much of monetary history, although monetary systems tend to rely less and less on the use of tangible money objects. Early bankers spent enormous time and effort on ascertaining the weight and metal content of the diverse coins circulating all over Europe. The quality of the coins counted. Were early bankers all gripped needlessly by some misplaced naturalism? If one compares older monetary systems with the contemporary ones, it is easy to see that the older ones indeed relied to a much greater degree on a sort of anchoring of institutional facts in physical facts. As an alternative, modern monetary systems require elaborate and – so it turns out from time to time – fragile and vulnerable organizational constructions for their support. However, even if money turns more and more into something so lofty that one is tempted to call it 'flying money',[53] we do move a lot of stuff and efforts, matter and energy, around with it, from one possessor to the next.

To conclude, the proposition that 'money *is* a social relation' is too simple. The basic social relations, between buyers and sellers, borrowers and lenders, constituting a monetary economy are relations mediated by commodities and/or tangible money objects. One may object that money nowadays does not need to take the form of tangible objects like coins or bills. However, money in most of its functions came in the form of tangible objects, if only as paper, at least until the most recent advances in information and communication technologies. To be sure, the concrete physical material used as the carrier of money functions – gold, silver, copper, paper – has turned out to be secondary. But even if we take into account that much of contemporary money comes in the form of numbers in accounts in data banks, that does not turn money itself into a social relation. Rather, regardless of its form, money is a visible, documented expression of the peculiar nature of social relations that it mediates in the DoL-PiP economy.

Since Ingham's proposition that money is a social relation is closely related to his concept of money as a relation of credit[54] – and since he shares this proposition with other important authors on money (Aglietta, Wray and others), this would be a good point to move on to the discussion of the proposition that 'all money is credit'. However, this discussion requires a careful analysis of the structure of monetary interaction as a preparatory groundwork. So the 'all money is credit' – proposition will be discussed in Section 3.5.

With the conclusion that money is not a social relation but a medium generated by and, in turn, structuring specific social relations, we can close Chapter 2. Starting from a clarification of the relation of money to language we have seen that communication with money differs from communication with language most clearly in two respects: First, money comes with a metric. When we associate money with an economic object by forming a price, we generate a quantitative representation of that object in the contexts of property and exchange. Second, monetary systems frequently operate as the give and take of tangible money objects. The metric, which originally seems to have borrowed much of its validity from similarity to physical measurement, has lost such anchoring in the physical world. In the contemporary economy it thus appears more and more as what it always was: an occasionally volatile social construction. Tangible money objects are crowded out by credit relations that are documented on paper, in computers, etc., and recorded by elaborate specialized institutions behind the back of the agents immediately involved. Despite drifting aloft, money is used ever more intensively and extensively to both form and 'realize' prices, as a social tool for calculation and for the appropriation and transfer of property.

In Chapter 3, I will try to lay the groundwork for a theory of money that can accommodate the problems and insights gained in Chapters 1 and 2. The idea is not so much to present a positive theory – that would be premature – but rather to discuss and prepare the basic ingredients of such a theory.

3 Elementary theory

3.1 Contingency and interaction

The sociological contribution to the theory of money has to explain monetary systems as social constructions. Recognizing them as such immediately gives the whole problem a rather uncomfortable twist. Social constructions are the outcome of actions and their interplay. Actions are always – at least to some extent[1] – contingent.[2] How can we find stability and order in an object of inquiry that is the product of contingent actions? We have seen, for example, that the acts of 'measurement' that supposedly take place in price formation rely on a socially constructed measure that never had – or, as some prefer, no longer has – any firm grounding in the non-social world. That means, if we accept the semantic of measurement, that prices are subject to contingency from at least three sides: What do we measure with? Who is doing the measuring? What are we measuring? So prices fluctuate not just because supply and demand vary, and with them the social significance of commodities, but also because the measuring instrument is unstable, because the agents doing the measuring are subject to moods, motives, contexts, that may lead them to modify their bids and offers and their willingness to reach an agreement, and, last but not least, because the commodities being measured vary in quality and setting. In short, the factors constitutive of an effective price are variable. What we can buy with a unit of money, say 1 euro, differs not only because production and market conditions for commodities change, but also because the monetary authority may choose a new policy, people may react to threatening events by hoarding, foreign currency exchange rates may fluctuate, and so on.

Given all these contingencies, why is the whole exercise of using money not merely futile and frustrating? On the one hand, most monetary systems must attain a sufficient degree of order so that agents are not deterred from using money. On the other hand, the needs that support the institution of money may be so overwhelming that all the difficulties involved in actual monetary practices are pushed backstage, suppressed, and held to be secondary except in times of severe monetary crises. As the financial crisis of 2007/2008 demonstrated, even severe crises are not sufficient to stop the use of money. German hyperinflation in 1923, deliberately induced by the government to get rid of the public debt accumulated during World War I, did not end because people were pushed to the point where they refused to use money, even though at the end you needed the proverbial pushcart full of bank notes to buy a loaf of bread. Rather, the government printing press ran out of the proper paper for bank notes. People switched to using locally created 'Notgeld' (emergency money) until a monetary reform[3] created a renewed currency on the national level.

Even disregarding such extreme events, the use of money is permeated by contingencies. A situation defined by contingency generates uncertainty[4] for the agents involved. Although Keynes did not have this general uncertainty surrounding money in mind when he asked: 'Why should anyone outside a lunatic asylum wish to use money …',[5] the general answer to Keynes's (improperly shortened) question is: The use of money is not just subject to all sorts of contingencies generating uncertainty, but it also creates certainty or: Money absorbs uncertainty.[6] To see how and why, we have to work our way from tracing contingency in basic interaction to contingency in a full fledged but still simple monetary system.

3.1.1 General setting: contingency and society

Any theory of money should start from a setting of interaction. Robinson Crusoe has no use for money.[7] Two players in isolation have no use for money, either. Edgeworth (1919: 329) made this clear with the story about two men bringing beer to a market, getting thirsty on the way and selling the beer bit by bit to each other with one coin going back and forth. At the end, they reach the market but all the beer is gone and the coin is again in the pocket of its original owner.

But two-player interaction, although insufficient to support money use, already implies the problem of 'double contingency'. As sociologists have emphasized with the theorem of 'double contingency', indeterminacy in the choice of actions due to cognitive uncertainty on the part of the agents involved is a basic feature of most social interaction.[8] So let us first clarify what this theorem says, then generalize it to more than two-person interaction, as contingency in interaction with more than two players involved characterizes the general background for the use of money.

Double contingency

When we distinguish the social from the physical or biological realm, we refer to events that involve at least two actors. Social relations, structures, systems exist only if more than one actor participates, where actors are human beings capable of goal-oriented behavior. Since the social realm starts with a minimum of two, it has appeared self-evident for social theorists to think about its constitution or emergence using models of a dyadic constellation: the mother-child dyad (Spitz 1957) in psychoanalysis, bilateral exchange, or Edgeworth's 'catallactic atom' (1881: 31n), in economic theory, the problem of 'double contingency' (Parsons [1951] 1964: 36f.) in sociology. Such models openly or implicitly tell a story about how the social world has evolved or, rather, what its conditions of possibility are. They involve a hen–egg problem: To explain the origins of the social world, should we (but how can we?) presuppose actors sufficiently competent to engage in communication? In the mother–child dyad, one actor, the mother, is competent, the other not yet. In the economics of bilateral exchange, the question is how two competent actors can complete an exchange and thus determine an exchange ratio for the goods that change hands. In sociology, however, it does not make sense to assume competent actors, if the ambition is to model a stylized primordial social situation. Where should actors have learned how to communicate if not in interaction? At the same time, the *problem* of 'double contingency' only arises if two competent actors face each other. An *ego*, conscious of the freedom to make choices, to follow wishes, to define purposes, runs into another being who is not just *alter*, the other, but someone in whom she recognizes the very qualities she assumes for herself: *alter ego*. 'Double contingency' results because the freedom to choose exists on both sides of the elementary social relation and both sides know this. Such knowledge potentially leads to paralysis. If the outcome of my action is dependent on your action and the outcome for you is dependent on my action, but neither of us knows what the other will do, it maybe unwise to even attempt a first move.

It is tempting to take such a stylized social constellation as a sort of zero point for social analysis. Everything interesting happens once this potential paralysis is overcome. What happens depends on how it is overcome. But it is worthwhile to keep in mind that modeling a social zero point should not involve the assumption of competent actors. Such competence must be socially conditioned.

In what follows, the reasoning behind the theorem of double contingency and its development will be sketched starting from the microeconomic analysis of bilateral exchange via game theory via Parsons' culturalist proposition to end with Luhmann's introduction of symbolic media of communication.

The 'catallactic atom'

Although the term 'double contingency' was coined much later in sociology, the *locus classicus* for the problem is bilateral exchange analysis in economics. We can refer to the well-known Edgeworth–Box diagram (Figure 3.1) to illustrate the argument.

The Edgeworth–Box depicts the allocation possibilities, given two goods and two players, in a rectangle whose dimensions map the available quantities of goods. The initial allocation is depicted by point t_0 in the north-west corner. Preferences are depicted by the indifference curves (for example I_A and I_B) relative to the two opposing, player-specific origins in the south-west (for A) and the north-east corner (for B). The indifference curves I_{A0} and I_{B0} going through t_0 mark the boundaries of the set of allocations that are feasible trading results according to the standard Pareto criterion, the 'better set'. Allocations are feasible if they are preferred by at least one of the players and leave the other one indifferent.

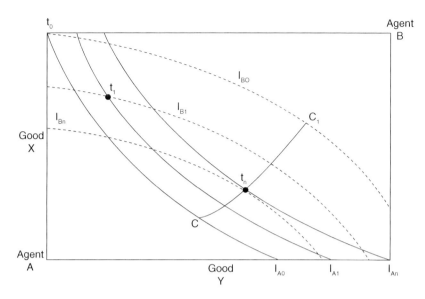

Figure 3.1 The Edgeworth Box.

The standard argument regarding possible outcomes of barter transactions is that the two players will bargain until they reach an allocation on the so-called contract curve (CC_1), the locus of all points of tangency of their indifference curves within the better set. Why? Because unless the contract curve is reached, there are still gains to be realized according to the Pareto criterion, whereas no such improvements are possible once the contract curve has been reached. But it is not possible to determine which allocation on the contract curve will be realized. The standard bilateral exchange model does not have a determinate solution in terms of predicting which 'price', i.e., exchange ratio, will be formed and which allocation reached by two players trying to maximize utility through barter.

Another way of arriving at the same point is suggested by Hardin (2003). He uses the term 'indeterminacy' to cover social situations for which established theories of strategic interaction cannot derive a determinate outcome. He is more radical than standard microeconomics where the indeterminacy of price in bilateral exchange is acknowledged: The standard argument about Pareto dominance used to arrive at the contract curve as the locus of all equilibrium trades is insufficient, according to Hardin. Once a player accepts a starting point suggested by the other player, all that can happen are moves that fulfill the Pareto condition: one of the players gets a preferred bundle of goods while the other remains at least indifferent. The repetition of moves according to that criterion will lead to the contract curve, where none of the players can improve without the other losing, so that no further moves are possible. But points on the contract curve clearly can favor one player more than the other. So how can a player accept a suggested starting point for bargaining if he knows that the final outcome, the point of arrival on the contract curve signifying an agreement, depends on the starting point?

In what became the dominant neoclassical tradition,[9] indeterminacy in bilateral exchange was seen as a disappointing deficit of price theory, so the emphasis was shifted away from bilateral interaction analysis to competition, by introducing more and more players on both sides of the barter relationship. The intuitive story was that these players would end up defining a determinate exchange ratio because they would make competing bids and offers, thus narrowing the range of exchange ratio variations. But it took the tools of game theory to formalize that intuition in the theorem of the core (for example, see Malinvaud 1972). Long before that happened, a redefinition of the problem took place with the development of the Walrasian concept of competitive equilibrium: Individual players were conceived to be of such small importance within the mass of all players that they could only adapt to prices. Since there was nobody left who could set prices, a mechanism had to be constructed so that prices could be varied systematically in response to observed excess demands until a unique set of equilibrium prices was generated: the tatonnement performed by the Walrasian auctioneer took care of price setting.[10]

But let us return to the 'catallactic atom'. The Edgeworth–Box diagram (Figure 3.1) illustrates well the unique perspective that economists have adopted. Two players are assumed to meet. They confront each other solely in terms of their individual utility calculus. If the condition of a double coincidence of wants is fulfilled and there is a 'better set', that is the chance of improvement of the welfare position for at least one of the players – according to the Pareto criterion – the two players are taken to communicate and negotiate. The Pareto criterion reflects the condition of all exchanges being voluntary, an implication of the players following the rules of private property, as well as their goal of maximizing utility. The bargaining implicitly analyzed in this way has a very restricted form: any offer that one of the two players makes is checked according to the Pareto criterion and accepted if it does or rejected if it does not fulfill it. On the one hand, this simple story is plausible when players are assumed to have given and fixed preferences – whereas much of empirical bargaining is about trying to hide your own and modify the other's preferences. On the other hand, this is not plausible insofar as the neoclassical players lack one basic capability that all non-autistic humans normally have: They are unable to see themselves[11] with the eyes of the other. However, this capability is at the heart of the double contingency problem, as we will shortly see.

Game theory

In 1935, Oskar Morgenstern published a paper entitled 'Vollkommene Voraussicht und wirtschaftliches Gleichgewicht' (perfect foresight and economic equilibrium). Referring to a Conan Doyle story in which Sherlock

Holmes and Professor Moriarty try to outfox each other in a life-and-death struggle Morgenstern demonstrated that the assumption of 'perfect foresight' in general equilibrium theory is inconsistent. For two strategically interacting actors, the possibilities of outguessing each other can be inexhaustible. Moriarty observes Holmes and Holmes observes Moriarty. But Holmes knows he is observed by Moriarty and Moriarty knows he is observed by Holmes. So Holmes tries to act in ways that are to influence Moriarty's expectations of what he is going to do and Moriarty tries to act in ways that are to influence Holmes's expectations of what he is going to do. Since both know that they are both extremely smart, they take into account these attempts to influence each other's expectations of expectations, etc. How can this end? In the story, it ends with the deaths of both Holmes and Moriarty, but read it yourself.

For Morgenstern's purposes, the story illustrates the impossibility of perfect foresight in strategic interaction. There is no logical end to the game of forming expectations of expectations. The problem can be transported into economic theory starting with bilateral exchange. Two actors want something from each other and they are not locked into a single exit situation by the anonymous forces of the market, as stylized in perfect competition. The reason why the standard treatment of bilateral exchange cannot lead to a satisfactory solution is that we are dealing essentially with a dual maximizing problem.

This indeterminacy can be understood as an implication of double contingency: If what I get depends on your choice and what you get depends on my choice, and if we are both free to choose, there cannot be a determinate result unless we introduce further factors allowing for a structuring of the situation. Without such additional factors, the situation is one of (Knightian) uncertainty, meaning that neither player can have sufficient information to form expectations of quantifiable outcomes. This may be paralyzing because both want to influence the choice of the other but do not know how to accomplish this effectively. Also, both must be wary of unknowingly taking an unfavorable first step. If they cannot find ways of bridging uncertainty, they cannot trade.

Morgenstern brought this problem into his cooperation with John von Neumann (Morgenstern 1976) that resulted in the pioneering *Theory of Games and Economic Behavior* (1953). Their argument took off from the proposition that economic actors are neither Robinson Crusoes facing a nonsocial environment nor price takers in perfect competition, but actors involved in strategic interaction. The game theory apparatus they developed uses several possibilities to reduce the contingency involved in interaction: The rational actors facing each other have limited strategic options. It is assumed that the set of outcomes of alternative strategies is known. It is also assumed that the outcomes are evaluated in a shared way. They can be entered into a pay-off matrix, as in the basic two-player-zero-sum game. Given these assumptions, von Neumann and Morgenstern were able to derive decision rules that ensure optimal outcomes relative to what the opponent does.

Parsons

When Talcott Parsons brought the concept of 'double contingency' into sociology, he was apparently influenced by the new game theory. His definition of
double contingency could easily pass for a description of bilateral exchange:

> there is a *double contingency* inherent in interaction. On the one hand, *ego*'s
> gratifications are contingent on his selection among available alternatives.
> But in turn, *alter*'s reaction will be contingent on *ego*'s selection and will
> result from a complementary selection on *alter*'s part.
>
> (Parsons *et al.* 1965: 16)

Parsons went beyond the game theoretical argument by undoing the exclusive
concern with rational action. He wanted to demonstrate that actors can overcome
double contingency only by relying on shared values and norms. Double contingency – to repeat – implies that actors are uncertain about what others will do, so
they are uncertain what they themselves should do. To form expectations, they
have to integrate each other into their meaning systems. In addition, these
meaning systems have to be complementary.

> First, since the outcome of *ego*'s action (e.g., success in the attainment of a
> goal) is contingent on *alter*'s reaction to what *ego* does, *ego* becomes oriented
> not only to *alter*'s probable overt behavior but also to what *ego* interprets to be
> *alter*'s expectations relative to *ego*'s behavior, since *ego* expects that *alter*'s
> expectations will influence *alter*'s behavior. Second, in an integrated system,
> this orientation to the expectations of the other is reciprocal or complementary.
>
> (Parsons and Shils 1951: 105)

Such complementarity is possible only if 'actions, gestures, or symbols have
more or less the same meaning for both *ego* and *alter*' (ibid.), which is the same
thing as saying that 'a common culture exist(s) between them, through which
their interaction is mediated' (ibid.). The common culture has normative force:

> The most important single condition of the integration of an interaction
> system is a shared basis of normative order... It must guide action by estab-
> lishing some distinctions between desirable and undesirable lines of action
> which can serve to stabilize interaction.
>
> (Parsons 1968: 437)

How do actors acquire the competence to recognize and follow the rules set by
the normative order?

> The most basic condition of such compliance is the internalization of a soci-
> ety's values and norms by its members, for such socialization underlies the
> consensual basis of a societal community.
>
> (Parsons 1966: 14)

It follows from this crucial role of socialization that Parsons does not use the problem of double contingency to model a social zero point: Actors have become culturally competent in socialization before they run into each other and into the problem of double contingency. Thus, the hen–egg problem mentioned above is avoided through the reference to socialization. The child learns from the mother who learned from her mother when she was a child. The constant in this process is taken to be culture. Transmitted by socialization culture is to structure and constrain actions that would otherwise lack order and stability.

Luhmann

Luhmann refers to double contingency in order to propose an impossibility theorem: 'Action cannot take place if *alter* makes his action dependent on how *ego* acts, and *ego* wants to connect his action to *alter*'s' (Luhmann 1995: 103). However, instead of seeing actors as being drawn into *n*th order outguessing games, which may indeed be paralyzing, Luhmann attempts to view double contingency as something productive: It cannot be eliminated from interaction, but it induces self-observation and reflexivity which, in turn, reduce the improbability of communication.

> In this way an emergent order can arise that is conditioned by the complexity of the systems that make it possible but that does not depend on this complexity being calculated or controlled. We call this emergent order a social system.
>
> (Luhmann 1995:110)

Double contingency stimulates the emergence of simple social systems if, in the two-communicator case, *ego* and *alter ego* agree: 'I will do what you want if you do what I want'. However, this deceptively simple rule is based on the possibility of not agreeing, on the freedom to go away. Thus, the emerging social system stays unstable. To handle the problem of instability, Luhmann adds media of communication to his argument. They increase the probability that a communication is not only understood, but accepted: *Ego* – appropriating the information given by *alter* – adopts it as the premise of her response.

While Luhmann convinces us that double contingency cannot be eliminated in social systems and that – instead of blocking communication – it can stimulate the emergence of stabilizing social constructions like media, the starting point of his argument is unfortunate insofar as he treats double contingency as a sort of social zero point. Double contingency only is a problem once actors are competent communicators. But once they are competent communicators and are observing each other, the axiom holds: 'One can not not communicate' (Watzlawick *et al.* 1967: 48).

To sum up, the concept of double contingency implies a clear criterion for the distinction between social and non-social phenomena. Neoclassical economics has neglected the social dimension of economic action and thus missed facing the problem of double contingency in a productive way. Game theory offers a remedy within the rational choice framework by starting from the proposition that strategic interaction involves uncertainty. But at the same time a strong dose of certainty is reintroduced with respect to the choice between *given* strategic alternatives and the *shared* evaluation of outcomes. Parsons extends this framework in the manner expected from sociology to include a common culture with shared norms and values as means to overcome the problem of double contingency. The mutually expectable choices of players are reduced by both following common rules, distinguishing between allowed and forbidden paths of action in a parallel manner. Finally, Luhmann emphasized that double contingency in interaction cannot be eliminated and is always a source of instability for social systems, but that this instability can be reduced through the use of media of communication. They increase the probability that a communicative offer leads to continuing communication.

3.1.2 Transcending the two-player framework

Interestingly, all four responses to the problem of double contingency involve reaching beyond the two-player setting to import some constraints from larger social settings: The neoclassical tradition shifts to the level of perfect competition among a finite but huge number of players to rely on the 'parametric function of prices' (Lange 1936/7) in the quest for determinacy. The theory of games reduces contingency by not only assuming known outcomes of strategic alternatives but also a shared mode of evaluating them: money-like pay-offs that are common knowledge among the players.[12] Parsons, of course, refers to values and norms, a shared culture that constrains the choices available, while Luhmann introduces media of communication that can, however, not be installed by only two players that find themselves in the double contingency situation.

We will have to see whether these responses to the problem of double contingency are helpful for the theory of money. In any case, interaction is characterized by contingency or indeterminacy more broadly than traditional microeconomic analysis takes into account. Interacting players have to find means to cope with the challenge of uncertainty. Promising responses seem to require moves beyond the two-player setting. But what holds for two players – that each is free to choose and that the outcomes of own choices depend on the choices of the other – *a fortiori* holds for $2+n$ players. In fact, we should speak of 'multiple' instead of mere 'double' contingency'. If that is so how can we expect expansion beyond the two-player setting to lead to reduced contingency? Perhaps extrapolating and combining the arguments proposed by the four theoretical approaches described above will help?

What we are looking for are constraints. Whereas contingency opens the space of possible actions, constraints reduce that space. Determinacy would be accomplished if constraints would eliminate all choice. If we can place agents, given their preferences and objectives, into 'single-exit situations', as Latsis (1972) aptly called them, we can predict their actions. Or, if each of n players has a decision to make that has an effect on the pay-offs that the other $n-1$ players receive as a result of the n decisions, and if we associate one degree of freedom with every player, constraints imply a reduction in degrees of freedom, in the extreme from n to 1, if all act as one in perfect coordination (Thalos 1999: 467).

So let us again go through the four arguments on double contingency suggested by the theories sketched above, now with an eye for constraints.

First, in traditional *bilateral exchange analysis*, double contingency is not explicitly recognized as a source of uncertainty or indeterminacy. But actions are constrained by applying the criterion of Pareto dominance to select feasible moves. Given the players' preferences and objectives of maximizing utility, they seek to improve their position by seeking consent for moves that must either improve the other player's position, too, or leave him indifferent at least. In other words, players are taken to respect each other as persons and holders of property rights. They do not use force.[13] Therefore, although this is rarely stated explicitly, any exchange rests on strong normative foundations ruling out some rather obvious, morally unattractive ways of dealing with one another. As we have seen, the implied constraints lead agents to agree to moves that result in an allocation on the contract curve, but the constraints are insufficient to determine where on that curve they will end up. An increase in determinacy is only achieved by leaving behind bilateral exchange to introduce additional constraints in the form of more players. This *social* expansion does not lead to increased contingency, as one could expect, given the additional degrees of freedom opening with each additional player. Rather, players are taken to narrow the range of feasible exchange ratios for each other as they compete by over- and underbidding. In addition, as proposed with the theorem of the core (for an application in the theory of money, see Gale 1982), they may form coalitions, so that many are acting as one. Taken together, there are three kinds of constraints introduced: a normative constraint eliminating certain types of actions, a constraint leading to price formation by approaching a situation describable in terms of the law of large numbers, and a constraint in the sense of individuals ceding their freedom to act to form a collective actor.

Second, in classic game theory, double (or rather multiple) contingency is explicitly acknowledged in the form of recognizing that exchange involves 'a peculiar and disconcerting mixture of several conflicting maximum problems' (Neumann and Morgenstern 1953: 11). The resulting indeterminacy is reduced by assuming a limited set of choices (in simple games like the 'prisoners' dilemma' a binary choice for each player will do: defect/cooperate) and a known set of possible outcomes. Although players cannot know exactly what the other players will do, they are able to anticipate all the outcomes resulting from all the alternative choices of all players. But not only that. It is also assumed that they can anticipate the significance of these different outcomes not only for themselves – each judging them in terms of their subjective individual utility – but also for the others. The reason for this rather far-reaching assumption is simple. If players cannot judge the significance of results for others, they cannot form expectations about the actions of others. To use chess as an example once again: If you play chess with somebody who does not want to win, you cannot anticipate your opponent's moves. Interestingly for the theory of money, von Neumann and Morgenstern were criticized for falling back on inter-personally comparable cardinal utility as a device to ensure this common evaluation of pay-offs,[14] raising the question of why they did not simply introduce pay-offs in terms of money.[15] We will get back to that issue when the possible role of money in reducing contingency will be discussed explicitly (see Section 3.2). Taken together, in classic game theory constraints are introduced explicitly by – sometimes severely – limiting the set of choices, by assuming all alternative outcomes to be known and by assuming a common standard for evaluating these outcomes. Clearly, the normative foundations of exchange noted above (sub a) are implicitly assumed to hold, too.

Third, as we have seen, Parsons introduces a common culture as the source of the shared norms and values that reduce the choices open to players by separating admissible from inadmissible paths of action. Players who have internalized moral standards can be expected to respond to situations in a more limited number of ways than players who are not constrained by moral considerations. If I trust that you will not cheat and that you will keep your promises, and *vice versa*, we can coordinate our actions much more effectively and easily than if we suspect each other to be opportunistic.[16]

Fourth, the sphere of economic actions is neither 'norm-free' nor is it conceivable without media allowing for communication, if only because institutions like property presuppose language, as we have learned from Searle. So the explicit introduction of money as a medium of communication, as suggested by Parsons and elaborated by Luhmann, is not a theoretical step that would amount to introducing a totally new factor into economic analysis. If we move down one level from language – as the most general medium of communication – we can understand the rationale of introducing other 'symbolically generalized media of communication' (Luhmann 1975): They constrain the set of possible actions and signal these constraints. When we enter a room in which ten persons are talking to each other, we learn within seconds whether we are in a meeting of local politicians, a pep-rally for encyclopedia salesmen or a seminar on Aristotle. We can perceive what is happening so quickly because communication is coded and we are able to distinguish the codes typically used in most social situations. Within language in general, special languages are 'nested' that simplify communication because participants – in using a code – can refer to specific shared problems in a sort of shorthand. Luhmann maintained that such codes have to be binary, functioning in terms of exclusive alternatives. For economic communication in general, the code refers to property. The question is always: *to have or have not*? For a modern monetary economy, the code is: *to pay or not to pay*? Such coding accomplishes the narrowing of communication and action possibilities in at least four ways:

1   For all participants, it is easy to form plausible expectations about the objectives pursued by all others. Everything else being equal, more money is

better than less money for all players.[17] The general expectation is that buyers want to spend less and sellers want to earn more.

2   The use of money by a player signals to the others that it is in their own interest to adopt a strategic, instrumental, calculative attitude.

3   Responses to adverse reactions are simple and quickly chosen and performed. Prices can be easily modified. You offer more or ask for less on the way to an agreement that implies action coordination with respect to property change.

4   If you do not have money and the others do not expect you to acquire some in the relevant future, you are excluded from the game of legitimate property change.[18]

Taken together, the responses to the double-contingency problem in economics and sociology suggest that there are several ways to overcome the difficulties for action coordination caused by contingency. They all involve transcending the simple setting of two-player interaction. Introducing more players may – as in the competitive process – increase determinacy instead of reducing it. Interaction may be framed and formed by a common culture. Players may know the range of their choices and form estimates of possible interdependent outcomes for others and themselves. Last but not least, they may use media to communicate in effective and efficient ways. There is no reason why the implied constraints have to be seen as mutually exclusive ways of reducing contingency. We will find out whether the use of money is a way of combining such constraints.

In any case, 'multiple' contingency and the implied uncertainty have to be recognized as the general background for the theory of money. The questions resulting are: Can the use of money reduce uncertainty? If so, how? Given the contingencies surrounding the use of money that we have noted so far, one issue even has to be whether the reduction of uncertainty can be genuine or whether it is merely generated by players ignoring their ignorance, so to speak.

However, before trying to answer these questions, there are two additional layers of contingency that we have to take into account. They result from the particular social infrastructure on which the monetary economy rests and from introducing credit relations that form specific links between the present and the future.

3.1.3 The DoL-PiP economy

What is the *larger social context* in which the money game is played? In most general terms, the game is about the transfers of property in an economy with a division of labor and private independent producers. Private property rights are applied to the part of the relevant resources that is appropriable (see the classification of goods, Table 2.1). The norms of private property prohibit the use of force and fraud. Property change is a peaceful affair.[19] This implies that resource transfers from one player to another take place on the basis of voluntary agreements.

Transfers of resources, whether in terms of property rights or not, are a necessary complement to any production system with a division of labor. If people produce not only for themselves, their families or households, but for – potentially unknown – others, there must be reliable mechanisms that can transfer units of good *a* produced by *A* to some agent *B* that needs or wants good *a*, and so on.

Karl Polanyi (1957: 47f., 1968: 148f.) has usefully distinguished three such basic mechanisms: reciprocity, redistribution, and exchange. *Reciprocity* refers to transfers in long-term face-to-face relations, as in mutual gift giving or care between generations in families. *Redistribution* presupposes a central authority that organizes property transfers, as when states tax and spend. *Exchange*, the social practice of *do ut des* (I give so that you give), is the dominant mechanism of transfer in market economies based on private property. Exchange does not involve money according to any kind of logical necessity, but in contrast to reciprocity, it involves a calculating attitude, the attempt to measure, quantify and fix the terms and times of give and take. Regular exchange takes place on markets. Markets become the more important as mechanisms of resource allocation the more the social division of labor is intensified to a level where most producers specialize in each producing a narrowly limited set of goods only so that hardly anybody can live by consuming only own products. In other words, most production[20] will be commodity production, for *exchange* on markets, in the DoL-PiP economy.[21] Production for exchange has been going on since ancient times, but it became a dominant feature of the economy[22] only in combination with money use and with the onset of 'occidental capitalism', some 300 years ago. More and more production for exchange implies that an increasing and – beyond some threshold – decisive share of the coordination of economic activities takes place *ex post*, after production has already occurred. We have seen that such *ex post* coordination involves an implicit social recognition or rejection of each privately produced good or service as a valid contribution to the overall economic reproduction of society. Someone who produces for exchange must attempt to anticipate the needs of others. This anticipation can be fully justified as correct or it can be totally rejected, or anything in between. The market is the social space where this happens.[23]

Producers enter markets with quantities of the commodities they want to sell and with price expectations. The reaction of others to their offers provides a dual feedback to producers, in terms of the quantities demanded and in terms of the prices offered. The two aspects of feedback are interdependent. By lowering the price per unit, more units may be sold, and so on. The interdependence between price and quantity is limited, however. Buyers try to observe and anticipate price movements, so they may not simply react to price variations according to the 'law' of supply and demand. Sellers must cover costs so that they can reappear on the market in the next period with their next offers.

Why does the system operate with dual feedback in this sense, why is not just one of the two, either quantity or price variation, sufficient? A possible but not very helpful answer may be: It is a dual system, in the sense of being powered by *two* operative intentions, to get something useful and to earn money. A simpler more technical answer would be: In many cases, quantity variation is not possible. If goods or services come in large units, there can be no bargaining in terms of quantity. Simultaneous price/quantity adaptations may be possible in many markets, but many are restricted to price variations as the form of adjusting supply and demand. The system only has the flexibility requisite for its reproduction if the trades that are its elements are not constructed as 'take it or leave it' propositions. Instead of 'yes' or 'no'-reactions to an offer or a rejection, it allows for 'yes, but if …' – or 'no, but if …' – reactions.

At the point of sale, money is the instrument of such social recognition or rejection. As commodities are sold, they are 'transformed' into money. As money is spent, it is 'transformed' back into commodities. So the degree of social recognition/rejection of private productive activities can be expressed in variations of the money prices of the commodities effectively sold in the market. This can be accomplished by any single transaction between two agents. It does not require a broader social consensus on the merits of the commodities sold or the acceptability of the prices paid. Any arbitrary person with enough money can buy or not buy, for whatever reasons. Some producers may simply be lucky, others not. Wherever a commodity is sold, however, an effective price results, expressing an agreement between buyer and seller. Such a realized effective price is not only relevant for the actual buyer/seller pair that has agreed on them. Markets tend to be public spaces.[24] Prices are observed by other market participants and inform their decisions. If they are believed to optimally exploit the 'opportunities of acquisition afforded by the market' (Markterwerbschancen) (Weber 1956: 48), they indeed acquire a sort of 'parametric function'.[25] So, as far as they are perceived as signals informing decisions, prices may lose the volatility they will have in random encounters of uninformed individuals. But market participants cannot be certain that the prices they observe today will be the prices they can rely on tomorrow. They may make a contract for tomorrow, eliminating uncertainty to some extent, but the meaning of the price/quantity couple specified in a contract can rapidly change with a change in the market environment. You may buy 100 barrels of Brent crude oil for x US dollars today, to be delivered a year from now. Assuming that the seller still is there next year to honor the contract, you have eliminated some uncertainty. You may even buy insurance against the defaulting of the seller and eliminate some more uncertainty. But you cannot know what the state of the oil market or the euro–dollar exchange rate will be a year from now. It is in this sense that the monetary economy adds an additional layer of contingency to the general contingency inherent in social interaction: We cannot know what the other market participants are doing or will do, even if we enter pair-wise binding obligations with a few of them. The DoL-PiP setting forces all market participants into a situation in which the returns for their efforts are uncertain in principle because we can control only a very limited subset of the activities on which our economic fate depends. However, this uncertainty concerns only the results of transactions, not the nature of the game being played.

Since the advance of capitalism with the rapid expansion of production for the market, the role of money in society has increased dramatically. Although money is much older than capitalism, it is only with the advance of capitalism that more and more and, finally, almost any economic activity is mapped, calculated, decided on in money terms.[26] As a consequence securing and maximizing money income and monetary wealth has become the *universal* objective of economic activity. The contrasting idea prevalent in economics, namely, that consumption is the one and only end of all economic activity,[27] is a rather romantic misconception, a touching contrast to the hard-nosed sobriety mainstream economists tend to display in their public stance.

However, criticizing mainstream economic theory, in this case including Keynes, as being romantic is not a substitute for a theoretical argument that can explain the dominance of the objective to maximize money returns over the objective of maximizing utility.

3.1.4 Double contingency and the double coincidence of wants

To construct such an argument, let us in a first step return to the basic exchange setting as depicted in barter models. The point of such a return is not to 'derive' money from the obstacles and frictions involved in barter. Rather, the idea is to see clearly the action coordination problems that money helps to tackle. These problems can best be identified in very simple interaction settings. We have already referred to Edgeworth's 'catallactic atom' to clarify the significance of 'double contingency'. Now, we can add the double-coincidence-of-wants problem to see that it has implications that generate more complexity than is depicted in models of barter as a simple yes/no issue.

Table 3.1 depicts a barter situation. Two players meet and the question is whether either one or both of the players have something the other player wants. The table shows whether – according to traditional analysis – they will cooperate or not. Cooperation – in the sense of starting a transaction – happens only when the Jevonian 'double-coincidence of wants' condition is fulfilled. By contrast, players will certainly not cooperate if both have nothing to gain from cooperation. The interesting cases are the 'semi-opportunities' for trading. One player has something the other player wants, but not vice versa. These 'semi-opportunities' remain unused according to the rules depicted in standard bilateral exchange models.

This approach can be modified if we introduce a new factor, communication. To start with, the question is – assuming agents speaking the same language:

Table 3.1 Do you have something I want?

Ego/alter ego	Yes	No
Yes	Cooperation	No cooperation
No	No cooperation	No cooperation

Can and will the players send additional signals, beyond 'yes' or 'no'? In the case of 'double coincidence', explicit communication is not necessary, at least not as long as the players know the basic rules of the game: Appropriation only with consent of the owner, no force, no fraud, no stealing, etc. The goods speak for themselves, as it were.[28] In the case of no coincidence, no communication to start cooperation can be expected. The semi-opportunities, however, mean: I have something you want, but you do not have anything to offer in return (*or vice versa*). Can such a semi-opportunity be used as the start of a transaction if players communicate? The constellations are asymmetrical in the sense that the player who wants something but does not have a quid pro quo to offer on the spot is in an inferior position and will have to make some extra effort to get a transaction going. If *ego* has a good desired by *alter*, *alter* can propose to *expand* the interaction, first of all in terms of time, or *temporally*: Let me take what you have now and I promise to bring something you want on the next market day. The implication of temporal expansion will normally be that the pair-wise inter-action will also be expanded *socially* and *materially*. A case of *social* expansion would be for *alter* to introduce a third player to perform a triangular transaction that circumvents the no-double-coincidence-of-wants condition. This social expansion simultaneously involves a material expansion in the form of introducing an additional good. So indirect exchange means that *alter* tries to exchange her own good for the goods *ego* wants.[29] The initiative for this may come from *ego*: You go and try to exchange your good for something I want. Then you can come back, and so on. Temporal expansion may also be combined with social expansion without indirect exchange: *Alter* can bring in a third player that pledges for *alter's* promise to deliver to *ego*.

How can *alter* convince *ego* that a promise to bring something tomorrow is as good as a quid pro quo on the spot? One can construct all sorts of cases in which symmetry between the agents is maintained or can be re-established. For example, because of production cycles both players know that *ego* will be in a position tomorrow like the one in which *alter* is today. However, because of the time passing between the promise and its eventual fulfillment, a promise *always* involves the risk that it will not be kept. Therefore, a promise will only be accepted if *ego* thinks that *alter*, as the one making it, not only has the ability to fulfill it, but also has additional reasons – in terms of norms, sanctions and rewards – for keeping the promise. The risk of *alter* just walking away with *ego's* stuff can thus be reduced. Sanctions may be informal – as in the private sphere of close communal relations where loss of reputation and status is sufficient to deter players from breaking their promises – or formal, for example, if the promise is in the form of a written contract and there is a legal system that sanctions breach of contract. A sufficient sanction can simply be the threat of discontinuing an ongoing, repeated interaction, if *alter* is dependent on continuing it. An important issue is whether the sanctions include attempts to materially compensate the lender for the loss incurred when the promise is not kept or whether they are just sanctions punishing the defector (Shubik 1999: 1, ch. 12).

In any case, the semi-opportunity constellations can induce players to find ways to deal with such situations that answer to the interests of both players. Despite the risk involved, to accept a promise may be mutually advantageous compared to the losses incurred by both having to fall back into autarky or by spending time and effort to find a more suitable trading partner. We will return to these questions when discussing credit (see Section 3.5).

Compared to coordination through promises, there seems to be a less risky solution, however. All that is needed to overcome the trading obstacles in the semi-opportunity constellations is an object that everybody wants.[30] What kind of object could that be? If it were a consumption or production good, it could easily happen that some players reach satiation and thus refuse to accept it in trades. So, at least with respect to any particular good useful for consumption or production, we are back to square one. The good that everybody wants, so that it can help overcome obstacles to trade, would have to be a good for which there is no satiation and thus unlimited demand. Described in terms of Searle's formula, the good 'X' that 'counts as Y', namely, as a means of exchange, does so because we can never get enough of X. Ironically and paradoxically, such an X will have to be something that everybody wants exclusively as a *tool in exchange*. It opens the access to all other goods because all their owners want it for the same use. Thus, everybody wants it because everybody knows that all the others want it. Clearly, this is a bootstrap phenomenon (Iwai 1996). The tricky thing about it is to explain how it can emerge in a social process where some players somehow must have the ideas and the power to introduce such an innovation.[31]

Return to Section 3.1.2. *Ego* has something *alter* wants, but *alter* cannot offer a means of consumption or production that *ego* wants. Instead, *alter* offers an object asserting that everybody else wants it, too, implying that it is a universal means of exchange. *Ego* takes it in his hands, sniffs at it, bites into it, turns it around, beats it with a hammer and so on. Nothing happens, no special quality.[32] But *alter* says that all others will find this means of exchange so attractive that *ego* would have no problems to acquire any desired good with it from one of the other players out there. Why should *ego* believe this? How could *ego* know that *alter* is not making this up? Instead of accepting *alter*'s offer, *ego* could react simply by saying: 'If you are so sure that all others will accept this thing in exchange for their goods, why don't you go yourself and get what I want with it? Then we can barter.' *Ego* would avoid risk and trouble.

If, on the other hand, *ego* is sufficiently certain that *alter*'s assertion is correct and that for some unknown, mysterious reason the thing is really what everybody wants and therefore a valid general means of exchange, it is plausible that *ego* will want it, too, and accept it. The advantages of – temporarily – holding a general means of exchange instead of acquiring a particular good are gains in 'degrees of freedom' (Parsons 1967: 307): Holding a universal means of exchange means that *ego* can select *when, where, with whom* and *for what* to trade. In the terms used above: the means of exchange permits the temporal, spatial, social and material expansion of the two-player situation. These additional degrees of freedom for money-holders also imply additional security in face of uncertainty because *ego* has a means to cope with all sorts of contingent events lurking in the future.

Given that the advantages of disposing over a general means of exchange are clear, we have two obvious explanatory problems: Where would such a universal social tool come from? How can players – as a condition for accepting it – gain confidence or even certainty that other players will accept it in turn? Of course, there is a third open problem. I have so far not considered the quantitative aspects of either bartering or buying and selling. Instead, by introducing the action coordination problems in barter as problems of communication, I wanted to demonstrate that the issue of determining exchange ratios or prices quantitatively is a second order problem.[33] But it is about time to discuss it.

3.2 Origins and acceptability of money

In this section, I will discuss the following partly overlapping questions: Can we explain the origin of money? Can we explain the acceptance of money? Do we have a complete theory of price determination? The answers to all three questions will be negative, but will nonetheless allow for a better understanding of the role of money in absorbing the uncertainty implied in the contingencies we have considered so far.

3.2.1 Origins of money

Evidently, to come up with a plausible story about the origins of money is a task for historians. Depending on the concept of money used such a story has to reach so far back that it does not seem likely that there is conclusive evidence for one and only one version of the story. It follows that claims by monetary theorists who invoke history as uniquely supporting their theory[34] are not very convincing. Whether the Babylonian *shekel* or the Egyptian *shad* ever played the role of initiating the transformation of 'hydraulic' (Wittfogel 1957) economies, relying extensively on redistribution (Renger 2011), into monetary economies with decentralized pair-wise exchanges in markets is unlikely to be decidable from historical evidence.[35] Rather, the reference to history seems to be matter of projecting contemporary theoretical argument into ambiguous historical evidence to increase the plausibility of a proposed theory of money. Instead of following that custom, let us leave the historical account of the origins of money to the historians and concentrate on the theoretical question: What are the conditions of possibility of money, given self-interested players involved in a game about the ownership and transfer of economic assets? How can they accomplish the installation of something like money? Since such an installation requires collective action, one major difficulty is to sort out the micro-foundations for such action according to the standards of methodological individualism. From Searle (1995), we have learned about the *form* such collective action has to take: There has to be a collective intention, describable according to the formula: We agree that 'X counts as Y in C'. From Pettit (2001), we have learned that collective intentions presupposes some organization to bring individual intentions in line for the pursuit of collective objectives. The requirement of organization does not preclude whether the organization in question is built bottom-up or top-down. If there is a sufficiently recognizable and strong common interest, one can expect a bottom-up process; if agents are caught in a prisoners' dilemma, it is more likely to be transformed top-down.

Another difficulty has to do with the *content* of the collective intention. In a world without money, somebody must have had the idea that something we now call money would be useful. This smart innovator had to convince a sufficient number of others. It was not enough for the cook to convince the king. Whatever power the king had, the coins he issued had to be accepted as a quid pro quo for goods or services by a sufficient number of his subjects in order to function as money. This would only happen if they saw some extra benefit in using these new things relative to settling affairs in the old ways. In short, to install money would not only have to benefit the innovator, but all potential money users.

Apart from the good old custom among impatient economic theorists to assume money falling like manna from heaven (Friedman 1969: 4), there are three basic versions of the origin story – sometimes combined:

1   Monetary system starts with the repeated use of one good as the *tertium comparationis*: some trader or administrator somewhere proposes to use a common unit of evaluation in barter or redistributive transactions. The others see the benefits of commensurability, accept the custom and follow suit. Subsequently, bargaining proceeds by evaluating whatever is offered or demanded as a quid pro quo in terms of the ideal unit of account. Exchanges take place according to the 'prices' thus expressed and agreed upon.
2   The emergence of a common means of exchange: Menger (1892) proposed that players learn to overcome the no-double-coincidence-of-wants problem by increasingly using the most marketable goods in indirect exchange and subsequently converging towards the use of one good as the preferred means of exchange.
3   Money is imposed from above by an authority, either in pursuit of its own interests or with the common good in mind.

All three versions share the problem that it seems difficult to imagine an agent, whether with authority or not, to convincingly predict at least some of the advantages of money use so that others will cooperate. Without the prior experience of using money, one has to think of perhaps unintended social experiments[36] with forms of 'proto'-money. In that respect, Menger's approach *(ad b)* is the most elegant because it suggests a gradual build-up of an institution by players who face a shared problem and therefore have a common interest in its solution. As to the suggestion *(ad a)* that money first emerges as a unit of account – for example, because players engaged in barter refer to quantities of a third good as a common reference object to state their demands in exchange in a communicable way[37] – it is not clear why a common unit of account would be needed in barter. The reference to a *tertium comparationis* cannot help easing the conflict between two traders about the barter ratio between their two goods. The conflicting interests of the two players can most easily be expressed directly in terms of each demanding favorable exchange ratios between the goods at hand. If means are sought for conflict resolution, help is not likely to result from a reference to a common unit in terms of a third object. It is more plausible that traders would look for a third player to act as a mediator,[38] where the third player might end up to act with the impartiality of an 'assembly of strangers' (Smith [1776] 1976a: 24). Or, what seems to be more appropriate historically, they would invoke customs and traditions. In terms of the Edgeworth-Box and Hardin's reservations (see page 65) with respect to the standard analysis of bilateral exchange, a neutral, trusted third person, the 'impartial spectator' (ibid.) may overcome the fear of both players that they could inadvertently accept a disadvantageous starting point for bargaining. Thus, a third player may push two persons on a path leading to the contract curve.

This kind of configuration also suggests a role for an authority in originating money that is more plausible than its introduction as a *deus ex machina* in (neo-) chartalism[39] (*ad c*). If 'private' players see a need for mediation or for standardization (see the example of measuring length, page 39) to create a truly *common* unit of account, but cannot easily agree on a concrete standard, a suggestion from a third party is helpful, the more so if the third party has legitimate and sanction-equipped authority to publicly declare a collective intention: 'X counts as Y in C', says the P, the Pharaoh. All others say: We accept, P has the power to declare: X counts as Y in C.[40] It follows that P can define and thereby install the 'shad' as the commonly used unit of account in old Egypt. That P is in a position to install a common unit of account in a performative act does not explain why P would do this, however. It would make sense in a redistributive economy where agents contribute to the common pool of resources that is administered by the center (for historical examples, see Renger 2011). Using a common measure to determine what has been contributed can, in turn, define claims for withdrawal, so that redistribution can take place according to a norm of fairness. Perhaps this allows the central authority to present itself as a public benefactor? But a precondition for such a redistributive mechanism is that generally acceptable transformation ratios between heterogeneous goods delivered and goods withdrawn can be defined. Without market exchange, how would a central authority accomplish this? Can it rely on own measuring efforts to propose equivalence, for example, by referring to something as opaque as an equal 'difficulty of production' (Ricardo [1823] 1986: 83)? Clearly, a money of account is useless without a complementary socially accepted mechanism for evaluating goods in some way or other. Market exchange is such a mechanism.

In any case, in general, installing a unit of account looks like the easier part of the process of establishing the use of money. If we follow Wicksell (1906, vol. 2: 7) the difficult problem is to explain the convergence towards a commonly used means of exchange.

Translating Marx's structuralist form of value analysis (Marx [1867] 1975, ch.1) into an action-theoretical frame suggests a possible synthesis of the unit of account and means of exchange stories. Starting from the assumed background of a DoL-PiP economy, all agents produce for exchange. The anticipation of exchange is guiding their decisions about what and how much to produce. The problem for any agent is to ascertain the potential 'weight' of her/his private product in a prospective exchange. To optimally exploit 'market chances' (Weber 1968: 91), each agent's aim is to find out as exactly as possible what his product is worth in the eyes of the others. They can only learn by doing. Agent A can take a first step in that direction by bargaining with an arbitrary agent B who shows an interest in A's good a, and perhaps they arrive at an agreement to barter. But the knowledge gained from this exercise is limited. Agent A now just knows what agent B is willing to give and can memorize this in terms of an $a = xb$ ratio (read the '=' as 'is exchangeable for', with x being a positive real number and assuming that barter ratios do not depend on the scale of transactions). What about agents C, D ... N with commodities $c, d ... n$? Repeating the exercise will result in barter ratios $a = xb$, $a = yc$, ..., $a = zn$. For agent A, this list (what Marx calls the 'expanded form of value') may be complete, but his (and everybody else's) knowledge is still too limited to make full use of all market opportunities or to protect himself from unfortunate decisions. As Marx suggested, to arrive at a 'general' form, agent A can simply read the list backwards and end up with 'proto'-price expressions: $p_b = 1/xa$, $p_c = 1/ya$, ... $p_n = 1/za$ (read: a unit of b can be 'bought' for $1/x$ units of a, etc.). Thus, for agent A, his commodity a serves as the means to express exchange ratios with all other commodities, based on trial runs in barter. In his own, individual perspective, commodity a turns into the 'general equivalent' for all other commodities, but this holds only for A. The other agents may arrive at the same status for their own respective commodities, so there will be as many 'general' equivalents as there are agents. Such 'proto-prices' are not very useful for communication because they remain idiosyncratic. Most importantly, what agents cannot do without further information about other exchanges *in which they are not involved*: They cannot check their p_b, p_c, ... p_n 'proto'-prices for consistency. For that, they need to perform triangular operations based on observing other agents trading the respective commodities. (We will return to that point when we discuss price formation in quantitative terms. The point is crucial because it can be used to show that it is not by following some mimetic instinct but because it is rational that agents try to observe what others are doing, given everybody wants to optimally exploit market chances.)

An action-theoretical translation of Marx's structural argument starts from the question: Given that the objective of agents in the DoL-PiP economy is to exchange, how can any agent know about her market opportunities given the particular bundle of commodities she is bringing to the market? The argument leads to a decisive threshold: Each commodity owner/producer uses his or her commodity as a general equivalent. But something has to happen for them to transcend their individual cognitive frameworks in order to install what Marx calls the 'universal equivalent', that is a commodity that all use to express whatever 'values' they want to express. How can *all* commodity owners converge on using one of the commodities[41] as a – then truly – universal equivalent? Marx did not answer that question in a satisfactory way (Cartelier 1991: 259f.). He proposed that in order to single out a universal equivalent commodity owners/traders must perform a 'social act' ('gesellschaftliche Tat'). Strangely, Marx then suggests that to accomplish that, they simply have to follow their 'natural instinct', so that 'they have already acted before they have thought' (Marx [1867] 1975: 86).[42] But 'instincts' are not a suitable factor in the search for micro-foundations. Instead, we can translate the problem into Searle's vocabulary. There must be a collective intention to the effect that 'X counts as Y in C', thus assigning the status function of 'universal equivalent' (Y) to a commodity (X).

With or without Marx, in terms of our search for a theoretical explanation of the 'logical' origins of money, a decisive link is missing: How can commodity owners not only agree on a common unit for expressing prices (or values, as Marx has it), but also on using a common means of exchange?[43] In contrast to this difficulty, there seems to be hardly any problem to explain the general use of such a unit to express prices and serve as a means of exchange *once it is installed*, as we will shortly see. But there is no satisfactory argument explaining how money originated in a context without money. Invoking collective intentions and function assignment in Searle's terms does not do the job, although both conceptual tools seem to be useful ingredients of the explanation sought.

So let us turn to the second question: How can we explain the general acceptance of money? Why is it used by everybody once it is available as a social tool?

3.2.2 Acceptance of money

Once money as an institution is installed, it is easy to see why any individual will use money. The advantages of doing like the Joneses do are obvious.

> Suppose we are tradesmen. It matters little to any of us what commodities he takes in exchange for goods (other than commodities he himself can use). But if he takes what others refuse he is stuck with something useless, and if he refuses what others take he needlessly inconveniences his customers and himself. Each must choose what he will take according to his expectations about what he can spend – that is, about what the others will take: gold and silver if he can spend gold and silver, U.S. notes if he can spend U.S. notes, Canadian pennies if he can spend Canadian pennies... whatever may come along if he can spend whatever may come along, nothing if he can spend nothing.
>
> (Lewis 1969: 7)

Frequently, the Nash equilibrium concept is offered as an explanation for such ubiquitous acceptance of money. A Nash equilibrium is defined as a combination of moves, one from each player, such that each one is a best reply on its player's part to the other players' choices. With respect to money use, that means that for each player the use of money is the best reply to the others using money. So a player will use money if he expects that the others will use money. The equilibrium is self-enforcing. No player has an incentive to deviate, given the choices of the others.

However, invoking the Nash equilibrium concept looks much like a tautology when considered as an attempt to *explain* an institution as a *result* of actions. All it says is: Once the institution is in place, it is best for everybody to act according to the rules defined by the institution. If player A sees that for everybody else the best response is to use money, and using money is the best response for player A, and everybody knows this, then using money is the best response for player A and everybody else, and so on. But how, in any given moment, can anybody be certain that the others will accept object X as money? Is this merely a case of confirming expectations that were unfounded in the beginning but became more and more backed by experience as life goes on?[44]

Let us be clear about the leap of faith required in any acceptance of money. Remembering Menger, we can construct two stories of indirect exchange. Both have in common that traders move from a utility position defined by their endowment to a better position defined by a target good bundle *via* an in-between position in which they neither hold their original endowment nor their target bundle. The first story seems to be simpler. Traders acquire a quantity of a third good to be used as a means of exchange that represents a utility increase compared to their initial position (e.g., Feldman 1973). However, this version of the indirect exchange story rests on the assumption that third goods as means of exchange are available which have the convenient property of not only being useful outside of exchange for the trader in question, but of also being more useful than their starting bundle. Intuitively, it would seem that the double-coincidence-of-wants condition for barter is merely shifted forward to apply to the good selected as means of exchange. This does not help much to understand how the obstacle of the double-coincidence-of-wants condition is overcome. Therefore, the second, more difficult and more adequate version of the indirect exchange story acknowledges that indirect exchange – whether with or without money – normally involves a temporary utility loss for the player performing it. Player A owns x units of good *a* and wants to exchange them for y units of good *b* held by B, given that A prefers y*b* to x*a*. Unfortunately for A, direct exchange is blocked because B does not want any *a*. A searches for and finds a potential way to transform x*a* into y*b* by first trading with C to acquire z*c* in order to then transform z*c* into y*b* by trading with B. A does not want commodity *c* for its own sake but only because he knows that B is willing to trade *b* for *c* at a rate acceptable for A (acceptability being defined by the condition that, for A, y*b*Px*a*, with '**P**' meaning 'is preferred to'). In this sequence, the utility of *c* does not matter for A, except that it must be the case that y*b***P**z*c*. If the intermediate good bundle acquired as a means of exchange had the same or greater utility as the target good bundle, there would be no reason for A to continue along the transaction chain. At the same time, the utility of *c* as compared to *a* – whether z*c***P**x*a* or x*a*P*z*c – does not matter for A, as long as A has sufficient reasons to assume that, for B, z*c*P*y*b. This implies that the utility of the commodity used as a means of exchange matters for A only, if A is *not sufficiently informed* about B's preferences with respect to that commodity. Given such insufficient knowledge, A will only use a commodity as a means of exchange that offers some protection against the risk of becoming stuck with something useless in case *B* does not want to trade *c* for *b* after all. Thus, the higher the uncertainty about the preferences of the owner of a target bundle of goods with respect to the selected means of exchange, the more this means of exchange must have some utility for its selector. However, as suggested by Menger, there is a way out of this obstacle to trade in the direction of *social* expansion: Protection against the risk of being stuck with an unwanted good can also be provided by using something as a means of exchange that is located high in the preference ordering of as many traders as possible. In other words, *B*'s specific preferences are less important for *A* if *A* can expect a sufficient number of other traders to accept the means of exchange selected by *A* under acceptable terms. This social expansion corresponds to Menger's criterion of 'Marktgängigkeit' (marketability): *A* will attempt to select a good as a means of (indirect) exchange that offers a high probability of being accepted by a large number of market participants. In this way, the requirement of *A* knowing the preferences of *B*, as the owner of the target good, can be loosened once *A* is sufficiently familiar with the preferences of *C*, *D*, *E*, … *N* to be able to select a highly marketable good as a means of exchange.

Thus, there is an inverse relation between the required utility of the means of exchange for *A* and *A*'s knowledge of the preferences of *B*. The utility of the means of exchange for *A* becomes less important the better *A* knows *B*'s preferences and *vice versa*. The implication of further social expansion is analogous: The more certain *A* is that the selected means of exchange will be desired not only by *B*, but also by *C*, *D*, *E* and so on, the less important will be the utility of the means of exchange for *A* himself. The more *A* learns from experience[45] that sufficiently many unknown others desire A's means of exchange with an intensity favorable for *A*'s trading chances, the less the means of exchange will have to have any utility at all for *A* (utility as a means of consumption or production, to be sure). The temporary utility loss incurred by *A* in indirect exchange, when *A* exchanges *a* for *c* in order to acquire *b*, would not matter. In this way, knowledge of the preferences of others can function as a substitute for the utility of the means of exchange for oneself.[46]

The theoretical gain implied in this account is, at least, that a plausible form of indirect exchange can help to understand one crucial feature of modern monetary systems: The intrinsic uselessness of money objects. It would be explained if we could generalize from the perspective of *A* to those of *B*, *C*, … *N*. *None* of the agents would have to care about the utility of the means of exchange as long and insofar as each can expect *all others* to accept it. But how can the collective arrive there? We are back to the origin question.

Without a story of emergence of a collective assigning the functions of money to some object, the observation that there is a trade-off between knowledge of the preference of others and usefulness of the means of exchange does not seem to contribute much, however. If *A* has to be certain about the preferences of *B*, *C*, ... *N* in order to afford ignoring the utility of the means of exchange for herself, could not the knowledge required simply be used by *A* to adjust her productive activities to fit those preferences? This would be a big step toward *ex ante* coordination of production. Products could be traded directly, without relying on indirect exchange and exposing oneself to the risk of being stuck with an unwanted means of exchange. But this would require anticipating both the kind and the quantities of goods/services demanded. With correct anticipations, *A*'s products would be perfect means of barter. The situation would be: *A* knows what *B*, *C*, ... *N* have to offer and wants their products. If *A* also knows what *B*, *C*, ... *N* are demanding from others, *A* can select a bundle of goods to produce that a sufficient number of the others are demanding. *A* can be a successful trader – by *creating* the double coincidence of wants with *B*, *C*, N through production. Indirect exchange would not be required. However, how can anyone anticipate what others want if these others are also trying to anticipate what the others want? The situation is one of multiple contingency. To gradually move out of that, agents have to position themselves in a division of labor that allows them to produce for the well-known set of needs of a roughly expectable number of others.

The less open the possibilities of gaining the required knowledge and of adapting own production activities are, the higher the uncertainty involved in specialized production for the market. Given some level of risk aversion, lower knowledge would imply fewer possibilities for and therefore lower gains from the division of labor. One would expect only staple goods to be produced for exchange, that is goods for which demand is easily predictable. Can the requirement of broader knowledge of the preferences of others be replaced by less stringent requirements for the conduct of indirect exchange? There seem to be several possibilities.

First, consider A as a 'representative trader' and perform the standard, somewhat dubious, generalization typical for much of current macroeconomics from such a representative to the aggregate. One could argue: If all traders know that all others always desire the good selected as a means of exchange, none of them has to care about the utility of this good – that means that it does not have to be a 'good' at all. Any object will do, as long as all select the same object. The underlying reasoning for each is: I don't really want that thing, but I can see that all others want it. So I will use and accept it, too. (But note that again, as with the problem of conceptually 'deriving' a Marxian universal equivalent, the crucial step from individual reasoning to social installation of a *common* means of exchange remains unexplained.)

Second, we can introduce mediators. Traders who buy A's whole output and sell it to B, C, ... N (Goodhart's (1989) 'market makers', Clower's (1995) 'marketors'). Such traders will have to offer A in return for her product a means of exchange that A can use in all further trades to acquire her target bundle of goods. At the same time, such traders will specialize and perform large numbers of transactions, so they can gain the broad knowledge of preferences required to form probability estimates of demand.

There must be a critical threshold beyond which a specialized trader starts being effective. The trader must mediate between a set of producers of the same type of good and consumers of that good. Why should the producers not trade directly? If we are talking about the double-coincidence of wants requirement, we could solve the problem by introducing selling points (Iwai 1996) for each good and injecting money into the system. Agents switch between producing, selling and buying. They need to coordinate their timing. Produce from Monday to Friday, go to the market on Saturday. If everybody wants to sell at the same time, there will be no one left to buy, so we arrange for producers to come in pairs like identical twins, with the first half of producers selling from 8 to 12 a.m. and the other half buying, and the second half selling from 1 to 5 p.m. with the first half buying. On Sundays, everybody can stay home and consume. Would a specialized trader be helpful in organizing a market like that? The producers must all sell and need time to buy, so they cannot spend their whole market time engaged in selling. An agent specializing in trade could wait at the market gate, buy everything from producers entering from 8 to 9 a.m., arrange the goods for sale and start selling at 10 a.m. Everybody could know where to go for selling and buying.

Finally, if a social constellation can be established in which the holders of a common means of exchange are always on the *short side* of the market, then these holders neither would have to have any knowledge of the preference orderings of others – beyond the conjecture that somewhere out there in the market there is normally is sufficient demand for whatever private individual agents tend to produce – nor would the means of exchange have to have any utility for anybody. Everybody would accept such a means of exchange.

What are possible arguments for stable short side position of money holders: Clower's cash-in-advance constraint (Clower 1969: 207f.) is not based on an argument, but introduced as an assumption characterizing a 'pure money economy'. Referring to the state and the obligation to pay taxes with state money (Wray, Ingham) does not help much. The state certainly is the major economic agent in most economies, but people tend to do more and other things with money than paying taxes. More promising is the introduction of capitalism and wage labor into the argument: Wage labor is a sustainable institution insofar and because access to goods is possible only with money. The moneyless have to sell their labor power. If – due to a sufficiently high rate of unemployment – buyers of labor power as holders of money are on the short side of the market more or less continuously, that will translate into a constellation where all holders of money are on the short side. However, all these arguments (with the exception of Clower's assumption) refer to the larger social environment of monetary systems, the state, capitalist enterprises and so on. This is beyond the range of my argument in this book.

Menger's puzzle of the general acceptability of useless objects as means of exchange can be approached by referring to Searle's arguments on the collective assignment of functions. The problem can then be formulated as the question: How and why do use functions and exchange functions separate?

Something useless can function as a means of exchange; something useful may not be exchangeable at all. This may appear puzzling – think of the classic value paradox – unless we bear in mind that any functions that appear to be inherent in objects are really assigned by *us*. They are not inherent in objects as physical objects. We know that bread in one version or another is useful for most people and we should also know that this quality of usefulness is nothing that emanates from the physical, chemical, biological properties of the objects alone. As physical objects they are what they are. They become useful only in relation to an agent. The same physical object can have several functions. When classical economists speak of 'use value' and 'exchange value', they speak about two different functions that may be ascribed to the same set of objects. The puzzle of alternating or separating functions dissolves once we see that these respective functions may be ascribed by different people: What is a use value for me is an exchange value for you. The same objects may also change functions for the same agents. Something may have been purely a use value for me yesterday and become an exchange value today. Utility can be a function of an object for only one individual with idiosyncratic tastes, but it is normally assigned by collectives. Take Searle's example: I can sit on the trunk of a fallen tree. I use it as a chair. We are three and sit on the trunk of a fallen tree. We use it as a bench. Is the 'bench' function the result of three individual function assignments? If I use it as a bench only because you use it as a bench and vice versa, the function 'bench' is the result of a collective function assignment.

Utility is a function that is ascribed by us to physical objects or processes that we then call goods and services. Once people start 'to truck, barter and exchange' (Adam Smith), the physical objects not only have utility, but are traded and thus are assigned the additional function of means of exchange by their owners. Again: Utility can be a function of an object for one individual only (Robinson). But in exchange, individual A works on the assumption that object *a* produced/owned/brought to the market by A is in some way useful for B, C, ... N. When something is brought to the market as a commodity, as a means of exchange, the offering agent acts on the belief that it is useful for others. Without that conviction, it would not make sense to bring it to the market. On the market, at the point of potential exchange, there will be communication, talking usefulness up and down according to the conflicting interests of buyers and sellers, but before the background of a shared conviction that the thing is useful for the potential buyer. So utility will be a collectively assigned function (although the concrete object traded may not be useful for the seller). By contrast, at least for a start, the object is a means of exchange only for the seller, thus this function is only assigned individually. Because A can anticipate that others will assign utility, A can use good *a* as a means of exchange. Good *a* may then come to be seen as a means of exchange by the potential buyer B, too, because in bargaining B will try to see the situation in the perspective of A.

In Searle's terms, we can understand the means of exchange function as being assigned as an *iteration* of the assignment of utility. The latter is the precondition for the assignment of the former, the means of exchange function. To define something as a means of exchange may be an individual act, but the individual has to anticipate a social constellation. At least one other agent is required to make the individual function assignment real.

We can see the contrast to money – and the explanatory gap in theories of money: The function of money objects as means of exchange must be collectively assigned by more than two agents right from the start. And, as it turned out in the long history of money, money objects do not have to be useful in terms of consumption or production. To understand collective function assignment without more than arbitrary physical underpinnings, as in various forms of money objects, it helps perhaps to think about their function in terms of abstract coordination problems. Two agents want to coordinate and they cannot communicate directly (the case of the interrupted phone call, or the case of losing each other in a crowd). They must take the perspective of the other and try to see the clues/focal points that the other might refer to in deciding how to act, although these clues may have no immediate relevance for the decision (the point is: There is nothing of such immediate relevance in the situation, otherwise it would be easy to reconstruct the decisions made by the other). Think of trying to anticipate the other's choices in 'heads or tails?' The probabilities are clearly 50/50, so there is no rational way of anticipating a choice. But if you are rewarded for making the same choice as the other, you will look for some clue that might guide the other. For example, in 'heads or tails?' you may choose 'heads' because the word comes first in the description of the choice situation. If you are successful you will stick to that choice in the hope that the precedent will motivate the other agent(s) to repeat their choices.

Can this kind of argument be applied to the collective assignment of the functions of money to physical objects that are useless? (cf. Lewis 1969). All you need is a common selection, the same selection by everybody involved. This need opens the way for a role, but a rather unimportant one, for some authority: Because the need is there already, it can ease the process of agreeing on a common selection by fiat.

So what exactly is the social constellation in which the two functions, utility and means of exchange, can separate? In a barter setting, what is a means of exchange for me has to be useful for you and *vice versa*. We each assign a different function: Something can be useless for me but serve me as a means of exchange because it is useful and *not* a means of exchange for you. When we consider modern money, however, this asymmetry in a symmetric constellation somehow changes into one where, to acquire useful objects from one another, we all use money objects as means of exchange that are totally useless for all of us. At the same time, we produce commodities as mere means of exchange, anticipating their usefulness for others.

Seen in the perspective of the standard neoclassical argument that the economy is, in the last instance, driven by desires to consume, this whole social arrangement looks weird: In order to get what I wish to consume, I produce something that I believe others will wish to consume. I bring this to the market, exchange it for something I cannot consume, namely money, then, if successful, I use the money to buy what I wish to consume. Shouldn't there be a simpler way to organize economic life? Why not produce what I want to consume in the first place? Of course, there are the advantages of the division of labor: higher productivity, more wealth on easier terms for all, etc. But how could agents who are assumed to be pure individual utility maximizers converge towards this weird social arrangement? It may have advantages, but seen from the perspective of individuals, the arrangement requires complicated agreements/conventions that imply relying on unknown others. The advantages have to be balanced against the costs, including the risks of wrong anticipations, of not being able to sell, or only at a price that will not cover costs, and so on.

In evolutionary terms, does it make sense to say that the original unity of functions in one object, the commodity, as object of consumption or means of production and means of exchange, has been replaced by a separation and differentiation of these functions? This appears to be the case with fiat money. But on the complementary side of commodities, it would be wrong to see these functions as being completely separated. The commodity *producer* still considers his products as means of exchange for himself and as a means to acquire the general means of exchange. To function as such, it has to be useful for others. Separation may be complete, on the other hand, for the buyer/consumer holding fiat money: Here is the money, there is the good I want to buy. The money object has no utility (for consumption or production). It can only be used as a tool in exchange. In short, the means of exchange function can be assigned as a separate, autonomous function to an object that everybody may consider to be totally useless in terms of consumption or production. This requires at least one additional iteration of function assignment based on a collective intention: '*We* count X as money in C'.

This differentiation of functions leads to a more complicated pattern of exchange transactions. They are split into purchase and sale. Instead of A trading y with B for x, A trades y for money with C and money for x with B. For this pattern to emerge, we have to know: Where did C get money? Why does B accept money? In other words, the development suggested is: Agents switch from two-person-barter interactions to triangular processes, selling to one, buying from another agent. Due to the use of money, these transactions are connected to form networks. They necessarily involve sequences, thus needing time. Money objects move on, from one transaction to the next, not just accidentally or occasionally. Rather, the acceptance of objects as money depends strictly on the expectation that they can be used in a subsequent transaction. This last point may sound innocuous, but it implies that it is simply impossible to understand money in the timeless, simultaneous mutual determination perspective of general equilibrium theory.[47] To do their work, money objects have to wander from one trade to the next. Or: the money leg of each transaction is seen by the participating agents themselves as an incomplete step in a time-consuming process. Why should B *accept* A's money if the money object has no utility in terms of consumption or production for either B or A, if not for the reason that it can again be used in a subsequent transaction?[48] *Acceptance* is conceivable as a rational act only because agents can anticipate the next round of activities in which a seller B can use the money object received from A to buy something from C, and so on. This anticipation is more than a simple wish for the future. It is based on the experience of a 'normal' way of doing things, a firm pattern of everyday life in businesses and in households, notwithstanding the fact that anticipations may be wrong from time to time.

Even if this is normally ignored in everyday life, in an abstract comparison the use of money objects without any utility involves a greater risk than barter for the owners of goods offered in a trade. In barter, you receive a quid pro quo on the spot or else there is no transaction. Given money objects (or monetary accounts) that are totally useless (or pointless) outside a given sphere of exchange, the risk of anyone acting as a seller is to receive such money and, subsequently, to not find somebody who will in turn accept it. One does not want to unwillingly end up with money objects instead of objects of consumption or means of production.[49] In other words, there seems to be a trade-off. In barter, we run into the double-coincidence-of-wants problem. With money, we run the risk of ending up with useless money objects.

3.2.3 *The minimal social setting of money use*

In buying and selling, just as in indirect exchange, there are at least four agents involved in a time frame that reaches beyond the present. The buyer (agent 1) must have received the money objects – normal players cannot produce them themselves[50] – from somebody else (agent 2) in a previous transaction (t_{-1}). The seller (agent 3) who accepts money now (t_0) does this because he expects a fourth agent to accept the money objects in the future (t_1), in a next transaction. As we have already seen, the expansion of the bilateral setting is threefold,[51] compared to the 'catallactic atom': *Materially*, for any agent to transform an asset (object 1) in a given endowment into a target asset (object 2) a piece of money (object 3) is used as an intermediary. *Temporally*, both the past and the future enter into the transaction: The buyer must have acquired the money previously and it is accepted by the seller in the expectation of it being usable again as money in the future; *socially*, beyond the pair involved in the current transaction, there must be at least two additional players, one from whom the current buyer got the money in a previous transaction and a second one who is expected to accept the money in the future that the seller is accepting now. What are the implications of letting elements of the outside world intrude into the 'catallactic atom'?

The least one can say is that the acceptance of money by any seller requires a large dose of confidence in the stability of institutional arrangements: When I accept your money, I must expect unknown others to do in the future as I am doing now.[52] There is no way to anchor such an expectation in the rationality of single-minded utility maximizers.[53] The standard economic explanation of an action consists of using a player's definition of the situation and his preferences to derive his decisions. (That a decision is not yet an action is usually ignored.) So in accepting money, the definition of the situation by a player must include the belief that business will go on as usual, that the money will in turn be accepted by (unknown) others.[54] This belief may be well backed by everyday experience. But as it clearly is a belief in a social fact, and social facts are the results of what we do, and whatever we do we can do differently, there is an irreducible element of uncertainty in the acceptance of money. How could it be understood in the terms of a purely individualistic rational-action explanation? *Ego* has to believe that an unknown *alter* will behave in predictable ways when confronted with money. How is such a belief formed? To what extent can it be rational?

If we consider the use of money as something we learn and rely on in the same way as we learn to speak and use language to communicate, this problem of circularity in the acceptance of money may seem to lose some of its bite. After all, the use of language includes a large dose of irrational or sub-rational elements, too. It is difficult to imagine an explanation in terms of rational actions for the fact that this animal is called 'dog' in English, 'chien' in French, 'perro' in Spanish, and so on. We simply use the word we have learned to indicate what we want to communicate about. Using the proper word works. Others who speak the same language can understand me.

Is not the use – and therefore the acceptance – of money an analogue to language use in this respect? In a way, yes. Just as the selection of the sound sequence for a word in a natural language is mostly arbitrary and is not necessarily related to its meaning, the selection of some physical object to serve as money appears to be arbitrary, apart from some well-known technical properties that have turned out to be appropriate for money objects (durability, difficulty to forge, divisibility, etc.). But, as noted above already, while we may say: 'Money talks', we also have to say: 'When money talks it says good-by'. Once you have learned the language, speaking does not require much effort, whereas each acceptance and use of money (other than in its function as a means of accounting) demands a sacrifice, as it were. You have to deliver something desirable or expend all sorts of undesirable efforts to get money in the first place. What you get is something you cannot use other than in a next exchange. You hope that by subsequently ceding ownership of your money, by giving it to a future trading partner, you will succeed to make him do what you want. If a subsequent exchange cannot be accomplished, the money object deteriorates into a piece of paper or a piece of metal, or the information in your account turns into noise. Given that this is a real danger, although it may not loom over us every day, how can we – as rational beings – stick firmly to the expectation that whatever we accept as money will be accepted by a sufficient number of other players in the next round? The 'bootstrap' answer is: We *all* stick to the expectation because somehow we all know that this is the only way to make the expectation come true. Do we have to presuppose an underlying *collective* commitment of money users? Yes, but only in the sense of Searle's collective assignment of functions. It is certainly not explicit and appears to conform to the observation that money works best when nobody thinks about how it works. Although this is true of language, too, the irrational element in money use has more weight than the irrational elements we can detect in language use. Nonetheless, empirically, even extremely clever real agents are evidently able and willing to ignore this uncertainty underlying money use in their everyday doings. The main reason for the successful suppression of the risk of painful losses ensuing from a breakdown of the collective function assignment supporting a given monetary system simply seems to be that we all grew into successfully playing the money game. The child learns that this is how we accomplish property change in a peaceful and mutually accepted, mostly frictionless way. It works reasonably well for the realization of our objectives so that we continuously and unquestioningly partake in the collective intentionality supporting it – although this has somehow slipped into what Searle calls the 'background' of our intentional behavior.

Apart from such own experience of successful money use, perhaps one reason for not questioning the viability of the money game in rational terms and rather unquestioningly partaking in the collective intentionality underlying it is that, in accepting or spending money in a given moment, we can see ourselves as building one more link in a chain of transactions that has started a long time ago. The 'we'-intentionality has immense historical depth. Imagine Croesus to be the first buyer, buying the service of one of his soldiers with one of his newly invented coins in the sixth century BC. The soldier then transmogrifies from a seller into a buyer, finding someone who sells him a house; the seller of the house buys a boat, and so on. If it were not for all sorts of things happening to the coin, like being buried, getting lost, losing weight, being melted and made into a ring, etc., and if it were not for the changes of monetary systems, the original piece of money could still be wandering from buyer to seller until today, with people easily understanding their respective intentions and thus being able to coordinate their actions by using the coin across many generations and spaces. Thus, the history of money use offers a practical proof of its own viability.[55] To say it in a first person perspective: I feel that I can safely continue playing a game that appears to have worked reasonably well most of the time for most people as long

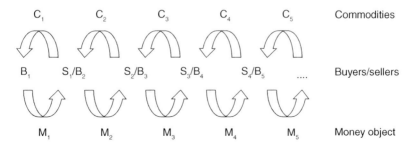

Figure 3.2 The chain of monetary transactions.

as the relevant others I observe do feel the same way. As individual players, we define ourselves as links in an ever-expanding chain of transactions. We can accept money because we see ourselves as forming such a link.

In a sequence in time, commodities move from seller to buyer, money objects move from buyer to seller and each player performs a role change from seller to buyer. Transactions are final.[56] Buyers may become consumers or producers. To become consumers is what keeps them alive. To become producers is what allows them to reappear in markets as sellers.

Switching back to the observer perspective, it is clear that to single out one such chain of transactions does not even come close to adequately depicting the complex workings of a monetary system. But the chain image can be used to demonstrate, first of all, the social, temporal and material aspects of money use. Compared to the catallactic atom, it involves expansions in all three dimensions. With the exception of the 'first buyer' (and the question how he acquired (or produced) money objects in the first place), each player is performing two roles in a sequence, interacting with at least two other players, selling a commodity *now* for a piece of money that comes out of the *past* with the expectation to buy another commodity in the *future*.

Second, the chain of transactions illustrates the way we gain experience in money use. When a seller turns into a buyer, she will carry the knowledge of the previous into the next transaction, so there is a built-in process of information collection and information use accompanying the movements of money objects through time, space and the social network.

Third, whereas commodities disappear into the private spheres of consumption or production where they are sooner or later used up, money objects – as long as they are to serve as money – reappear in the semi-public space of what is somewhat misleadingly[57] called 'circulation', that is, they move from one player to the next with more or less speed. After each transaction, the money holder has the choice of spending or saving.[58] If we imagine many such interwoven chains of transaction and some event that will shock a sufficient number of sellers and stop them for a while from turning into buyers, the whole social metabolism accomplished through the change of ownership of commodities can be seriously disrupted.[59]

Fourth and most important, each transaction is a locus of price formation. Each buyer/seller pair can negotiate and may or may not agree on a price. Price formation will be influenced by the fact that transactions are interdependent along the chain. Money not only has to flow, but it is flowing in definite amounts between each buyer and seller. Buyers are constrained in their offers by what they previously received.[60] Players form links, have memories and will observe other, similar transactions when forming prices. In addition, all this is happening in the framework of a division of labor, of specialized production for sale that creates material interdependence in the form of input–output intertwinements. Nonetheless, in principle, because each buyer/seller pair is interacting in a setting of double contingency and, given their respective assets, is free to fix whatever price the two players agree on,[61] each transaction is to some degree independent of all the others.

3.3 Quantitative price determination

This mixture of inter- and independence of transactions results in a loosely coupled system.[62] To further understand how it works, we can introduce variations in the tightness or looseness of coupling. The coupling is loosened, for example, if we introduce credit relations. Adding some institutional frame, the spot payments depicted in the transaction chain above may be replaced by promises to pay, so that the time structure of transactions becomes more flexible and more complex. To start with, buyers can spend more than they have previously earned, but they have to pay what they owe at some time later on or go bankrupt.

In contrast, some sort of cross-tightening is generated by the fact that each player is part of several transaction chains. A seller does not have to turn around and spend his monetary returns in one lump to buy some quantity of a single other commodity. In a division of labor context, any producer will sell one type of commodity, his product, and then become the buyer of a whole basket of diverse other commodities. So each player is acting as a node in a network. Players do not just represent one link in one chain. The material objective for each player is to acquire an optimal target bundle of commodities in terms of their usefulness for consumption or production. The fact that the acquisition of commodities according to criteria of use is accomplished through monetary transactions, however, implies that each player tries and will be expected to maximize monetary returns as a seller – as a precondition for realizing consumption or production plans that may be framed in terms of utility and usefulness – and to minimize spending on each item as much as possible as a buyer.

Economic models have been constructed so as to use either individual decision making in terms of consumption and production plans (in general equilibrium theory) or systemic material reproduction requirements plus a distributional variable (in linear models of production) as the means to arrive at quantitative price determination. In both alternatives, agents are assumed to select their actions under constraints that are tight enough to result in determinateness. The modeling trick is simply to eliminate the freedom to choose that agents using money actually have in their decentralized market activities. They are thus seen as completely subjected to a system-logic imposed by equilibrium conditions, whether with regard to efficiency of allocation or use of resources to secure aggregate reproduction. In our terms, however, the tightening of constraints achieved in this way means that a loosely coupled system is modeled as a rigid, determinate system governed by assumed strict interdependence. Thus, attempts to model quantitative price determination appear to be successful only if money and decentralized decision making are squeezed out of the model. Alternatively, can we improve our understanding of money price formation in a loosely coupled system?

Again, imagine a participant in the DoL-PiP economy entering the market with the commodities produced for sale. Assume that money is an established institution. What our player must first do is to define an asking price for the commodity in terms of the money that everybody knows and uses. Leave aside the reasons for choosing one price or another at this point. Our player will announce an asking price in the market. She may get some reactions, but she also may get none at all. Depending on the reactions, she may conclude that the asking price was too high or too low, but this is not easy to find out. After all, what she is offering is something quite complex: a commodity bundle with a – perhaps recognizable – given quality offered in some – perhaps variable – quantity at a price that may or may not be negotiable. Players interested in buying will have to find out about these matters and may start probing and bargaining. If a buyer appears and offers to buy the whole lot for the asking price on the spot, our player cannot help but feel that she has made a mistake. The asking price is too low, but given the rules of the game, she cannot retract. If nobody shows up, the asking price is too high and she can revise it downward. Given this asymmetry, in general, it is better to ask too much, but in a range that attracts at least some buyers and opens the possibility of bargaining. If she tries to avoid such guesswork, she will need information about what others are doing in similar transactions, involving similar or same commodities. If there are competing buyers, she will get relatively useful information rather quickly. Buyers will outbid each other and selling to the highest bidder cannot be all that wrong. If there are competing sellers, there will be pressure to adapt the asking price or – with more time – change the product given that other sellers are more successful in finding buyers with their asking price.

All this is familiar and apart from the tools of standard partial equilibrium microeconomics, there are interesting sociological contributions to reconstructing the social logic of market formation (White 1981; Salais *et al.* 1998; White 2002; Beckert *et al.* 2007). But they have mostly neglected to examine the role of money in the structuring such market transactions. Can understanding money use help us to determine effective prices, given the institutions of a monetary economy and the usual data (initial endowments, preferences, technologies, players' definitions of the situation, a distributional variable)? Clearly, money use introduces some structure into trading situations in the following ways:

First, in announcing an asking price, players refer to a common standard, easily understood by all money users. Second, in market encounters of money users mutual expectations concerning their objectives are easy to form, as we have already seen: Sellers want to earn as much and buyers want to pay as little money as possible. So they are both programmed, as it were, in a definite and mutually expected way. 'To pay or not to pay' (Luhmann) is the binary code. Third, the issue then is for both to convince the other that the bid or offer is acceptable, fair, legitimate, correct, appropriate, favorable, etc. How can they do this? As they operate in a social context, the easiest way is to refer to other prices in comparable transactions. The use of money directs bargaining communication away from exclusive concern with the utility of the commodity to be traded and the persons present. Money is not comparable to commodities in terms of utility, so it does not make sense to directly compare the two objects traded when one of them is money.[63] Attention of the players is shifted to observing prices: This is how much is being paid for a comparable commodity in the market, says the seller. Depending on market conditions, perhaps she may add: If you buy from me, I will give you a better price. The buyer may ask for an even better price, depending on who is on the 'short side' of the market and so on. The conclusion is: Any reference to prices is primarily a reference to observations in the market. Any two players will seek orientation and support for their bargaining position within their one-on-one transaction by referring to what others out there in parallel situations are doing or have done in terms of observed effective prices. Fourth, the – perhaps implicit – normative claim channeling communication is: You have to treat me at least as well and maybe a little better than the others we are both observing are treating their respective trading opponents. This equality claim will be backed by the freedom to go away, the threat of breaking off negotiations, switching to the competition or refraining altogether from buying or selling the commodity in question. Except in cases of strong asset specificity (Williamson 1985: 30) no one is obliged to do business with a given single trading partner. With a minimum of competition, i.e., more than one buyer or seller of a commodity, there is always an exit option built into transactions. Thus, the freedom to choose enforces the equality claim. Money is instrumental in creating both the equality and freedom associated with markets because expressing bids and offers in terms of money allows for an easy comparison between options *and* because money can be used in all trades, so that no money-holder is bound to one single seller.[64]

Does all this help to construct a theory of price formation that enables us to derive determinate prices as dependent variables from a set of independent variables? Rather not. The idea that economic theory could be used to determine prices is too ambitious, even if all the standard non-price data describing an economy were available. The deterministic approach to a theory of prices and money is not compatible with the conception of the monetary economy as a system that is self-regulating through decentralized decision making.[65] Such a system needs 'slack' so that agents can adapt – not only in terms of quantities traded, but also in terms of prices – to externally or internally generated contingencies coming forth in a more or less unpredictable fashion. However, to reject deterministic ambitions does not mean that theory has nothing to contribute to the understanding of price formation. There are at least two distinct and well-known processes that create some order in price formation: competition and arbitrage.

3.3.1 Competition

The first is competition, of course, but competition in the commonsense meaning of overbidding by buyers and underbidding by sellers, not in the sense of 'perfect competition' as modeled in general equilibrium theory. Competition carries with it the threat of exclusion from transactions. It forces potential buyers and sellers to observe each other and to adapt to observed and expected market trends. It results in two kinds of pressures: First, the well-known pressure to respond to a change in market conditions through price changes. As a tendency, every trader of commodities that are close substitutes for each other is forced to move in the direction described by the 'law of one price'. Prices for uniform commodities can be brought to converge. Second, players may duck the threat of exclusion by trying to offer unique commodities, aiming to create a stable niche for themselves in markets consisting of several such niches where similar commodities are produced and traded, but product differentiation in terms of quality is associated with price differentiation (White 1981).

3.3.2 *Arbitrage*

The second type of process imposing order on price formation is perhaps best described as the result of actions reflecting an advanced level of experience and learning in markets: Arbitrageurs observe market prices for inconsistencies and exploit the resulting chances to gain by pure trade. Arbitrage operations will impose an order on prices insofar as they support a tendency towards a consistent price system. Given complete decentralization and independence of transactions, the number of possible pair-wise trades defines the degrees of freedom in the system. By contrast, given a consistent price system, the degrees of freedom are drastically reduced because all prices are strictly interdependent. Due to decentralization, consistency may never be attained, but due to arbitrage, it will be an 'attractor' for a price system despite the fact that transactions are decentralized.

How does arbitrage work? It requires players to perform a new role in the market game. If they see an opportunity of gains from pure trade, they will become active. To spot such opportunities arbitrageurs have to observe price relations in triangles, as it were. Take as an example the type of recent international speculation called the 'carry trade'. It was based on the rather stable interest rate differences between Japan on one side and Europe and the United States on the other since the 1990s. A player borrows Japanese Yen at extremely low Japanese interest rates, exchanges the yen for euros or dollars that can be invested in assets bearing the higher interest rates in those currency areas. As long as exchange rates do not turn against the arbitrageur to wipe out potential gains and as long as other transaction costs are sufficiently low, the arbitrageur can realize the higher interest income and recover his principal in Euros or dollars and repay his Japanese debt plus interest in yen and retain a profit. The price-'triangle' exploited here is made up of two different interest rates and a currency exchange rate.

Arbitrage is not something restricted to financial markets. Schumpeter refers to arbitrage in an argument supposed to demonstrate the advantage of indirect exchange over barter. Indirect exchange is supposed to increase the

> attainable maximum of utility for all participants. If, for example, we have three commodities – A, B, and C – which are exchanged only directly, so that on each occasion only two are exchanged against each other, there will arise three markets, on each of which will be established between two

commodities an exchange ratio which could be independent of the exchange ratios on the other two markets. Hence, it could happen that, if we let a, b, and c represent units of the commodities, on Market I, 3a might be given for, say, 2b; on Market II, 3a for 1c; and on Market III, 4b for 1c. But in that case, the possessor of 4b who wishes to have C will obviously do better, if, instead of acquiring his 1c for 4b on the market of B for C, he would go first to Market I – where he gets for his 4b, in the first instance, 6a, which, to be sure, he does not want, but for which he can get 2c on Market II: this is the essence of arbitrage.

(Schumpeter 1991: n8)

Schumpeter is wrong in maintaining that the arbitrageur contributes to a 'maximum of utility for all' in this context, because his gains will be the result of somebody else getting less, but leave this aside. The important issue is to see whether a decentralized exchange system can evolve towards consistency or, which is the same thing, towards a system of equivalence relations in which all possible gains from trade are eliminated. The argument usually is that the attraction of sufficiently high gains from arbitrage will draw more players into this kind of market sub-game, leading to shifts in supply, demand and exchange ratios, so that arbitrage possibilities tend to dwindle. This will happen if none of the players is able control the respective markets – in contrast to classic monopolies in colonial trade, for example. In a competitive context, the 'suicidal stimulus of this gain would always make it disappear', as Schumpeter (1952: 61) once put it.[66] Why?

If arbitrage possibilities are eliminated, a price system is a system of equivalence relations. Equivalence, as seen in mathematics or formal logic, presupposes the symmetry, reflexivity and transitivity of the respective relations.[67] While the reflexivity property does not make much sense as a part of a description of exchange processes – why should x_i be exchanged for x_i? (Beckenbach 1987) – symmetry is evident in that if x_i is traded for x_j, x_j must be traded simultaneously for x_i. The interesting property is transitivity: It is realized in a market for a given set of goods if for any three goods x_i, x_j, x_k, if x_i is traded for bx_j and x_j is traded for cx_k then x_i will be traded for $(bc)x_k$. Walras pointed out the implication of interest for us:

> Hence, if one wished to leave arbitrage operations aside and at the same time to generalize the equilibrium established for pairs of commodities in the market, it would be necessary to introduce the condition that the price of either one of any two commodities (chosen at random) expressed in terms of the other be equal to the ratio of the prices of each of these two commodities in terms of any third commodity.

(Walras 1954: 161)

In economic terms, equivalence relations in exchange imply not only that gains through arbitrage transactions cannot be realized, but, more importantly, that exchange transactions are no longer independent. Although buying and selling takes place in a decentralized form between traders who are supposed to determine prices according to their pair-wise consensus as the outcome of the free will of both, at a given time in a given space, the outcome of these bargaining processes is supposed to be a system of prices that are consistent. But if prices are to be consistent, they certainly cannot all be determined independently on the spot by the agents directly involved. Why should agents cede some of their freedom in price formation? And how can they know what the price to be determined in a concrete transaction would have to be in order to fit into the larger system? What would be their interests in – knowingly or unknowingly – establishing a consistent price system?

Let us use Schumpeter's example quoted above to throw some more light on this problem. The point Schumpeter seems to overlook is that all three agents have equal reasons and possibilities to exploit the inconsistency of exchange rates. If they attempt to do that, each will not use one of the three markets and engage in indirect trade instead. This will mean that all three will attempt to turn 'the wheel of commerce' in one direction only, but this direction will be blocked because each wants to exclude the direct trade with the unfavorable exchange ratio: The possessor of *a* will avoid market I and attempt to approach the possessor of *b* indirectly via *c*, the possessor of *c* will avoid market II and approach *a* via *b* and the possessor of *b* will avoid market III and approach *c* only via *a*. This means that arbitrage in the way suggested by Schumpeter can only work for the possessor of *b* if the possessors of *a* and *c* do not perceive and attempt to exploit the exchange rate inconsistency, too.

Schumpeter neglected the possibility that all agents in a given trading network will react to inconsistent prices. This is inappropriate because:

1   In an inconsistent price system, arbitrage possibilities are open for *all* players. There are no privileged positions in a transaction chain/ring/ network.

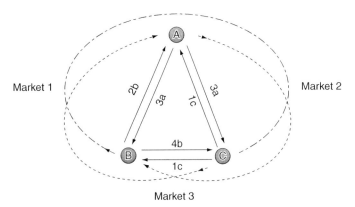

Figure 3.3 Schumpeter's arbitrage example.

2   If all players know about these possibilities and want to use them simultaneously, they are blocking all trades because they will try to use indirect
trading possibilities in mutually exclusive ways. Thus, once *all* players
observe the arbitrage possibilities inherent in an inconsistent price system
and want to use them, they cannot trade at all. So they either have to find a
set of consistent prices or fall back into autarky. Of course, this stark alternative emerges only in the unlikely case that *all* players know about arbitrage
possibilities and want to benefit from them by choosing indirect trading
paths. That only a system of consistent prices leaves open the possibility of
trading while inconsistencies threaten every participant with the exile into
autarky provides a strong, shared motive for finding a consistent system,
however. The easiest way to bring this about is to make all exchange ratios
instantly comparable by expressing them all in terms of one money of
account. Inconsistencies will be not only easily detectable, but will also lead
to bargaining patterns in which each buyer/seller insists on being granted a
price no worse than what they observe in other transactions. Such bargaining creates pressure towards consistency, but we do not have to assume that
an equilibrium defined by such consistency is ever reached.

By contrast, if we follow Schumpeter and assume that only a minority of
players are active arbitrageurs, would they exert pressure towards more consistency in a given price system? Take Schumpeter's example, again. The direct
exchange ratios are assumed to be fixed. Assume total quantities offered in the
three markets to be fixed, too. If we consider sequences of trades – which is
implied because a player using indirect exchange has to take two trading steps
instead of one – a likely outcome is rationing: The arbitrageur has picked up a
quantity of the good he will use as a means of exchange that is larger than what
he wants to use as a consumer or producer. Thus, the direct trader cannot get as
much as he wants at the exchange ratio announced. The seller of the good for
which there is an excess demand notices that the exchange ratio he has asked is
too low. He could have acquired more other goods by asking higher ratios, so he
realizes that there is an excess demand for his good. If the same trading pattern
were repeated, that trader could keep demanding a higher exchange ratio, until
demand would match the supply he is willing to offer (assuming that he does not
overshoot). The exchange ratios arrived at in this way would no longer allow for
arbitrage. Given such activities as a regular pattern, agents pursuing arbitrage
profits are constantly working to 'attain the "arbitrage-free" state' (Mirowski
1991: 576) of the economy. It is not the intended result of their actions and never
reached completely. Nonetheless, all agents use observed prices and price
changes as the primary means of orientation, as if they were valid indicators of
potential equivalence, or as if Schumpeter's 'suicidal stimulus' had done its job.
When producers, consumers or traders form their strategies, they build in
observed prices and anticipations of their movements. In doing that, they must
implicitly assume that most relevant prices are sufficiently close to consistency.
Prices are used as 'an artifact ... for 'reading' the consequences of our actions in

the economic sphere'. In using them as such 'some forms of change have to be ignored, or bracketed, or exiled to the margins' (Mirowski 1991: 579).

The self-elimination property of arbitrage can help explain how the 'working fiction of a monetary invariant' (Mirowski 1991: 581) can be maintained: If markets with arbitrage have a built-in tendency towards consistent prices that would *no longer* allow for gains from trade, agents acting on given market prices assume that the risk of failing to realize possible returns from trade is low. They believe that they can 'read' prices as signals of 'real' demand–supply constellations. As long as arbitrageurs are continuously monitoring the market for potential gains from indirect exchange and move to use such opportunities whenever they open up, this belief will be self-confirming. The price system cannot stay too far away from consistency. There may still be all sorts of factors and events triggering price changes, but at least there is only a low risk that endogenous market forces will be responsible for surprising price changes all the time. In other words, there is less uncertainty involved in taking prices as parametric – which is what agents will have to do with the subset of prices immediately relevant for them when calculating their strategies.

With regard to money and uncertainty the implication of arbitrage is, in sum: Money makes it not just easier, but – in the case of a sufficiently large number of commodities – only the combination of effective prices and a stable unit of account makes it possible to recognize arbitrage possibilities. If, in addition, arbitrage operations are self-eliminating, the resulting price system will approach consistency properties that in turn make it feasible to reach a higher level of rationality in the construction of market strategies. Such strategies will normally be based on calculations in which an important subset of money prices is taken as given, including probability of change estimates. Or, to put it the other way around: If markets do not show any tendencies towards uniform and consistent prices, the precariously founded general conviction that the metric of money can measure anything cannot be sustained.

> Money is only a 'measure of value' if there is some confidence (some minimal confidence) in price-stability.
>
> (Hicks 1967: 28)

At one extreme, where prices fluctuate wildly, one obviously cannot estimate the purchasing power of a unit of money. But once no one can even approximately know the purchasing power of money, it is hard to see why anybody would accept it in exchange. Money would disappear. At the other extreme, where prices are uniform, stable and consistent, everybody could design strategies on transparent and solid foundations. Money would not be needed. Monetary systems move between these extremes.

In sum, as far as they are realized, competition and arbitrage generate order in price formation. But monetary economies are driven by contradictory requirements: price formation is supposed to be both decentralized and to lead to consistency. Therefore, there cannot be a guarantee that a tolerable degree of order will always emerge. Modeling such a system should not be guided by the aim of quantitative price determination in the traditional sense pursued by economic theory. Instead, models should throw light on the processes that generate both order and disorder.

3.4 Money and uncertainty absorption

> Money is only of use in a world where things are not certain, are not completely known or even knowable, where the fantasy that all knowledge can be had at a cost does not prevail.
>
> (Shackle 1974: 4)

Everybody knows that our knowledge is limited. Concerning the past, any history text is at best an exercise in illuminating an island of knowledge in a sea of ignorance. Concerning the present, all of us have to make decisions whose outcome depends on what expected or unexpected actions known and unknown others are taking – so we are constantly reminded that we do have insufficient knowledge as we attempt to form strategies for reaching our goals. Concerning the future, we are to some extent willing to bet that a good part of the world tomorrow will be like the world as we experienced it today and yesterday. But certainly, the problem of not knowing is aggravated when we turn to non-observables – and, on principle, that is what future events, objects, processes are relative to the past and present. So when economic theorists assume that the population of their models should be equipped with perfect information,[68] whether about the past, the present or the future, what are they doing? In a way, they try to ignore their own ignorance by endowing *homo oeconomicus* with cognitive superpowers.

This holds even after 'uncertainty' was introduced into general equilibrium theory in the 1950s (Malinvaud 1972: 273). The ersatz assumption for perfect knowledge now became: common knowledge of all possible states of the world.[69] Agents in general equilibrium models with 'uncertainty' do not know which of these states will be realized. But as they all know the set of all possible future states of the world, they can prepare for all eventualities by making contracts for buying or selling 'contingent' commodities.[70] For example: It may rain or not rain in Des Moines, Iowa on 28 June 2042. I can make a contract now with an umbrella seller, obliging her to sell me an umbrella for the price $x in case it does rain and I am in Des Moines. Spinning out the example (What if seller and buyer are not alive anymore? Why should a rational agent be bound in 2042 by a contract concluded in 2008? What if there are innovative new rain protection devices? What if I choose to be at some other place in the world?) demonstrates that the way the theory is supposed to cope with uncertainty is based on an even more extreme assumption about knowledge than the traditional perfect information assumption. In a perfectly known world, all the variables relevant for an individual's decision have only one value. Given 'uncertainty', all these variables have n (with $n > 1$) possible values. As a consequence, the number of contracts to be made is: number of variables multiplied by number of their possible values, covering states of the world from now until some arbitrarily fixed date.

There is nothing wrong with the *logic* of replacing the assumption of perfect knowledge of the world by the assumption of perfect knowledge of all possible states of the world in some finite future. But if introducing 'uncertainty' in this way was guided by the intention to give general equilibrium theory a touch of realism, something went wrong: The new knowledge assumption and its implications – cognitively in terms of information processing and socially in terms of making contracts – looks even more implausible than the assumption it replaced.

In a sociological perspective, as we can already see in the limiting case of 'double contingency' in interaction, assuming cognitive super-powers turns out to be contradictory with regard to the objective of determining the strategies agents will devise. If two or more agents have opposing interests and know that the results of their own actions depend on what the others do, more information does not help, at least not if it is symmetrically distributed. If more information does not help, agents need other means to cope with the uncertainty endogenous to interaction. This is where money enters the picture. Money is a 'social contrivance' that allows us to cope with uncertainty, albeit to a limited extent. To recognize uncertainty generated in interaction should be the starting point of any theory of money, as a considerable tradition of heterodox monetary theory has asserted. But how can uncertainty in economic matters be 'absorbed'[71] by using money?

Economists have taught us since Bentham that we are all and always trying to maximize utility. But even in extremely simplified exchange models this general orientation does not narrow the range of *alter*'s objectives sufficiently to enable *ego* to form expectations about *alter*'s strategies.[72] Economic theorists assume monotonicity of preferences, implying that everybody knows about everybody else that to have more of anything that is useful is better than to have less. But this general attitude is applicable to the whole commodity space, as it were. When *ego* enters into a transaction with *alter*, *ego* cannot know to what degree *alter* prefers pears to apples to tennis balls, and so on, not least because hiding your true preferences is an important ingredient of bargaining. So, while economic theory suggests common knowledge that everybody is always trying to move upward on the '*colline de plaisir*' (Pareto 1909), uncertainty remains as to where any player is located and which of the many paths upward any player will choose. *Ego* cannot know the directions and intensities of *alter*'s concrete desires *ex ante* and thus *ego* has insufficient knowledge about the alternative transaction channels in which *alter* may become active when trying to transform her endowment through exchange into her utility maximizing target commodity bundle.

How can this uncertainty be reduced by using money? There are several ways:

1   First of all, the use of money creates a uniform informational horizon for agents involved in exchange. In contrast to barter as an alternative, splitting

good-for-good transactions into purchase and sale means that in each resulting semi-transaction, the objectives of players are radically simplified: Whatever the commodity involved that is traded for money, buyers want to *pay as little money* as possible and sellers want to *earn as much money* as possible. The general objective of accomplishing a utility enhancing transaction is subject to the constraint of maximizing money holdings. This general condition defines the underlying conflict of interests in exchange unambiguously and, thus, establishes a shared cognitive frame in which a compromise on price has to be found. For the sake of brevity, I will refer to the objective of maximizing money retained (buyer) or money received (seller) in each market encounter as 'maxM', it being understood that this does not necessarily involve maximizing hoards of money objects as the only adequate form of wealth.

In other words: In buying and selling, the utility aspect of goods partially disappears behind the '*veil*' of money. In barter models, goods are compared according to their utility by both parties involved, as depicted in the Edgeworth-Box diagram (Figure 3.1). In buying and selling, the utility of the good or bundle of goods is important for the buyer, but the seller simply wants to maximize the monetary return, whereas the buyer cannot compare the utility of goods to something like the utility of money.[73] He will simply try to pay as little as possible for any bundle of goods in question. He can only compare what he will get for his money – given a price has been negotiated – in this transaction to other potential transactions or, perhaps, to the effort it took to earn the money to be spent.

Does that amount to assuming a general 'money illusion'? No. It means assuming that all agents know of each other that, *ceteris paribus*, for each more money is better than less money (Hardin 2003: 72). This does not necessarily contradict the neoclassical axiom of utility maximization: If having more money simply allows players to buy more of the things they believe will maximize their utility, to strive for more money is a rational intermediate step on the way to any target commodity bundle, provided the general acceptability of money is not in question. However, the result of such mediation is that players observe each other as maximizers of monetary returns. While each may presume that utility maximization is still ruling 'behind' observed action patterns of maxM, each player forms strategies built on what is observable, namely, that all others are striving to maxM in each transaction.[74] In terms of uncertainty absorption, this is a decisive reduction of complexity. Instead of trying to identify the full range of the concrete needs and desires of others, it is sufficient to observe how much money they are willing to give or take for any concrete bundle of commodities or for whatever else is the object of bargaining.

2 One important implication of the simplification of expectations among money users as maximizers of monetary returns is the establishment of a simple social hierarchy. Those who dispose over more money can dominate those who dispose over less not just as competitors in buying, but in many

socially important respects.[75] As far as differences in command over money are visible or known, interacting players tend to rank themselves according to these differences, at least in economic terms, but very likely also in terms of status, and so on (Bourdieu 1979).

3   Money allows us to cope with uncertainty about unknown adverse future events: It can serve as a 'security blanket' (Davidson 2005). An important reason for saving money or accumulating claims to money is to increase security in the sense of being protected against future mishaps. This can take place in the form of buying insurance in cases where the probability of such a damaging event is calculable. But if such events are truly uncertain, insurance will not be offered. One way to protect oneself against them is to increase disposition over money as a general means of coping with unforeseeable adverse events and possible economic damage. Thus, to save is a way of 'buying' protection: We increase our money reserves in the expectation that the money can be used to escape or diminish the damage if an unwanted event occurs.[76] Saving can happen in non-monetary forms, such as the hoarding of durable goods. Services cannot be saved. The point in saving money, by contrast, is that one does not have to predict the type of adverse event that will require protection. Whatever can be bought will be available when needed, requiring one transaction. Non-monetary assets can only help if we can predict that we are going to need them (which is the case with stable needs like housing). Otherwise they will be ranked according to their 'liquidity': How much time and effort, how many transactions does it take to transform them into what is needed? Due to its liquidity money offers extra protection in terms of the speed and simplicity of relief.

> In essence, liquid assets are efficient time machines that savers use to store and transport savings to the future. Unlike savers in the classical system, real world savers do not know exactly what they will buy, and what contractual obligations they will incur at any specific future date. As long as in the world of experience money is that thing that discharges all contractual obligations and money contracts are used to organize production and exchange activities, then the possession of money (and liquid assets that have small carrying costs and can be easily resold for money) means that savers possess the ability (a) to demand products whenever they desire in the uncertain future and/or (b) to meet a future contractual commitment that they have not foreseen. Liquid assets are savers' security blankets protecting them from the possibility of hard times in the future.
>
> (Davidson 2005: 27)

Money is most liquid because, everything else being equal, it is transformable into all other commodities in one step and it has the lowest carrying and transaction costs among all assets. However, it does not yield interest if it is held in the maximally liquid form.[77] The prospect of additional gains in the form of interest payments lures agents away from holding cash or demand deposits.[78] Choosing less liquid forms of savings in order to gain interest implies increasing the risk to be stuck with non-money assets that cannot easily be transformed into whatever one needs. In a credit crunch, what is needed above all is money itself.[79] So all sorts of non-monetary assets will go on sale when nobody wants to buy. They lose their capacity to protect quickly as their prices fall. A credit crunch, a type of event that can occur only in monetary systems, is exactly the type of adverse event for which money is the optimal 'security blanket'.

But even held in the most liquid form as cash, money is far from perfect as a means to protect oneself against unforeseeable adverse events. You need others who will respond to money offers. In settings of extreme need, for example, for water in the desert, others may not respond to money offers. Or, as discussed in debates on pension reforms, the number of persons one can address with money offers may shrink when the economically active of a population declines relative to the retired part. In addition, if money is to serve as a 'time machine' to transfer claims into the future for savers, the monetary system has to be stable. People must expect that everybody will continue to use money and that the currency they use will retain some relevant purchasing power. This is why precious metal coins were preferred as money objects.[80] They offered more protection against loss of purchasing power due to manipulation and forgery than other forms of money. By contrast, contemporary money users have to rely on steadfast, enlightened governance of monetary systems. Historical experience suggests that such governance is more likely if management of the monetary system is somewhat removed from the reach of the 'furies of private interests' (Marx). But the representatives of the state, though declared to be responsible for furthering the public interest, are easily tempted to manipulate the monetary system if that promises to solve some of their own problems, like the financing of wars or of populist policies, and so on. To what extent the recently fashionable 'autonomy of the central bank' provides an escape from such dilemmas remains to be seen. One can have doubts, as the mandate given to autonomous central banks to maintain monetary stability is a goal that is not beyond serious political conflict. As Keynes (1936) and Kalecki (1943) have argued, monetary stability is not a goal that is equally high on everybody's list of goals. Rentiers tend to like it much better than wage-earners threatened by unemployment. However, this is not the place to discuss the policy implications of the need to sustain a stable monetary system. In terms of the issue of uncertainty and the use of money, it is clear that the uncertainty absorption capacity of money depends to a crucial extent on the ability of agents, including monetary authorities, to roughly maintain the stability of the monetary system.

The function of money as a 'security blanket' reinforces the hierarchy generating function of money (see point 2). Those who feel more secure than others because of their superior money holdings also tend to be more assertive in interactions. In short, in terms of uncertainty absorption, more money is better than less. In reverse, to live in a monetary economy without money drastically increases uncertainty because it increases the exposure to contingent events.

4   Money use leads to the reduction of degrees of freedom in market interactions: Coding all transactions in terms of money makes them easily comparable, thus increasing the pressures of competition and arbitrage towards uniform prices for uniform commodities and towards consistent price systems. The asymptotically approached but never reached target state is the realization of equivalence relations in prices. They imply that all one-on-one transactions are firmly linked into a network, limiting the freedom of traders to make their own decentralized decisions to quantity adjustments. In terms of theory, one can only choose between recognizing the importance of decentralized decision making for price formation on the one hand and spelling out the implications of equivalence relations as an essential feature of equilibrium on the other hand. In practice, decentralized transactions may tend towards, but never realize equilibrium as traders closely observe each other and read observed effective prices as signals when forming their strategies, thus either confirming their status as parameters or exploiting price differentials, as in arbitrage.

5   Money further simplifies social interactions in markets in two important ways: first, by depersonalizing them. You do not have to trust the other person, you only have to trust her money. The other person does not matter, what matters is the potential money flow emanating from that person. Second, money simplifies social interactions in markets by wiping out history. *Pecunia non olet.* It does not matter how the other person earned the money you accept. Thus, a segment of memory in which agents store information about other agents may become redundant.[81] To be sure, this disappearance of persons behind their money is not likely to happen outside of markets, too. For example, the aspirations to gain social status by disposing over ever more money may be blocked by backlashes against the *'nouveaux riches'*.

6   As long as the 'working fiction of a monetary invariant' (Mirowski) is maintained, money opens the possibility of monitoring your own and others' activities by measuring success or failure in terms of money. Observing own actions and the actions of others in terms of money means relating costs to returns. MaxM means searching continuously and in all directions for improvements of net returns. Regular accounting, especially in the form of double-entry bookkeeping, imposes a degree of 'formal rationality' (Weber) on economic activities that was unknown in pre-modern societies. Better means of data processing and communication support ever-increasing 'formal rationality'. This general calculating attitude made possible by money leads to increased discipline,[82] both that imposed on oneself and that imposed on others. In turn, such discipline allows for ever more extensive calculation to form more extensive and elaborate new strategies. As long as

the assumptions made about the disciplined behavior of others hold, strategies may be successful.[83] For each agent's own past actions, the information on costs and returns can be (quite) complete, offering certainty in terms of records. Learning from past successes or mistakes can lead to guidelines for decisions on what to do and what to avoid. Future actions, however, are present only in the realm of expectations. In between is the set of 'half-actions', so to speak, when costs have already been incurred but future returns cannot yet be known. This constellation is crucial for understanding the need to acquire money as such, as a means of payment without a substitute in the world of goods. There is certainty about the costs, but no certainty about the returns. The constellation becomes even more interesting when it is embedded in a credit relationship (see below).

7 Money offers ways of re-formatting complex issues and conflicts in all sorts of social relations. All sorts of interests in non-economic, non-monetary matters are articulated simply as demands for more money or their rejection. In marital conflicts, for example, hurt feelings and lost love are channeled into the objective of getting the most out of a divorce settlement. In industrial relations, grievances about working conditions are redefined as demands for better pay, and so on.

In sum, given that money has these uncertainty absorbing capacities, the fact that money is used ubiquitously in contemporary society loses some of its improbability. However, an explanation of the continued – and basically unquestioned – use of money in modern societies that relies on its uncertainty absorption capacities presupposes that the latter must somehow dominate the countervailing *uncertainty generating properties* of monetary systems. Such increases of uncertainty inevitably result, first of all, from the simple fact that money is socially constructed. A monetary system can function only if and as long as money users can rely on the metric of money. That presupposes a considerable degree of stability, but such stability is unlikely to be permanently achieved in the social world, with its conflicts, contentions, intended or non-intended changes and cumulative feedback effects. Monetary stability in part turns into a 'make believe' problem. A sufficient number of people must believe that the money they use is a sort of invariant, that deviations from conservation and equivalence are moderate. In older forms of society, people could be convinced by 'naturalizing' money: Although money always was and is a social construction, the monetary unit was defined as a quantity of some natural material and money objects were made of or somehow connected to such material – gold and silver were the favorites. This suggested stability, durability, plus unquestioned desirability as long as humans remained humans. As it turned out in the history of money, finally in that of the gold standard, monetary stability could neither be achieved nor maintained in this way. The definition of the monetary unit in physical terms simply does not and cannot preclude shifts in its significance in the social world. Not only were precious materials relegated to the role of reserves for circulating paper or cheaper metal. Banks learned how to 'create' more or less private money (see below).

Once all sorts of things could become money objects, however, new possibilities of manipulating monetary systems were discovered and used, on the one hand. On the other hand, the unlimited desire for more and more money became a social obsession, first in the upper layers of society, then 'trickling down'. Starting with events like the Dutch tulip mania or the South Sea Bubble (Kindleberger 1989), this desire drove a repetitive dynamic of speculation that periodically resulted in crises, reasserting the need for stable money. The resulting pattern of boom and bust, of crises and restructuring has dominated monetary history at least since the beginnings of occidental capitalism.

In general, instead of a universal 'monetary invariant', we observe many monies in systems of occasionally extreme volatility. In view of this turbulent history the main question to be answered about money may have become the following: Why is the need for the 'monetary invariant' so overwhelming that it seems to block the general insight that a monetary invariant can never be more than a 'working fiction'? A preliminary answer is suggestive: Even if limited, the uncertainty absorption properties of money are so important for coordinating economic actions that the countervailing uncertainty-amplifying properties of money are periodically forgotten and recognized again only in crisis periods. In other words, money can only become a means of coping with uncertainty as long as the fact that it also generates uncertainty is mentally suppressed by most money users. Perhaps both the tendency to ignore money in mainstream economic theory and the shape and content of most theories of money are part of this suppression?

At this point in my argument, it would not only be difficult but also decidedly premature to draw a bottom line and balance the uncertainty generating *versus* the uncertainty absorbing effects of money use. Before attempting such balancing, we have to explicitly introduce modern forms of money that are more complex than the simple forms (coins or state paper currency) examined so far. Above all, understanding modern money requires understanding credit relations. They can be considered as responses to some of the constraints imposed by simple monetary practices. They introduce more flexibility but at the same time more possibilities of abuse and therefore less transparency and less stability of monetary systems. They also imply a wholly new dimension of uncertainty.

3.5 Credit

3.5.1 Basic credit relations

First, a warning. To describe and explain the forms and modes of operation of the contemporary financial system would require a separate book, or even more than one. The system is complex and opaque, mostly because the agents involved create iterations of collective function assignments all the time. Not only do extra layers of mediators deal with extra layers of ownership paper, but parts of the financial system seem to have degenerated into a kind of bookmaking operation where you can not only make debts but also bet on your ability to repay them. For a while it was claimed that contemporary forms of credit and their management by enlightened central banks had led to the so-called Great Moderation (Bernanke 2004). The temporarily observed streamlining of business cycles and reduced volatility of global economic development that had purportedly started in the 1980s ended promptly with the extra-size crash of 2008. As the crash laid open, the financial system crossed a threshold into enhanced speculation in the Great Moderation period. People were invited to borrow money, their loans were sold as securities while side-bets were placed on their ability to pay back these loans. The circularity involved generated self-propelling positive feedback – a 'bubble', once again. For a while such positive feedback increased asset prices and bank profits and thus fed the increased trading of 'financial products' that were designed with the conviction that the uncertainty generated in the interaction of the agents buying and selling them could be transformed into calculable risks. That turned out to be wrong, first of all for the small but decisive part of the system concerned with financing housing. The lesson that the crash taught was once again that risks in financial markets are not independent and that there is no insurance against highly correlated adverse events – even if somebody sells it.

In any case, the recent crash and crisis is not the issue at this point. What follows is a modest attempt to explain some basic features of the credit system and its role in creating contemporary forms of money. The aim is to extend the argument on how money both generates and absorbs uncertainty so as to take into account credit relations in their basic forms.

Compared to the structure of simple monetary interactions, credit is primarily a way of loosening budget constraints. To see the difference, return to the chain of transactions diagram in Figure 3.2 (Section 3.2.3). Without credit, each buyer is constrained in the amount of money she can spend as a result of her previous success as a seller. Given the possibility of credit, buyers and sellers can assume the additional roles of borrowers and lenders. When the buyer cannot pay now, the seller may nonetheless let her take away the goods for a promise to pay in the future. At first sight, this appears to be simply a case of temporal expansion of the pair-wise interaction. As we will see, however, the temporal expansion is feasible only because it coincides with further material and social expansions. But not only that. While credit relations may evolve as a simple temporal modification of the basic buyer–seller relation through deferred payment, functional differentiation leads to pure borrower–lender relations. Once there is the foundation of a basic monetary system – say, the use of coins – agents can specialize in the role of lenders. As selling for a promise to pay is a risky affair, normal sellers may refuse and – instead of extending credit themselves – push their potential buyers to seek a money lender. The lender will be a specialist in calculating and handling the risk of not being repaid. The role is feasible only if the lender is somehow rewarded for his activity: Interest will be charged, whether openly or covertly.[84]

Before pursuing such questions further, it is useful to address some ambiguities in the discussions on money and credit. As Schumpeter once put it, there are monetary theories of credit and credit theories of money, meaning that either credit relations are seen as a subset of monetary relations or monetary relations are seen as a subset of credit relations. Within the latter school of thought there are those who, like Schumpeter, would hold that the subsuming of monetary relations under credit relations is a historically rather recent phenomenon, but also those who argue that credit is older than money, so that the first forms of money evolve out of pre-existing credit relations. I will discuss these views by first addressing the 'credit is older than money' proposition, then the 'all money is credit' proposition, and, finally, Schumpeter's argument for a credit theory of money instead of a monetary theory of credit. All these propositions are inappropriate. They contribute to confusion about the nature of money. I will argue that the first proposition implies ignoring the difference between a monetary and a non-monetary economy, that the second proposition is based on a misunderstanding of the role of money as a means of payment, and that Schumpeter's argument rests on the assumption that the acquisition of money cannot be a goal in itself.

3.5.2 Monetary relations as a subset of credit relations?

Social practices of giving without simultaneously taking have been widely observed in societies that do not use money, so they may rightly be held to be not only older but also more widespread than the use of money. But apart from the apparently common constitutive role of promises in both the practices of gift giving (Mauss [1922] 1990) and of buying on credit, the credit relations typical for monetary economies have little to do with such more general practices. They should remain conceptually distinguishable. A plausible distinction can rely on Polanyi's distinction between 'reciprocity' and 'exchange' (see Section 3.1.3). The context of reciprocity is a community in the sense of the term proposed by Tönnies ([1887] 1922): 'Community' refers to social units based on face-to-face contacts, with personal ties and corresponding obligations, in contrast to 'society', in which contractual relations based on shared interests are dominant. Members of a community are likely to mutually support each other spontaneously, be that in terms of services or the transfer of goods. There is little calculating attitude behind communal give-and-take. Symmetry, as in returning a favor, is expected, but only roughly and in the long run. In contrast, the exchange transactions typical for 'society' are entered with an instrumental attitude, requiring symmetry of give-and-take[85] in the peculiar way of combining opposing and converging interests in the formation of effective prices. Participants aim for quantitative calculability, both in terms of the objects exchanged and the time structure. Using money answers the needs, desires and strategies involved in exchange, as money allows for both the calculation and the precise realization of the symmetry of give and take.

To distinguish between the reciprocal relations involving – perhaps only implicit – promises to compensate for services or goods one has received and credit relations that involve promises to pay, we can simply apply the criterion of money use: A credit relation is constituted by the acceptance of a promise to pay an amount of money in the *future* in return for the performance of a service, the transfer of a good, of an ownership title or of a sum of money *now*. This proposition reverses the ordering suggested in some credit theories of money: Credit relations are a subset of monetary relations, not the other way around. Given the possibility that elements of reciprocity may play an important role even in monetary relations, the proposition should not be read to mean that the use of money necessarily implies the dominance of instrumental attitudes among the agents involved.[86] But in general, the *differentia specifica* of a monetary economy – and the credit relations inherent in it – is that its reproduction does not seem to require more than instrumental attitudes in the social relations constituting it. Only if we set aside relations of reciprocity where trust between persons is taken to prevail are we led to the question crucial for understanding credit relations in a monetary economy: *What can make a promise to pay acceptable among buyers and sellers or borrowers and lenders who merely have an instrumental interest in each other?* This question is circumvented by theories in which credit relations are held to underlie all monetary relations and are thus seen as a subset of reciprocal relations governed by morally defined mutual obligations. To simply assume such a moral dimension to constrain credit relations in the modern economy is rather daring. Frequently, this notion of credit as a form of reciprocity is combined with the second proposition mentioned above: All money is credit. The effect of this combination is the – at least implicit – conjecture that all monetary relations involve reciprocity. This implication is manifest in the radical version of the 'all money is credit' proposition suggested by A. Mitchell Innes (1913), an author recently rediscovered by neo-chartalists (Wray 2004; Goodhart 2005).

> Money… is credit and nothing but credit. A's money is B's debt to him, and when B pays his debt, A's money disappears. This is the whole theory of money.
>
> (Innes 1913: 402)

Innes suggests that whenever we pay, we pay with a promise to pay. The only way to accomplish a 'final' payment is to transform the buyer and seller relationship into a debtor and creditor relationship that can then, in turn, be extinguished in clearing operations that imply repaying the debt with a promise to pay issued by the creditor himself. The creditor has made the promise as a buyer or borrower from a third person (Innes 1913: 394). In other words, the picture of the monetary system drawn by Innes is derived from the way in which traders do business using written promises to pay a fixed amount at a fixed date for a specified commodity. The simplest case suggested by the description given by Innes is circular: A cedes ownership of a good to B, B 'pays' with an IOU, A uses B's IOU to 'pay' C, C uses B's IOU to 'pay' the debt he has to B. There are likely to be more agents involved, so that more transactions may be accomplished using B's IOU. The contracts may be more complicated by obliging third persons to act as intermediaries. But in the end, B will be paid with his own IOU. The IOUs that served as 'money' disappear. The system works because: 'Debts and credits are perpetually trying to get in touch with one another, so that they may be written off against each other' (Innes 1913: 402).

This touching inner urge of debts and credits to create harmony through mutual extinction is supported by the banker, whose business it is 'to bring them together' (ibid.). If they do not clear, the banker may step in as a second order lender. While Innes adequately described the procedure among traders using promissory notes, it is quite daring to suggest that all monetary transactions follow these same patterns. The contortions required to pull through such an argument indicate some over-generalization. Operations that have nothing to do with credit have to be read as if they involved credit. Thus with coinage:

> By issuing a coin, the government has incurred a liability towards its possessor just as it would have done had it made a purchase, – has incurred, that is to say, an obligation to provide credit by taxation or otherwise for the redemption of the coin and thus enable its possessor to get value for his money.
>
> (Innes 1913: 402)

To repeat: 'By issuing a coin, the government ... has incurred .. an obligation to provide credit by taxation ...' It takes some strange way of thinking to view taxation as a way for a government to provide credit for the redemption of the very coins issued by that government. If we assume that the government is not only the operator of the mint,[87] but also the original owner of the coins that it produces there, the government can use them to make purchases. To do that, it has to find a seller willing to accept the coins. Acceptance will depend on the expectation of sellers that other sellers will accept it in their turn. Since acceptability is a frequent problem, one may argue at this point that general acceptability is conditioned (Ingham 2004) or enhanced by the government declaring that it will in its turn accept the money it issues when taxes have to be paid.[88] But it is simply redundant to read credit relations into all this. Taxation is a government's way of appropriating resources in a monetary economy. Instead of the direct appropriation of resources (as in tributes, tithes), the government takes money and uses it to buy them, thus transferring them from the subjects to the sovereign. Whether that is accomplished by taking the resources in kind, as in pre-monetary economies, or by taking taxes in money form is secondary compared to the fact that taxes are imposed one-sidedly by political fiat. Taxation cannot be reduced to voluntary exchange. Once tributes are defined in money terms and have to be paid with money, there is a clear connection between the monetary system and taxation (Ingham 2004). Whatever the form and amounts of money objects, a state that does not accept the money objects it issues when they come back as a means of payment of taxes will clearly undermine the very monetary system it intends to control and maintain, apart from issues of legitimacy.[89] But this is a question that is quite independent of whether the money objects used are coins or central bank notes, whether they enter circulation through the mint or through the public debt and credit relations.

Taxation or not, it is important to distinguish between money and credit instruments. That Innes fails to do so seems to be the result of seeing money in the not entirely disinterested perspective of a banker. He reads the operation of depositing money in a bank as 'selling your credit' to that bank. When discussing the adequate response to monetary crisis, he argues for abolishing the law of legal tender. Innes wants everybody to 'realize that, once he had become a depositor in a bank, he had sold his credit to that bank and was not entitled to demand payment in coin or government obligation' (Innes 1913: 405). But why should anyone deposit money in a bank if the bank will not guarantee to pay it back on demand? Innes wants his readers to ignore – quite conveniently for the banks – that the bulk of the operations of a commercial bank consists of profitably transforming the short-term liabilities it has towards its depositors into long-term assets it holds against its borrowers. Such operations evidently involve the risk that too many holders of short-term deposits may demand their money back when the bank has lent the money to somebody else. Innes wants to convince his readers that such demands to get back what you put in, namely money, are illegitimate.[90] If one has to admit that depositing money is the same thing as 'selling your credit' to the bank, depositors who have done so have relinquished their right to demand back exactly what they deposited. All they should get in return is a promise to pay issued by whomever the bank chooses, since what they deposited was not more than a promise to pay in the first place, even if it was a promise given by the state or the central bank. Innes's world-view here looks decidedly non-chartalist and much more like that of a banker reflecting on the drama of a run on his bank. If the banker could weasel out of the obligation to give depositors back on demand exactly what they gave him, a run would not cause headaches. By contrast, state intervention into the banking business to protect depositors is a cause of crisis for the banker. Even by merely defining what can serve as 'legal tender', the state is unnecessarily restricting the responses of banks to depositors' demands. 'No law is required; the whole business regulates itself automatically' (Innes 1913: 406).

For Innes, it follows from the proposition that all money is credit that a 'sale ... is not the exchange of a commodity for some intermediate commodity called the "medium of exchange", but the exchange of a commodity for a credit.' Once that much is accepted, to abolish something as archaic as coins appears to be a mere matter of convenience, because there 'is absolutely no reason for assuming the existence of so clumsy a device as the medium of exchange when so simple a system' (i.e., buying and selling with promises to pay, HG) 'would do all that is required' (Innes 1913: 391). Innes reduces the various ways to accomplish buying and selling to the alternative of either using the 'clumsy device' of a commodity serving as the medium of exchange or of using promises to pay in credit operations, only to find credit operations everywhere. Stretching that argument a little further, contemporary neo-chartalists like Ingham suggest that debt–credit contracts underlie even the most ephemeral everyday cash transactions: 'It should be noted that "spot" monetary exchanges also involve short-term debt "contracts" in which a coin is handed over, for example, to settle a debt incurred in contracting to buy a newspaper. (Ingham 2006: 261). With that kind of argument, one can see credit contracts everywhere. Real life is much simpler. As Chuck Berry sang:

> Drop the coin right into the slot,
> you've got to hear something that's really hot.

With most everyday cash payments, there is no need for a contract, especially not a contract as conceived in the common law tradition that stresses offer, consideration and acceptance as constitutive elements of a contract. The reason why a contract is unnecessary is that paying with a coin or with a central bank note implies an immediate transfer of purchasing power to the amount stated on the money object, with no further strings attached. There is no need to extend the given spot relation between seller and buyer in the temporal, material or social dimension. In contrast, the way Innes describes purchases and sales, the relationship between buyer and seller *cannot* end with the transfer of the items exchanged. Rather, it must continue as a creditor–debtor relationship because there is no such thing as a final payment. So he assumes a temporal expansion even when the buyer uses cash in a spot transaction. But there is no such expansion. The origin and the form of the objects used as cash do not matter. What matters is the finality[91] of the transaction. The buyer–seller relationship ends when 'money says good-by' to the buyer.

By contrast, Innes seems to see everyday monetary transactions from the banker's point of view, thus obscuring rather than explaining the relations between money and credit. In view of such confusions, one wonders why it is attractive to refer to authors like Innes in current controversies. Perhaps it is because Innes can be used to construct a tradition, and not just that, but a tradition claiming historical depth[92] by combining the 'all money is credit' proposition with the 'credit is older than money' proposition.

> What we have to prove is not a strange general agreement to accept gold and silver, but a general sense of the sanctity of an obligation. In other words, the present theory is based on the antiquity of the law of debt.
>
> (Innes 1913: 391)[93]

By referring to the 'sanctity of an obligation' as their common background, Innes placed monetary relations in the same class as the reciprocal relations of help among kin and neighbors in old forms of community life. Thus, this type of theory overlooks the qualitative differences between monetary and reciprocal relations.

In sum, neither of the two propositions, namely, that monetary relations are a subset of credit relations and that all money is credit, is convincing. With regard to the first proposition, there is no doubt that borrowing and lending are older and more widespread than the use of money. But such pre-monetary relations have little relevance for understanding money and monetary relations of credit. With regard to the second proposition, it should be modified. Money, in the sense of cash, whether coins or fiat paper, is not necessarily and in general tied into relations of borrowing and lending, quite the contrary. However, there is no question that modern central bank money is credit money (in a sense to be clarified) and that the modern financial system has made it increasingly difficult to distinguish money from credit instruments – except in times of crisis. While the 'all money is credit' – proposition is not valid in general, it may hold in a more restricted way for contemporary forms of money. This seems to be the position of Schumpeter who has greatly influenced this whole debate with the suggestion to stylize it as a controversy between 'monetary theories of credit' and 'credit theories of money'.

3.5.3 Monetary theories of credit vs. credit theories of money?

Schumpeter does not argue that all money is credit. He asserts a priority of coins as money historically and he distinguishes such money, including state paper currency, from credit instruments. However, for Schumpeter this distinction does not imply that we have to understand modern money by considering it as a result of the evolution, modification and development of older forms, because

> logically, it is by no means clear that the most useful method is to start from the coin – even if, making a concession to realism, we add inconvertible government paper – in order to proceed to the credit transactions of reality. It may be more useful to start from these in the first place, to look upon capitalist finance as a clearing system that cancels claims and debts and carries forward the differences – so that "money" payments come in only as a special case without any particularly fundamental importance. In other words: practically and analytically, a credit theory of money is possibly preferable to a monetary theory of credit.
>
> (Schumpeter 1954: 717)

This is a rather guarded statement, but one referring to a substantial reason for 'possibly' preferring the 'credit theory of money': the modern capitalist financial system works largely without money in the sense specified. Clearing institutions set off claims against debts. If an imbalance remains, it is carried forward until the next date for clearing. The need for money payments, to balance whatever cannot be cleared, arises only as a special case 'without any particularly fundamental importance' (ibid., my italics, HG). *Ex negativo*, one can conclude that Schumpeter would *not* prefer a credit theory of money to a monetary theory of credit if money payments *did* have such 'particularly fundamental importance'.

In an earlier section of his *History of Economic Analysis*, Schumpeter proposes a second argument for his theory option, making a much stronger claim. Money, Schumpeter tells us, is the only case in which a:

claim to a thing can, within limits, to be sure, serve the same purpose as the thing itself: you cannot ride a claim to a horse, but you can pay with a claim to money. But this is a strong reason for calling money what purports to be a claim to legal money, provided it does serve as a means of payment.

(Schumpeter 1954: 321)

What are these 'limits' for a claim to money functioning as money that Schumpeter refers to? His criterion for counting something as money despite it not being 'legal money' is that it serves as a means of payment. So are there any differences in the ways in which this function is fulfilled? Apparently not:

> Bank notes and checking deposits eminently do what money does; hence they are money. Thus credit instruments, or some of them, intrude into the monetary system; and, by the same token, money in turn is but a credit instrument, a claim to the only final means of payment, the consumer's good.
>
> (Schumpeter 1954: 321)

Thus, when credit instruments serve as means of payment, they turn into money 'and form part of the supply on the money market' (ibid.). Their entrance affects the nature of money itself: It turns into just another credit instrument. The reason, then, why Schumpeter prefers the credit theory of money is that neither money nor credit instruments are *final* means of payment. Therefore, the historically justified distinction between money and credit instruments no longer matters and can become obsolete. For Schumpeter final payment can apparently only be accomplished by 'the consumer's good'. With this reasoning, Schumpeter relies on an all too familiar romantic reductionism prevailing in mainstream economic theory: What matters in the end even in a monetary economy are 'real' consumer goods. In their distinction and distance from consumer goods, money and credit instruments are one and the same. They both *cannot* be consumed. Therefore they cannot be final means of payment.

This argument misses the crucial difference between a monetary economy and the neoclassical barter economy (Dillard 1987). It implies the proposition that 'money is a veil', which in turn implies the proposition that 'money is neutral'. Enough has been said on this, but let us question Schumpeter's proposition: Can only consumer goods be final means of payment? If two traders agree on a contract, specifying deferred payment and the means of payment to be used, the buyer (the borrower) can accomplish a final payment. He just has to deliver the agreed upon means of payment in the correct amount at the correct date. If the contract is in terms of money, money will be required – unless the seller (the lender) agrees to accept some substitute. If Shylock insists on payment with your own flesh, as promised, you have to pay with your own flesh. *Pacta sunt servanda*. The distinctive property of money – as opposed to credit instruments – is precisely that it is the means to fulfill contracted obligations between any two agents once and for all. The agent receiving the payment may or may not feel satisfied, may or may not transform the money received into a consumer good. That is of no concern for the payer. 'Payment is in some sense final' (Shackle, as quoted in Goodhart 1989: 26).

In view of everyday monetary practices, Schumpeter's argument that one cannot distinguish money from credit instruments because neither – in contrast to consumer goods – are final means of payment, is not only romantic in reducing an economy geared to the acquisition of money to a utility oriented economy. It is simply wrong. Finality of payment has to do with ending a specific social relation, not with the individual deriving ultimate satisfaction, as from eating porridge. Nonetheless, Schumpeter's distinction and his preference for the 'credit theory of money' instead of the 'monetary theory of credit' has been widely accepted.

One can certainly imagine better arguments for a credit theory of money. It neither has to rely on the idea that there is an implicit relation of credit and debt even when we use cash; nor on the idea that consumption, 'to repeat the obvious' once again, is the sole end of production, with the implication that only 'real' and not 'nominal' magnitudes matter. The Schumpeterian proposition that monetary relations have turned into a subset of credit relations wrongly presupposes that the lender–borrower setting characteristic of credit relations is inherent in each contemporary monetary transaction. This would imply that the more extensive social, temporal and material expansions of the catallactic atom characteristic of credit relations are shared by all modern monetary relations. This is not plausible at all if we think, as a contrast, of a typical everyday cash transaction, especially with regard to the temporal expansion that the buyer–seller relation undergoes when it turns into a lender–borrower relation: For example, it rains in the big city. Umbrella salesmen appear on all street corners. You buy an umbrella for $10 and walk away, protected from the rain. Neither the umbrella salesman nor you have any reasons to waste a second thought on a transaction that took about five seconds. It is final. There is no deferred payment. The seller has the money. The buyer has the goods.

The only question with regard to credit that an observer may have is: What has been used as money? It may indeed have been credit money (in a sense to be clarified), but that does not change the fact that the simple transient buyer–seller transaction in which an umbrella and $10 change hands does *not* imply a credit relation. People can use credit money as cash, without entering into a borrower–lender relationship. The time structure of the credit relation is more complex than that of the cash transaction because borrower and lender agree now (t_0) that the borrower will pay (back) later (t_2), with the borrower engaging in further transactions in the meantime (t_1) to acquire the means that will allow her to fulfill the payment promise (at t_2).

It follows that a credit theory of money has to focus on the *form* of modern money. And it would be preferable to a monetary theory of credit if indeed the modern credit system had left behind the constraints characteristic of older payment systems.

3.5.4 *The structure of credit relations*

To see the difference between a monetary and a credit transaction, let us use the former as the reference case. Using money pure and simple, what you can spend depends on what you have (earned, inherited, stolen, won in a lottery, received as a present, etc.). If a potential buyer does not have the money to pay the price negotiated, the transaction does not take place. In contrast, the credit relation starts from such a constellation. The buyer does not have the money and offers a promise to pay

A *credit relation* is constituted by the acceptance of such a promise to pay. It involves an agreement on the amount of money to be paid at a fixed date in the *future* in exchange for the ownership of a good, the provision of a service, the transfer of an ownership title or a sum of money *now*. Imagine a dialogue to illustrate the type of difficulties involved in accepting a promise to pay.

BUYER: I want what you have and I am willing to pay xM. But right now, I do not have xM. Will you accept a promise to pay $(1+i) \times M$ at time t_2 instead of spot payment xM now, at t_0?

SELLER: How good is your promise?

BUYER: You know me. I have always kept my promises. I have a solid reputation in our community ...

Alternative:

BUYER: You don't know/trust me, but I can give you references ...

SELLER: What about collateral, or a pledge in case of your failure to fulfill the promise to pay?

BUYER: OK. Let us write a contract. In case of my failure to pay at t_2, you will gain possession of my asset a_b, worth at least $(1+i) \times M$.

Alternatively:

SELLER: What about a guarantee by a third person?

BUYER: There will be a payment to me of $(1+i) \times M$ by C, due at t_1. C has a good reputation, you know C. Here is his written IOU as proof how much and when he has to pay.

SELLER: Why don't you give me C's promise to pay as a collateral?

BUYER: OK, but if I do, why should I still be involved? You can get the money I owe you directly from C.

SELLER: OK, but if there are any problems with C, I will get back to you. Please sign C's IOU here to indicate that you will still have to pay me in case C fails to pay.

Note that the dialogue starts from a general problem and ends with suggestions of various specific solutions (relying on reputation, collateral, pledges). These solutions in turn offer starting points for more complex transactions emerging as iterations and generalizations of specific action patterns. Now, remember Innes: If the buyer in turn uses C's IOU to pay the next seller, and so on, a whole network can be built. But it requires sufficient knowledge among the agents involved, namely, that they all know about C's solid reputation or sufficient collateral. Also, the in-between buyers will remain debtors as long as C has not paid.

One crucial difference between the monetary and the credit transaction consists in the *additional* uncertainty involved in the latter. It results from the nature of a promise: It is a commitment to do something in the future. The future is unwritten, so nobody can know for sure whether the commitment will in fact be honored when it is due. However, there are various factors influencing the acceptability of the promise. They may help to transform the uncertainty into calculable risks. The probability of promises being fulfilled can be enhanced: Failure to keep the promise can lead to appropriation of a collateral, or to claiming the pledge given by a third person, or to legal sanctions, or to losses of reputation that damage the ability to obtain credit in the future, and so on. The gains to be made by accepting the promise will be compared to the potential losses. Both gains and losses can be modified by additional factors brought into the transaction.

In contrast to the cash nexus among buyers and sellers who do not have to trust each other but rather have to trust the money being used, the characteristic sociological aspect of credit is that players revert to personal relations in which trust and reputation play a major role despite the basic instrumental attitude prevailing among agents.[94]

As we have considered them so far, credit networks are 'know-who' networks (Shubik 2001: 5). In such a network, promises to pay can serve as means of payment, as illustrated above with the example of promissory notes circulating among traders. Insofar as the debtor has a good reputation, his promise to pay will be accepted as a means of payment within a given 'know-who' network. It can therefore be used, with the proviso that the failure to keep the promise by the original debtor will reinstall as debtors the intermediate buyers who used it as a means of payment. This reliance on knowledge of the personal characteristics of the traders sets clear limits for the extension of this type of credit network. As long as means of communication are primitive, these limits will also be spatial. Nonetheless, a 'know-who' network may bridge long distances[95] in both space and time if its links are repeatedly used and thus tested and reliable. They involve 'relational' contracting.[96] However, in such credit networks, sooner or later the question arises: How can the limits set by the requirements of personal 'know-who' be extended?

There seem to be two major ways: First, a network can link persons who do not know each other and can thus be more extensive than the 'know-who' network if membership in the network is subject to strict, broadly known but locally applied criteria, so that members will trust each other without further knowledge of the other person. The trust is based on the knowledge that the others have passed through the same sort of social 'filter' in order to gain membership in the network. Max Weber gave a classic description of such a mechanism when he tried to identify the reasons for the economic success of members of Protestant sects in the USA in the nineteenth century.

> When a sect member moved to a different place, or if he was a traveling salesman, he carried the certificate of his congregation with him; and thereby he found not only easy contact with sect members but, above all, he found credit everywhere.
>
> (Weber [1905] 1970a: 305)

A second way of extending credit networks proceeds through mediation by third persons or organizations. Deferred payment with bills of exchange can illustrate the mechanism. A bill of exchange is an order written by the buyer to a third person or organization to pay a specified sum of money at a specified future date to the bearer of the bill. At first sight, it seems unlikely that such mediation can increase the acceptance of a promise to pay. How can the seller, the person to be paid, expect the order to be effective? From the seller's point of view, instead of reducing uncertainty about the fulfillment of the buyer's promise to pay, the insertion of a third agent into the buyer/seller interaction could increase uncertainty, simply because the seller now has to deal with two other players instead of one. He needs more information (cf. Goodhart 1989: 40f.) and in terms of trust has to make two selections instead of one. The transfer of the obligation to pay from the buyer to an agent of the buyer can only reduce uncertainty if – compared to the buyer – the agent is better known and has a more solid reputation, so that there are less doubts about his ability and readiness to pay. An additional factor may be that a seller would rather accept a promise to pay instead of a real payment because he may fear the potential loss of regular money objects, for example, during long and risky voyages. In terms of contemporary credit systems, one can add: if the third agent *guarantees* payment regardless of what the buyer does – as credit card issuers do – the relations of buyer and seller to the credit card issuer is inserted to mediate the relation of seller to buyer.

An additional way of overcoming the limitations of credit relations imposed by the requirement of personal mutual knowledge is tied to the secondary use of a bill of exchange as a means of payment. The original seller, as the person to be paid, can quickly turn into a buyer by using the bill as proof of an incoming payment, demonstrating credit-worthiness. The next seller will accept the bill as a – provisional – means of payment if she expects to be able to use it in the same way as a buyer. The use of the bill thus accelerates transactions: Nobody has to wait for 'real' money to come in. The written promise to pay, the indicator of an expected payment, demonstrates credit-worthiness, backing up a second, third, fourth ... transaction in which the promise to pay is sufficient to accomplish the transfer of commodities that can be used now (for whatever purposes) and paid for later. In a trading network in which agents habitually use such bills, a given promise by A may be obtained from B and used by C to fulfill an obligation to pay A – as described by Innes above. If, in a given time frame, each buyer/borrower is also a seller/lender, the bills can be collected and cleared against each other by special agents who charge a fee for this service. If an agent has more outgoing than incoming promises in a given period, the deficit has to be dealt with in some way (Cartelier 1996). Again, this may be done with a promise to pay, but it will be more difficult to establish the credibility of such a secondary promise that is supposed to take the place of unfulfilled first promises. Collateral or pledges by third agents may be demanded, etc. Insofar as such debts are carried forward, as Schumpeter and Innes would agree, there is no special role played by money (in the sense of cash, of legal tender) in such a credit network. Just like gold reserves in nineteenth-century international trade had to be used only occasionally in international trade to even out imbalances, money would be used occasionally in case clearing was impossible and the imbalance could not be carried forward.

Does that mean, 'that "money" payments come in only as a special case without any particularly fundamental importance', as Schumpeter (1954: 717) argued? In the normal run of things, yes. In a monetary crisis or a credit crunch, no. When anticipations of incoming payments in the form of promises go wrong for a critical number of traders, the credit network breaks down and only money payments count. The need to pay forces agents to attempt to acquire cash through 'fire sales', but almost everybody needs cash and those who have it want to keep it. Hardly anybody wants to buy. Prices of assets will deteriorate rapidly, so their role as collateral is undermined when everybody wants or needs cash. Without intervention by central banks, there simply is not enough to be had to fill the gaps left by unfulfilled promises. Markets stall. Pricing becomes impossible for many assets. Bankruptcies abound. Strangely, in terms of the proposition that money is a symbol, it turns out in the crisis that only the symbol matters, whereas what the symbol is supposed to merely 'stand for', namely, assets, commodities, 'real' values, all have to be sacrificed to acquire the symbol that counts alone as the effective means of payment.

In sum, the sociologically interesting aspect of credit relations is how the lender's person-specific trust in the borrower's willingness and ability to (re-) pay is extended and re-addressed. Not least through the use of written documents it turns into 'trust' in more or less known third agents and, finally, into trust in the 'system'. The result is a network of credit relations that connects many agents who actually do *not* know each other sufficiently well to trust each other. But as long as such business on credit is pulled through smoothly, it would look foolish to insist on tighter conditions for granting a credit. One would voluntarily exclude oneself when everybody is making money. As a prominent banker excused himself for continuing speculation right into the subprime crash: 'As long as the music plays, you have to dance.'

In basic credit transactions, the lender has to assess the risks and uncertainty involved in accepting a promise to pay. Normally, this is a relevant obstacle against the over-extension of credit. However, this obstacle is circumvented if agents can shift risks onto others at little or no cost. Such third parties will take on these risks on the assumption that the originator of a loan has performed a proper risk assessment. But the originator may not have assessed risk properly precisely because he can shift it. The buyer of a share in a fund composed of such loans will therefore be exposed to more risk than he opted for. The ability to repackage and 'sell' the originator's reliance on promises to pay by others as an ownership paper therefore introduces grave moral hazard into the credit system.

3.5.5 Credit money

How do credit operations result in credit money? There seem to be three principal ways.

First, think of early banks. Bankers were coin experts, determining the value of all sorts of coins of different origins relative to a standard unit and changing foreign coins into the local ones and vice versa. At the same time, they offered the service of safeguarding your coins, so one could deposit money objects with them and use them only when needed. From there, it is easy to imagine the steps in an evolution at the end of which a certificate of deposit by the banker or a letter advising the banker to pay from the deposit to the bearer of the letter could be used as means of payment. The 'real' money remained in the coffers of the banker but changed ownership as documented by written statements. It is also easy to imagine that the banker would expand his role in two ways, first, by turning into a money lender, for example, when a depositor needed a sum larger than the one deposited; second by learning that, on average, the sum of the requests for paying out some of the money deposited remained well below the total deposited. So with a low risk that he would be unable to honor the promise of paying out deposits on demand, the banker, charging interest, could lend out a large share of the money that others deposited with him. This possibility increased with the share of monetary transactions that were accomplished without agents having to resort to cash payments themselves. In the end a multiple of the 'real' money deposited could be used in the form of accounts managed by the banker, where buyer A would write a check, a letter advising the banker to pay xM to B, the bearer of the letter, and the banker would simply transfer the respective amount from account A to account B. No cash would be used, so for all practical purposes, it does not need to exist.

Does such credit 'creation' amount to creating money? Their experience with patterns of deposits and withdrawals encouraged bankers to open accounts on credit: Entrepreneur E comes to the bank, has no money but has a great business plan. E convinces the banker. The banker 'lends' money to E by opening an account for E, with some maximum amount of money at the disposal of E. The banker thus places a bet on the ability of E to earn enough money not only to repay the amount borrowed but also an additional amount charged as interest. Is the banker 'creating' money out of nothing? That depends, but much of the emphasis (Riese 1995) on 'creatio ex nihilo' looks misplaced. In the bank's accounts, the money lent to E is booked as an asset (payment outstanding, to be received), with a corresponding liability (obligation to pay, to honor the checks written by E).[97] For sure, the holder of the new account can pay somebody else by writing checks without ever having deposited money. The banker will honor these checks with the expectation of eventual repayment by E. Meanwhile, the banker has to take care that the bank's total liabilities and assets remain in some sustainable relation to the bank's capital. If E has spent but cannot repay, the banker has to write off the corresponding assets, suffering a loss.

Of course, the banker expects the borrower to use the money so that eventual repayment will be possible. But the banker has limited control over how E spends the money. The credit could have been extended in an optimistic mood, with the banker supporting a speculative business venture in a boom.

The rather harmless practice of lending out other people's money can turn into a highly risky activity in this way, lured by the gain of extra interest income. The problem for banks that arose from time to time and is still with us today, usually with some drama, is the relapse from the use of promises to pay that offset each other to the use of 'real' money triggered by some event causing a chain reaction of failures to pay. Bad rumors can be enough to set off a run on a bank and the conviction that it is unable to pay will turn out to be self-fulfilling.

Second, discounting bills of exchange is a further distinct source of credit money. Traders using bills of exchange as means of payment frequently run into the problem that a bill may not be accepted beyond a given know-who network. So instead of waiting for the desired transaction until they receive generally acceptable means of payment or exchange through sales etc., they use a bank to transform the bill of exchange into a more readily acceptable credit instrument. Banks offer – against a fee, for sure – to transform bills of exchange with limited acceptability into their bank notes with a wider acceptability. In the underlying credit operation – the bank is the lender, the trader is the borrower, the bill of exchange functions as a kind of collateral – the interest has the form of a discount. What the banker pays for a bill of exchange is less than the full sum stated on the bill of exchange. How much less depends on the time until payment is due and on the going rate of interest. The banker assumes the risk of not receiving payment as promised on the bill of exchange. The trader can use the bank note, as far as it goes, to buy in the know-who network now extended through the bank. The bank itself may iterate the same operation with a more widely known bank, for example, a regional bank may re-discount with a nationally operating bank. The evolution of such a system tends to generate a central bank, with the state adding the legal tender property to central bank notes. But whether a banknote is issued by the central bank or by a bank in the lower ranks of the banking hierarchy does not change the operation: The banknote as a promise to pay replaces the bill of exchange as a promise to pay. In the end, promises to pay serve as means of payment. But the central bank's position is special, at least within a national context. A more credit-worthy agent or organization does not exist, so its notes can serve as a final means of payment, even when convertibility (into silver or gold, according to the legal definition of the monetary unit) is suspended.

Third, when states moved from minting coins to simply printing paper money, no credit relation was involved.[98] However, modern states use the central bank in a dual position, apart from delegating the political task of maintaining monetary stability. On the one hand, it functions as the bank of banks (the lender of last resort) in the context of a banking system operating with the currency of the nation-state; on the other hand it is the banker of the nation state. Instead of simply printing money, states 'borrow' money from the central bank: fiat money, which is a debt of the government only nominally because it does not involve payment of interest or principal. By contrast, government securities sold by the central bank to the private sector are debt certificates. On these, states pay interest. The debts are periodically paid back, but mostly by refinancing, by incurring new debts. The whole operation relies on the promise of future tax revenues.

In this way, modern central bank money has to be seen not only 'as a creature of the state' (Lerner 1947), but also as credit money. Credit relations are its origin, but this does *not* mean that all the transactions in which such money is used are automatically credit transactions. Central bank money is used to make final payments.

3.5.6 Credit, money and uncertainty

As credit is a way to soften budget constraints, the disciplinary force of the simple monetary system is weakened. Whoever receives a loan can buy or has bought without having first sold. On the one hand, the ability to pay with a promise to pay increases current certainty for the borrower – in terms of the availability of commodities or money *now*. On the other hand, contingencies for tomorrow increase. Promises can never be as certain as cash or a commodity in hand.

Wicksell (1906: 24) states two conditions under which a promise to pay is just as good as a medium of exchange: 1) It must be 'properly secured'. 2) It must be 'redeemable at will'. It is not difficult to understand the meaning of 'properly secured': The promise must be backed by a recognizable ability to pay, be that in the form of expected income, collateral or pledges by third parties. But what is the meaning of 'redeemable at will'? It amounts to a guarantee of instant liquidity for the lender who has accepted the promise to pay. However, if instant liquidity were available, why settle for a promise to pay in the first place? 'Redeemability at will' must be a fiction. Of course, one can understand how it was concocted by remembering the guarantee of redeemability as stated on older bank notes. The promise was that the presenter of the note would receive a specified amount of precious metal. But whenever the promise was seriously tested by too many holders of notes, it turned out to be empty precisely because it is the business of banks to transform deposits into loans, short-term liabilities into long-term assets. The working assumption is that increased uncertainty is balanced by increased rewards in the form of returns for transactions based on credit. However, this assumption may turn out to be wrong.

The basic borrower–lender relationship is iterated to form chains and networks of borrowers who receive loans because they are expecting payments and can show (written) promises to pay to prove this. The borrower–lender relationship constituted by a transfer of the power to purchase is not only iterated, but also reversed. Short sellers find buyers to whom they can sell without owning the object sold. In terms of uncertainty, this means that credit partly destroys the uncertainty absorption function of money. Going through the ways in which money absorbs uncertainty and reconsidering them as credit is used, we can see that the whole system becomes even more ambiguous in terms of a balance between the creation and the absorption of uncertainty.

There is no change in (1) the function of money to create a uniform expectational horizon: Whether they use credit or not, agents interacting in a monetary economy maximize their disposition over money and they expect each other to do just that. But the function of money (2) to establish a social hierarchy according to money holdings is certainly perturbed: credit allows agents to make others belief that they are wealthier than they actually are. So, as in the fairy tale about the emperor's new clothes, a world of make-believe may be established – until the proverbial child calls out that the emperor is naked. With regard to (3) the function of money as a 'security blanket', the ambivalence introduced by credit is especially drastic. Access to credit can be a substitute for access to cash for the borrower in need of liquidity, but what the borrower may gain, the lender may lose. The lender who suddenly calls in loans may be in for a bad experience. Access to credit may seduce agents to engage in speculative transactions. The build-up of positive feedback loops leads to bubbles. When bubbles burst, only cash counts. This is a return to the original role of cash in the absorption of uncertainty. Mere promises to pay are no longer acceptable. The function of money (4) to create pressure towards the uniformity of price and a consistent system of prices may be enhanced by credit, as the example of arbitrage financed by credit illustrates. But, at the same time, speculative build-ups of bubbles certainly distort prices, destroying their signaling function. With regard to (5) the dual function of money to depersonalize and de-historize social relations, credit introduces a reversal. In a credit system, the lender wants the credit history of any potential borrower. In a cash economy, there is no role for credit rating. As to the (6) function of money to enhance formal rationality, a generalized calculating attitude and the ensuing discipline in self-governed or imposed activities such as work, the first effect of credit, the softening of budget constraints, appears to undermine that function. However, there is a secondary effect that at least partly compensates for the softening of budget constraints. Once in debt, agents are under much more pressure to increase the (formal) rationality of their actions and perform in disciplined ways. One could argue, additionally, that a credit system induces people to think more and more in terms of risks and probabilities and to apply this kind of thinking to all areas of life.[99] Finally (7), the function of money to allow its users to redefine conflicts and problems as issues of demanding or offering money, thereby reducing complexity and thus uncertainty, seems to be unaffected by the use of credit.

Many of the transactions characteristic of the contemporary credit system can be seen as attempts to transform or redefine uncertainty into calculable risks.

Derivatives and their use have been praised as ways to exclude or minimize risks in the normal operation of business. However, in all these operations the aggregate outcome cannot be the elimination of uncertainty. Rather, agents may succeed in transferring parts of the risks they are taking to others, because there is a mutually complementary interest in doing so. Think of hedging in futures markets as the simplest, original case. As recent and previous financial crises have demonstrated these attempts to push back uncertainty have actually led to higher levels of risk-taking. If all agents think that they can shift some of their risks onto others, they feel free to undergo further risks. Thus, hedging may generate ubiquitous moral hazard that, in turn, works in a positive feedback manner and destroys the very possibilities of calculating these risks. The financial crisis is a drastic reminder that uncertainty cannot be eliminated in a system that operates on the fragile grounds of contingent actions.

The major effect of a credit crisis ironically turns out to be that everybody falls back on the one social tool that promises more certainty: money. 'All you need is cash' was the title caption of the *Economist* in November 2008. Thus, while the monetary system may become invisible or a minor sideshow when the 'great wheel of commerce' is turned by easy credit, the self-induced crises of the credit system demonstrate that when the pyramids built out of promises to pay crumble, everybody turns back to rely on the monetary system pure and simple.

To conclude: *Not all money is credit.* A modern theory of money must nonetheless be a credit theory of money, but in a different sense than suggested by Schumpeter. All modern money is credit money insofar as the state issuing it follows a procedure that lets the central bank take on the role of lender while the state mimics a borrower. As a result, the central bank holds as assets payment obligations by the state. The central bank notes 'created' in this way then serve the state as functional equivalents of cash: Payments made with these notes are final. In this way, the credit operation underlying the 'creation' of modern state money loses its significance. What money users use as cash counts as cash. Its use generates loose networks in which each buyer–seller relation may be transient and impersonal. In their pair-wise transactions only the validity of the money objects and the quality of the goods and services count, not the other person/ agent.[100] By contrast, credit relations – as relations between borrowers and lenders who define the time, form and size of payment obligations – persist as long as the payments have not been made. They are entered only if the lender believes that the borrower can service and repay the debt. This requires information about the credit-worthiness of the borrower composed of knowledge about past performance, assets serving as collateral, belief in future payment capability, and so on.[101] Thus, what Keynes said about money in general, namely, that it 'is, above all, a subtle device for linking the present to the future', can be further specified. Whereas the link between the present and the future in the use of money as cash only exists in the belief of the seller that the money object accepted in a sale will be accepted by unknown others in the future, the link between the present and the future in a credit relation exists as an ongoing relationship between lender and borrower, based on the belief that the borrower will be able to pay in the future.

This difference between monetary and credit relations may appear to be rather trivial. But it involves very different types of social relations with very different ways of coping with uncertainty and therefore, very different potentials of both enhancing and reducing the level of economic activities.

In sum, there can be no doubt that credit relations may generate uncertainty beyond the contingencies implicit in interaction in general, in the *ex post* coordination through markets and in simple monetary transactions in particular. Credit relations involve not only the more or less calculable risk for the lender that the borrower will fail to fulfill his promise to (re-)pay, but also genuine uncertainty. The roots of this uncertainty are systemic. What may appear as a calculable risk on the micro-level of lender/borrower interaction can and – judging from historical experience – will regularly lead to crisis on the system level. The combined effects of individually rational action based on calculation of risks destroy the presumed calculability of risks.

3.6 Money, credit and crises

To explain crises in general and the big crisis of 2007/2008 in particular cannot be the purpose of the following sketch. Its purpose is to underline the role of money and credit as conditions and causes of crisis, as the backside of the uncertainty absorption achieved with money and credit.

The use of money is a condition of possibility of economic crisis. Against 'Say's law', money separates sale and purchase: Nobody is forced to buy just because she has sold. If money 'freezes', that is if an increasing share is held as a liquid asset instead of being spent, fewer sales than expected can be completed. The economic process is slowed down, the level of activity decreases, growth may stop and turn into shrinkage and crisis. Investments slow down, unemployment increases, demand declines, a downward spiral can be set in motion.

But the use of money is not just a condition of possibility of crisis, it can also be a cause. Depicting the economic process as a circular flow shows how money income streams are generated as production proceeds. Wages, profits and rents are earned and flow back to firms if production and sales are successful. On the side of households, money income streams are directed to consumption and savings. Savings may or may not translate into investment and growth. If they do, capital will be accumulated.

Without credit, investment possibilities are limited by own earnings. Banks in their role as collectors of excess money holdings may facilitate growth by granting credits to investors. In addition, banks or other lenders may 'create' credit in excess of the deposits they have collected. In this way, they place bets on growth possibilities discovered by entrepreneurs who negotiate with banks for the financing of their projects. If the projects are successful, the entrepreneurs are able to service their debts. (Schumpeter 1939: 223) The growth resulting from their investments justifies the credit creation in retrospect. But the projects, especially if started in the late phase of a boom with the expectation that the boom will continue, may not be successful. Keynes described the ambivalence of the situation and the role of money inherent in it:

> There is a multitude of real assets in the world which constitute our capital wealth – buildings, stocks of commodities, goods in course of manufacture and of transport and so forth. The nominal owners of these assets, however, have not infrequently borrowed *money* in order to become possessed of them. To a corresponding extent the actual owners of wealth have claims, not on real assets, but on money. A considerable part of this 'financing' takes place through the banking system, which imposes its guarantee between its depositors who lend it money and its borrowing customers to whom it loans money with which to finance the purchase of real assets. The interposition of this veil of money between the real asset and the wealth owner is a specially marked characteristic of the modern world.
>
> (Keynes 1931:151)

This 'veil of money' is more than a veil, because the 'nominal owners' of capital assets owe money to the banks, not 'real' assets. They have to service their debts out of the monetary returns on their investments. Whether they are successful depends on demand for their products, that is, on market conditions normally beyond the control of both the enterprise and the bank that financed the investment. Note that the agents entering into mutual obligations are dealing with money in time. The flow of money from the bank to the enterprise is conditional to the expectation of future profits, whereas the flow of money back from the enterprise to the bank depends on realized profits. Whether the return flow can take place depends on aggregate demand, which in turn depends on aggregate investment, which in turn depends on expected profits.

This circular structure means that expectations may be self-stabilizing to some extent. But such a game of expectations can only produce a relatively fragile constellation. If expectations are not fulfilled to a sufficient degree, the whole system will be destabilized. In contrast to assumptions maintaining that there is such a thing as 'rational expectations', all expectations on the basis of which money now is traded for money in the future are unavoidably speculative. They motivate actions despite uncertainty. But it does not make sense to diagnose 'money illusion' if the alternative is not attainable.[102] Whatever happens, at the end of the day, money has to be paid. That is the one certainty.

Of course, the degree to which expectations are speculative varies. Minsky suggested an instructive threefold classification of economic units, engaged in 'hedge, speculative, and Ponzi finance'. They all have payment obligations. Hedge financing units – operating with low leverage – can service their debts out of cash flows. Speculative financing units, while able to pay interest, 'need to "roll over" their liabilities', making new loans to repay maturing debt. Ponzi units cannot meet their obligations out of cash flows. They borrow because they anticipate increases in the prices of the assets they buy. To service their debts, they have to sell assets or borrow again, lowering their equity and increasing their leverage. (Minsky 1992: 6f.) When a critical mass of projects turns out to be not successful, obligations to service the debts incurred for financing their projects will move economic units from the hedge finance class to the speculative finance class and from there to the Ponzi class and from there to bankruptcy. We have a debt deflation crisis.

The probability of such a crisis increases with banking operations that imply the separation between the originator of a loan and the lender. A bank is the originator, a person buying ownership paper issued by the bank is the lender. Wealth owners buy 'securitized' assets, shares in some fund or other ownership paper. They rely on the seller of the paper that the money borrowed and lent in the original transaction is used to finance some economically worthwhile project. The seller, say a bank, has a strong interest to earn money by making loans. If asset prices and equity increase and the bank is aiming for constant leverage (the ratio of assets to equity), it will offer more loans. The bank expands its balance sheet, financing more acquisitions of assets. This creates upward pressure on asset prices. A positive feedback loop is created (Adrian and Shin 2007).[103] To expand the loans despite the constraints of capital requirements, the bank will try to get the loans off its books. However, the more successful the bank is in 'selling' the (repackaged) loan, as a share in a fund or as any other form of ownership paper, the more the bank is exposed to moral hazard. As the originator of a loan it no longer has to care about the long-term economic prospects of the project financed by the loan as long as eager 'investors', lured by promises of high returns, pick up whatever the bank offers as ownership paper. At the same time, the buyers of the paper rely on the reputation of the bank or the fund managers for selecting promising projects.

These transactions can become more refined and less transparent. The crisis of 2007/2008 turned out to be such a big one because it was fed by the belief in the transformability of uncertainty into risk. New types of ownership papers were constructed by repackaging loans according to estimated risk, with these risks being positively related to promised returns. The transformation of subprime mortgages into triple A-rated papers is the prominent example (Carruthers 2011). Unfortunately, the risk estimates went wrong. Potential systemic effects of micro-activities were neglected. If – on the micro level – everybody bets on rising house prices, house prices will rise because more people will try to buy themselves into the game and reap a share of the gains. When – given a variety of potential causes (slow-down in demand, clever people cashing in their chips, some external shock) – the 'upper turning point' in the respective asset market is eventually reached, the whole structure starts to crumble. It becomes manifest that the originators of the loans or mortgages did not consider whether the borrowers would be able to service their debts in case house prices would no longer rise. The layers of paper start flying. They were pasted over non-sustainable borrower–lender relations based on overpricing assets as collateral.

Consumers were lured by easy credit, supporting a period of 'privatized Keynesianism' (Crouch 2008), in which private households – instead of governments – went into debt and supported aggregate demand. A decisive factor in the build-up of the crisis was the disregard of established rules for viable investments, amounting to widespread serious cognitive deficits. Investors seem to have lost the criteria and capability for checking how their individual strategies add up in the macro context. The questions they should have asked are simple. How many participants in a given market can realize double-digit income gains in a context of comparatively low 'real' growth? How many can continuously gain by more and more aggressive leveraging? People were lured by seductive theories promising that financial markets would behave like perfect markets and suggesting that decisions could be based on rational expectations. Thus, the crisis turned out to be a 'moment of truth' for theories of money and credit. Unless they start from the premise of uncertainty, they share the responsibility for the next crisis.

Remember that the word 'credit' comes from '*credere*', to believe. The term thus underlines the point that any credit operation requires faith in the borrower's willingness and ability to repay. Any lender has to overcome uncertainty. Who knows what the future will bring? Who can be certain that a borrower will keep his promises? In part, this uncertainty may be reduced by building safeguards into credit contracts (collateral, third agent pledges), by installing sanctioning institutions for breach of contract and by lenders collecting information about borrowers' prospects and personalities. But there always remains an indelible block of uncertainty to cope with. The roots of the term 'credit' indicate that, lastly, such coping is accomplished with faith.[104] Faith functions as a substitute for the certainty, most basically for the certainty gained by laying hands on a tangible quid pro quo in return for whatever one has given away.[105] As a complement to lenders' uncertainty, there is uncertainty on the side of the borrower, too. On the one hand, the borrowers know for sure that they will have to service their debt. But on the other hand, they cannot be certain that their the expectation of future income streams sufficient for the servicing and repayment of the loan will be fulfilled. Who can know?[106]

'Action involves a suspension of disbelief ... and economic success foster[s] such a suspension' (Minsky 1996: 2). Such reliance on faith is difficult to incorporate into a theory that assumes all action to be rational and utility maximizing with given individual preferences. As credit relations are the foundation for all modern forms of money, assuming straightforward rationality instead of 'a more bumbling kind' (Simon 1955: 117) in spite of this faith component is a rather daring theoretical device. Its continued use suggests that economic theory itself has become part of the general social strategy to ignore the shaky foundations of the modern monetary economy. For a better theory, it would be wise to acknowledge that straightforward rationality cannot possibly rule our economic activities. Rational economic action is a myth that serves to suppress the knowledge that all we are relying on in our economic activities are rather shakily founded beliefs in the stability of monetary institutions.

Conclusion

> People are often reproached for wishing for money above all things, and for loving it more than anything else; but it is natural and even inevitable for people to love that which, like an unwearied Proteus, is always ready to turn itself into whatever object their wandering wishes or manifold desires may for the moment fix upon. Everything else can satisfy only *one* wish, *one* need: food is good only if you are hungry; wine, if you are able to enjoy it; drugs, if you are sick; fur for the winter; love for youth, and so on. These are all only relatively good, [Greek: agatha pros ti]. Money alone is absolutely good, because it is not only a concrete satisfaction of one need in particular; it is an abstract satisfaction of all.
>
> (Schopenhauer [1851] 2004: 23)

How do we live with money? 'The possession of actual money lulls our disquietude' (Keynes [1937] 1973: 116), but not only that. Most of the time, monetary systems operate so that they provide footholds secure enough for money users to perform their economic transactions in calculable patterns. Much uncertainty is absorbed. However, at the same time, uncertainty is generated by two impulses ultimately resulting from the generally unlimited desire for *more* money. *First*, this desire implies – historically uniquely strong – incentives to innovate, to rationalize, to find new ways of doing things. Innovations lead to 'creative destruction' (Schumpeter 1943: 82), creative destruction generates uncertainty (Deutschmann 2009). *Second*, using money involves both the need and the willingness to speculate. The distinction between normal business and speculation is shady. Any normal business in everyday life involves faith, trust, believing in and accepting promises. It is based on expectations that things will turn out as planned. Money adds to this speculative element because even the simple use of coins[1] involves faith in the acceptability of these metal things as money objects. Speculation here means that – despite repeated historical evidence to the contrary – we rely on money as a social fact as if it were a natural fact.[2] The speculative component is more manifest in the unquestioning acceptance of fiat money: You accept it because you believe – normally without thinking – that others will accept it, too. The speculative element becomes dominant in much business on credit: You accept a promise to pay because you believe – again without much thought – that it will be fulfilled. You may in turn use the paper stating a promise to you in writing to 'pay' third persons – who in their turn add a strong dose of speculation by believing in your promise that the original debtor's promise to you is 'as good as gold', and so on. These elementary patterns of speculation involve bets on events in the future, events that are unknown in principle. However, to use a distinction made prominent by Donald Rumsfeld, these forms of speculation are about 'known unknowns'. When they are multiplied and iterated to generate additional layers of paper stating contingent claims, as in the contemporary financial system, however, the system may switch to generate 'unknown unknowns': You try to hedge your bets and others make a business of selling you comforting securities, speculating on the possibility to shift and spread the risks involved so that they cancel out on the system level. But if they do not cancel out because positive feedback pushes some crucial elements of the system out of line, as in an asset speculation bubble, there will eventually result a domino effect, destroying the safeguards against the 'known unknowns' (Taleb 2008). The result of speculation is that the invisible hand works in cyclical patterns only. The system's capacity to absorb uncertainty is undermined by waves of speculation. If a crisis is deep enough, states will step in to try and rescue the system that private players have ruined.

In short, we do and can rely on the working of the monetary system most of the time but, periodically, we have to face more or less catastrophic disturbances or breakdowns. These breakdowns have never been final. While we do know of moneyless societies, we do not know of any monetized society that has re-switched to the moneyless state, not even after severe crises. Crises only mean that, after the winners have been separated from the losers, everybody returns to playing the money game. Its advantages seem to outweigh its disadvantages, although the distributions of both are rather uneven.[3]

So this is how we live with money. We use it as a way to escape uncertainty while – admittedly or not – we also know that all our calculations, strategies and projects may turn out to be castles made of sand. The escape from uncertainty is provisional. In the speculative games induced by promises of certainty some will be rewarded excessively, some will be suddenly ruined. In quieter times, most people play the money game to earn more, while, when something goes wrong, they will do anything to avoid falling into a moneyless position. The effect is that the vast majority of the population in a monetized society is just struggling to stay in between the high flyers and the poor.

Looking back, what did I accomplish with this book in terms of the goal to contribute to monetary theory from a sociological standpoint? It has turned out to be mostly a critical examination of existing theories of money, with a focus on traditional economics and its failures. Much of the argument was conducted as a conceptual analysis on the level and as close to the standard assumptions of microeconomic analysis as I found feasible. The deviations turn out to be important, however, so it is worthwhile to present them in a summary way as a conclusion for purposes of further theorizing.

Roughly, standard microeconomic reasoning uses the following set of conceptual tools:

- Utilitarianism (U): Agents maximize utility.
- Rationalism (R): Agents are rational (meaning mostly that they have given, consistent preferences and use the best available means to achieve their ends).
- Individualism (I): Agents are self-interested individuals. Collective agents must be explained as composed of such individuals, whether voluntarily or not.
- Equilibrium (E): The interplay of individual activities is considered in terms of the question of whether it will result in or, rather, whether it is compatible with an equilibrium state.

Although one can certainly be skeptical about all these tools and their combination (URIE), I started with the idea of clearly defecting only in terms of two, utility maximizing and equilibrium.

Against the *utility maximizing* assumption I hold that in a monetary economy, agents maximize monetary returns (maxM). The rule of buying cheaply and selling dearly can be explained as the combined effect of the quality of money as the 'absolute means' and the fact that it is always available in limited quantity only. By contrast, utility maximizing is a correlate of the absence of money illusion. But money illusion cannot be absent if agents have to make payments in money terms in situations with uncertainty.

Since such maxM is an open-ended, never to be completed project – there is always more money to be had and striving for it generates cumulative effects – *equilibrium* in the traditional static sense of a sort of resting place for a social system is not a relevant concept for understanding the processes characteristic of a monetary economy.

I did not anticipate problems with the other two tools, the *rationality* assumption and *methodological individualism*. They should be seen as heuristic devices in the tradition of Max Weber (1964: 92, 101). But it turned out that the meaning of rationality changes drastically once one takes uncertainty seriously. It implies the rejection of the traditional perfect foresight, complete information assumptions, including the Arrow/Debreu version of 'uncertainty' with its implication that agents know all the possible contingent future states of the world. Given uncertainty, one can use Weberian justifications to assume that agents are *intendedly* rational in a world that leaves lots of opportunities for errors and plans that go wrong. Such an assumption of moderated rationality is useful in exerting pressure on explanations to not flee prematurely into some half-baked sociology and invoke unexplained norms to make sense of seemingly non-rational actions. Beyond that, it turns out that the traditional conceptual triangle of rationality, information and foresight starts to wobble once serious uncertainty is introduced. 'How on earth can you have all the facts when the most important ones refer to what other people will do (Shackle 1990: 107)?' How much rationality is possible when information is weak and foresight is based on extrapolating from past experience? Should we say that maxM is a rational reaction to situations with weak information and low foresight in a monetary economy? Certainly, that cannot be maintained in general and the whole issue needs more attention than I have been able to devote to it.

As to *methodological* individualism, I take it to mean that explanations of social facts referring to *unexplained* supra-individual agencies (social systems, the state, the community, collective memory ...) should be rejected. This implies starting social analysis in a micro-perspective, moving from simple to more complex patterns of interaction, and giving logical priority to actions over their results, like social structure or institutions. More narrowly, in the theory of money, methodological individualism turns into an issue when we consider what Schumpeter called the 'logical' origins of money. How can rational agents come to an agreement to introduce and use money? Neo-chartalists invoke the state or some central authority in their answer. Unless they can explain what the state or some other center of collective action does in terms of the participating individuals, referring to it does not give a satisfactory answer to the 'origins' problem.[4] I have favored an answer suggested by John Searle, but despite his deference to methodological individualism, the reliance on 'collective intentionality' leaves open many questions with regard to its roots in individual intentionality. Methodological individualism simply means that we do not skip over the fact that whatever a collective may do and intend, it cannot operate beyond the minds and intentions of the individuals that are the elements of the collective.

So the result as to the toolbox for further research on money is the modification of URIE: maxM instead of the maxU; intended instead of perfect rationality; a modest version of methodological individualism; disregard of equilibrium issues.

To conclude and in sum, the main result of my examination of – mostly economic – theories of money in a sociological perspective is that mainstream economic theory lacks two features required for understanding money. First, economic theorists are not in the habit of analyzing economic processes as *social processes, as interactions*. This may appear strange because, after all, the analysis of bilateral exchange is traditionally one of the core concerns of economic theory. But the theory neglects or ignores the capabilities and continuous efforts of human agents to see the world, including themselves, with the eyes of the other(s).[5] To take account of that capacity and thus move beyond simplistic individualism (in the manner affirmed by Mises, see Section 1.1) is not only a necessary requirement for all social science, but also an essential ingredient of any explanation of money. The capacity to take the perspective of the other allows one party in a transaction to use something as a means if it can be anticipated to be an end for the other party, and *vice versa*. I can use something as a tool in exchange that is useless for myself once I know that it is an object of need for you; you can do the same with me. This simultaneous duality of function ascription in simple interaction lies at the root of money, but with a paradoxical twist. Once we both know that we can manipulate each other by anticipating the other's desires and needs and using the objects promising fulfillment as instruments, we can also agree on using things as means of exchange among the two of us that are useless for both of us, if only we expect that third agents will desire them. This leads to the paradoxical money constellation: Everybody can use something useless as a means of exchange to acquire useful things. Once human agents understand this possibility, they can move to handling their transactions with money objects that are mere symbols, signaling what game is being played. But along with this move, these objects turn from simple means of acquisition into what Simmel called the 'absolute means'. A society is fully monetized once money is what everybody always wants, whether one has to clamber to get it for satisfying daily needs or whether one wants it to stay ahead in parades of conspicuous consumption. Even at the uppermost end of the distribution, there are no natural limits to acquiring wealth in this abstract form. Satiation may occur in terms of owning houses, yachts, jewellery, art, and what not, but all this does limit the desire for money.[6] You will always want more if you find more ways to spend it and it is easy to find new ways to spend it because there are all these people scrambling to offer something new and exciting to you in order to get your money.

Second, because mainstream theory does not sufficiently take into account interaction, it also misses (or suppresses) the essential role of *uncertainty* in economic life. Uncertainty is not only part of the human condition because we have to cope with unknown events generated by nature. It is produced and reproduced by us in every interaction every day. Of course, I can expect what you will do and you can expect what I will do. But such expectations are formed before the background of the knowledge that we both can do something else and that we can do that unexpectedly. We may surprise each other positively by creativity leading to beneficial innovations, or we may surprise each other negatively by opportunism leading to destruction of the commons or by suddenly being forced to renege on our promises, perhaps because others do the same to us.

Again, how does money fit into this general picture of uncertainty in social life? Because money is the 'absolute means', it is one of the most important devices we can use to influence each other, thus limiting the scope of relevant actions by others, confirming expectations, reducing uncertainty, accomplishing coordination. However, because of this very nature of money and because of the unlimited desire for it, it is not only such a powerful instrument for absorbing uncertainty, but at the same time also the reason for formidable explosions of uncertainty. When the strive for ever more money leads to ever more risky speculative activities, bubbles build up. They burst sooner or later. In the ensuing crisis, everybody who is exposed to the effects of the breakdown of chains of payment is running for cover. Where? The best cover is provided by money: it is great to have cash when everybody else urgently needs it. So, in a paradoxical way, the very fact that the monetary system generates crisis confirms and strengthens our need for money.[7]

To repeat, money is a social fact. In our daily activities, we construct and reproduce the monetary system. We are 'doing' money. It is not something imposed on us by some outside force. It is not part of an inescapable fate, of the human condition. It is a social fact and as such something we can change, develop, destroy or what not. But while some indelible background uncertainty is the birthmark of social facts, the success of money as a social construction rests on its function to absorb uncertainty. Ironically, this holds even when monetary systems fail and suddenly generate steeply increasing uncertainty. The general need for security grows simultaneously. As there are few alternatives to money to answer this need – think of the precarious roles of alternative 'stores of value' or the risky reliance on agents like families or states in providing social security – we hang on to money even when its uncertainty generating features dominate its uncertainty absorbing features. Because of this paradox, the monetary system is, in the jargon of systems-theory, 'ultra-stable': By generating crises it confirms its own reality.

Appendix

A.1 Money and inequality according to econophysics

A rather fundamental proposition on the social consequences of money use stems from recent applications of ideas from physics to economic matters. They come under the label econophysics (for a survey, see Yakovenko 2011)

The economy is presented as a network of interacting agents using money. The system is closed in the sense that neither the number of agents nor the quantity of money change. The initial distribution of money is arbitrary, but the most stimulating set-up starts from equal endowments with money. Agents engage in pair-wise transactions in which money objects change hands, subject to a local constant sum condition: The sum of money held by two agents after their encounter is equal to the sum they held before their encounter. The resulting distribution of money holdings is analogous to the distribution of the temperature of particles running into each other at random, a so-called Kirchhoff/Gibbs distribution emerging after a not too large number of repeated rounds of transactions. Econophysicists have experimented with all sorts of restrictions and constraints: no debt, limited debt, savings, capital–labor relations, taxation. The result invariably is a distribution of money holdings that is independent of agents' properties like talent or effort: The exponential Gibbs distribution is combined with a Pareto-power law distribution, the latter having the property that, as the amount of money owned increases, the share of the population owning that amount is reduced by a constant factor. Monetary wealth 'in every case is always owned disproportionately by a small fraction of the most wealthy, but as the number in the fat-tailed pattern grows smaller, the concentration of wealth becomes more pronounced' (Buchanan 2002: 193).

What can we learn from econophysics – even if we are reluctant to accept the analogy of agents and particles?

- Monetary systems, because of their network structure and transaction pattern, automatically produce strong inequality of money holdings. This raises a political issue: What can be done to weaken the trend towards strong inequality? There is a role for the state to be played, first of all simply because the state is such a uniquely big player in any economy; second, because taxation and redistribution can be simple and effective instruments to prevent the degeneration of the money distribution into gross inequality.

- Econophysicists simply take the requirement of a monetary invariant as given in those models (assuming a closed system with a given aggregate quantity of money). In reality, the monetary invariant is a 'working fiction' (Mirowski), as we have seen. The interesting question then is: How can such a fiction work? The most likely answer is: Because there is a system-inherent need for it – without a monetary 'conservation principle', there would be no metric, without a metric, there would be no market transactions and strategic calculations, no 'formal rationality' (in Weber's sense), and so on. Does the installation of a conservation principle imply that the influx of additional money objects into an economy has to be controlled and should be a stable, transparent process, as quantity theorists have proposed? The issue is too complicated to be boiled down to a matter of the quantity of money, to be controlled at the 'source'.
- One irony that emerges when juxtaposing economics and econophysics is that economists of the orthodox kind start what is meant to end as a particular kind of social analysis by assuming as given a very barren physical world (see even the contributions of search theorists of money by Kiyotaki and Wright 1993; Kocherlakota 1998). In the assumed n-dimensional commodity space (R^+) the traces of individual actions can be identified, but individuals are not visible. They only react to given constellations in an equally invisible market (there are no social interactions, no institutions). By contrast, the econophysicists start from money and specify typical transactions between pairs of agents *without* any reference to the physical world. It does not matter what is traded, it only matters that money is used. But, of course, they rely on analogies, as between the stationary distribution of energy in a closed system and the distribution of money, or between T (temperature) and money holdings.
- If read correctly, the physics approach, using statistical mechanics, demonstrates that discussions of money should aim for the level of the rules of the game, specifying a macro-mechanism as the result of interactions, rather than starting from individual behavior, with individuals facing a non-social environment (Cartelier 2002: 8).

Quite clearly, applying results from physics to a social realm that, in evolutionary terms, has some emergent properties not present in the physical realm involves constructing analogies that may not be fitting. As a first rough indication of the difference between the physical and the social realms, we can say that the latter is more about the use of information and something philosophers call intentionality and less about energy. But the analogy may be justified if, when using money, the social realm seems to simulate the physical one in the sense of societies installing a conservation principle analogous to the principle of energy conservation in physics. This is the case when money is used: In any pair-wise monetary transaction, regardless of its further content, the sum of money held by the participating agents will be the same before and after their transaction. This is the simple reason why the econophysics models can produce interesting results. If we want to know how money is likely to be distributed after a sufficiently large number of monetary transactions, we do not need to know more about these transactions than that they are constrained by a local constant sum condition, apart from assuming a closed system (given sum of money, given number of agents, some initial distribution of money). So the point is really *not* to propose that there are no important differences between the physical environment and the economy, but rather that in the case of money, the information that transactions are governed by a conservation principle is sufficient to derive the resulting probable stationary distribution of money. It turns out to be drastically unequal.

In sum, the issue raised by econophysic models should not be whether their use of analogies is reductionist, treating social processes as if they were physical. Rather, it should be: How much information about economic processes is sufficient to determine the probable distribution of money? It turns out that it is surprisingly little information – if the physicists are correct, which I think is very likely.

So what is the result of our excursion into econophysics? Monetary systems, unmodified by countervailing powers, tend to generate a sharply unequal distribution of money holdings among participants. They produce a social division into two classes, a vast majority with very little money and a small group with extremely high money holdings. More specifically, the form of the probable stationary distribution will be a combination of exponential and power law distributions.

This result adds a few new questions to the theory of money. The most important one seems to be: If this strong inequality increasing effect of simply using money were well known, why would the resulting, almost moneyless majority of a population, given a democratic political system, tolerate a monetary economy? Why would the majority not vote against an economic system that leaves them relatively poor?

But let us leave that question to political scientists at this point and concentrate on the issue of relating money use to capitalism. What the econophysics argument suggests is the following connection: On the one hand, everybody needing or wanting to participate in a monetary economy has to have money. On the other hand, the simple use of money sooner or later generates a distribution of money holdings that leaves a vast majority with little or nothing. This situation is ideal for capitalism in the sense of forcing this majority to do almost anything or, at least, almost anything that is legal, to earn some money. The exit option out of moneylessness is: Work for money! So a monetary system continuously generates the willingness to work – for pay.

A.2 Money and the state

Charles Goodhart (1998) has stylized one major continuing controversy in monetary theory as a battle of ideas between Mengerians and neo-chartalists. The latter have contrasted their own views, according to which all money, with its primary function being that of the means of accounting, is credit money and is installed by the state, against traditional economic thought that is purported to hold that the means of exchange function is primary and emerges as a property of a selected commodity in exchange transactions of private individual agents on markets. This stylized contrast is misleading in several ways. First of all, it is not clear why there should be a need to ascribe ('logical') priority (Ingham 2004) to any one function of money. Whatever is used as money has a bundle of functions. The question is not whether we can select one of them and derive all others from the primary one. Rather, the question should be, as Richard Seaford (2004: 16) put it: What properties must an 'X' have in order for us to call it money? The answer is a list of properties among which, right from its historical origins, some are attributable to the state (or a state-like authority) and others are the result of spontaneous function attribution by private agents in their transactions. Whatever counts as money in a given political realm is not only the means of accounting, but also the means of exchange, the means of fulfilling payment obligations, a 'store of value', and so on.

The substantial issue in the controversy between Mengerians and neo-chartalists is not whether all contemporary '(m)oney is a creature of the state' (Lerner 1947). Empirically, there is no question that nation-states install and attempt to manage their currencies. The euro indicates that supra-national currency systems may replace national ones. Alternative monies, emerging bottom-up, exist only in niches.[1] The substantial issue is that the concepts of money and the strategies to explain monetary systems differ, with Neo-chartalists shifting much of the explanatory burden to the state, while Mengerians emphasize the role of markets and argue in line with methodological individualism. They face the underlying theoretical problem of collective action as a presupposition of money straightforwardly, whereas Neo-chartalists run into this problem only once they do not take the state as a – most likely benevolent – agent as given: In either case, explaining money involves indicating how agents solve a collective action problem. If money is a social fact whose possibility stems from a collective agreeing on: 'X counts as Y in C' à la Searle, the puzzle is to find out how and why all agents 'count' in the same way. Searle invokes 'collective intentionality' and that remains a problematic concept. Neo-chartalists seem to circumvent this problem by referring to the state (or some state-like authority) imposing the collective intention required to 'count X as Y in C'. However, this merely shifts the theoretical problem from the level of spontaneously interacting individuals to the level of a collective agent assumed not only to be given, but equipped both with the knowledge to anticipate the benefits of something like money and with the power to coerce its subjects into using it. In short, neo-chartalists run into the same type of explanatory problem as Mengerians, but they run into it as a general problem in the explanation of the state, whereas Mengerians run into it in the specific form of explaining the spontaneous emergence of a means of exchange as the rudimentary form of money.

Notes

Introduction

1 As Wesley Mitchell (1950:171) put it: 'Money may not be the root of *all* evil, but it is the root of economic science.'
2 'Contingency' refers to the modal property of something being both possible and non-necessary.
3 In the sense of Knight's distinction between (insurable) risk and uncertainty: 'Economic life necessarily involves much uncertainty or risk, in the loose sense, due to the vicissitudes of nature. Not all of this could theoretically be covered by insurance, and for much more insurance is impracticable. Enterprise economy adds to this the far greater uncertainty associated with the almost universal production of goods in anticipation of the wishes of consumers' (Knight 1933: 486).
4 While there certainly are different approaches to economic sociology, I share the view that the distinctive contribution of economic sociology to the understanding of economic life rests on recognizing uncertainty as the driving force of institution building (Beckert 1996).

1 Problems and their setting

1 The concept of uncertainty absorption is taken from March and Simon, who introduce it as follows: 'Uncertainty absorption takes place when inferences are drawn from a body of evidence and the inferences, instead of the evidence itself, are then communicated.... Through the process of uncertainty absorption, the recipient of a communication is severely limited in his ability to judge its correctness. Although there may be various tests of apparent validity, internal consistency, and consistency with other communications, the recipient must, by and large, repose his confidence in the editing process that has taken place, and, if he accepts the communication at all, accept it pretty much as it stands' (March and Simon 1958: 165). We will see below how communication with money is based on such processes of uncertainty absorption.
2 See Section 3.6.
3 In view of this crude fact, governing the everyday life of so many people, it remains a mystery why so many writers on money assume that its primary function is that of a means of accounting.
4 See Goodwin (1989) for how to combine Marx, Keynes and Schumpeter for a theory of capitalism, and Keen (1995) for an extended Goodwin model that includes finance.
5 'Social history in the nineteenth century was thus the result of a double movement: the extension of the market organization in respect to genuine commodities was accompanied by its restriction in respect to fictitious ones. While on the one hand markets spread all over the face of the globe and the amounts of goods involved grew to unbelievable proportions, on the other hand a network of measures and policies

was integrated into powerful institutions designed to check the action of the market relative to labor, land, and money' (Polanyi 1957: 76).

6 'In its pure form, neoclassical theory is a theory of relative prices. Monetary theories vaguely related to it in spirit can be grafted onto it, but none have succeeded in achieving a genuine synthesis' (Arrow 1974).

7 Does this view inform monetary policy? Former Federal Reserve Governor Larry Meyer is frequently quoted as stating that 'money plays no explicit role in today's consensus macro model, and it plays virtually no role in the conduct of monetary policy (Woodford 2007: 1).' Woodford in turn is reported by the Economist (9 June 2007: 88) to argue 'that inflation can to all intents and purposes be modeled and controlled without paying any attention at all to money'. Of course, Meyer and Woodford merely meant that central banks do not have to pay attention to the aggregate quantity of money in their conduct of monetary policy, but is it accidental that their language is misleading in suggesting that money as such does not matter?

8 'It [money, HG] is none of the wheels of trade: It is the oil which renders the motion of the wheels more smooth and easy' (Hume [1752] 1970: 33).

9 Such abuse is a constant possibility, of course, which is why extremist economists like Hayek (1976a) are convinced that money, too, should be privatized.

10 See Schmitz (2002) for an instructive comparative listing of such assumptions.

11 Note the normative twang: 'should … if … rational'!

12 Max Weber's term 'effective price' (1964: 194) is useful because we need to distinguish between the desired, estimated or imagined prices all around us (for example, on price tags in a shop or in accounting) and the prices that have been 'realized' in the sense of somebody actually having paid them.

13 Keynes clearly described the potentially immobilizing effect of ignorance and the ways in which it is overcome:

> By 'uncertain' knowledge … I do not mean merely to distinguish what is known for certain from what is only probable. The game of roulette is not subject, in this sense, to uncertainty…. The sense in which I am using the term is that in which the prospect of a European war is uncertain … or the position of private wealth owners in the social system in 1970. About these matters, there is no scientific basis on which to form any calculable probability whatever. We simply do not know. Nevertheless, the necessity for action and for decision compels us as practical men to do our best to overlook this awkward fact and to behave exactly as we should if we had behind us a good Benthamite calculation …

Keynes goes on to list three techniques that allow us to save our faces as rational, economic men. 'First, despite bad experience we use the present as a guide to the future and ignore the prospect of future changes.' Second: 'We assume that the *existing* state of opinion as expressed in prices and the character of existing output is based on a *correct* summing up of future prospects.' Third: 'Knowing that our own individual judgment is worthless, we endeavour to fall back on the judgment of the rest of the world which is perhaps better informed.' Dealing with uncertainty in these ways has costs, however: 'a practical theory of the future based on these three characteristics … is subject to sudden and violent changes' (Keynes 1937: 113f.).

14 As Marx pointed out, the possibility of crises is inherent in the splitting of transactions into sale and purchase. The fact that you have sold does not force you to turn around and buy. Once money is used, supply no longer creates its own demand.

15 'Money is a symbol. It represents in some measurable way some command over goods and services' (Firth 1963: 124; as quoted in Codere 1968: 559).

16

> However, purer than by some kind of 'coin' the concept of money is represented by an intrinsically valueless commodity, like a paper imprinted with signs, a

commodity which not only has its meaning but also its value *assigned solely* by the society.

(Tönnies [1887] 1922: 45, my transl. HG)

17 Schumpeter (1991: 536f.) attempted to avoid this difficulty by defining 'value' in a way that would make the term unusable for expressing such a hidden intrinsic property of commodities:

> By 'value' is to be understood here 'exchange value' expressed in money: hence, whenever what is involved is the quantity-unit commonly used in the market for a commodity – a material commodity or a service – 'exchange value' means its unit price, or, if what is involved is a quantity other than the quantity-unit, 'exchange value' means this price times this quantity. Thus, if one says that money functions as a 'measure of value', one usually means, in *this* context, that the exchange ratios of commodities with one another are replaced by the exchange ratios between each of them and money.'

Unfortunately, this brings Schumpeter very close to the view that money is merely a medium to uniformly express relative prices that are formed without money.

18 For a critical discussion of the sociological concept of money as a symbolically generalized medium of communication, cf. Ganssmann (1988).

19 Starting the explanation of money by referring to markets as locations of social encounters and interaction is meant to exclude neither solitary exercises in the use of money, like accounting, nor occasional barter-like market transactions. But it is meant to reject the (neo-)chartalist idea (Aglietta 2002; Ingham 2004) that some time way back money was somehow pumped into transactions by the state or some 'sovereign authority'. Roughly twenty pages into the Bible (Genesis, 23, 15) we learn that Abraham in foreign lands refused the gift of a piece of land with a cave he wanted for burying Sarah and rather bought it by paying 400 shekel of silver to the Hittite Ephron. There is a reference to customs, to a contract and to a public of merchants, but not to any state. The silver is measured by weight, not coined, so – following Knapp ([1905] 1923, ch. 1) – one may be reluctant to call the shekel money.

20 For recent contributions to monetary theory that start with descriptions of the 'physical environment' of the economy, while treating social facts like goods, utility functions, expectations and trades as elements of that 'physical environment', see Kiyotaki and Wright 1989 or Kocherlakota 1997, or: 'It is somewhat standard to describe a model in two parts. One is the *physical* environment – people and their preferences, resources and the technology, and the information structure. The other is the equilibrium concept – the rules governing interactions among people' (Wallace 1998). The idea seems to be that one can separate the actions (that may or may not lead to equilibrium) from the situation, the means and the agents. But it is somewhat hard to swallow that 'people and their preferences …' are part of the 'physical environment'. There is no such physical fact as a preference and the role of information is not reducible to its physical aspects.

2 Clarifications

1 The nature and number of these building blocks vary a bit. Based on Searle (1995), Meijers (2003: 170f.) distinguishes 'four conceptual tools:

1 the distinction between constitutive and regulative rules;
2 the imposition of function, according to the formula 'X counts as Y in context C';
3 collective intentionality; and
4 the background of intentionality, which consists of non-intentional skills and abilities.'

Searle (2005) only uses three, leaving aside the 'background', which I will do, too, in this chapter. But note that the 'background' may include *social* skills important for using money.

2 Searle is very careful to show that his concept of collective intentionality does not contradict the postulate of methodological individualism that 'there cannot be a group mind or group consciousness. All consciousness is in individual minds' (Searle 2002: 96).

3 Money objects usually have three components, the material (paper or metal), the inscription of a number stating how many units of money the objects represents, and engravings and other refinements that are supposed to prevent forgery.

4 Of course, there is also an official status assignment imprinted on many bank notes. But this only serves to confirm or support the status assignment required by users of the notes.

5 More about this later, but it is clear that the use of money involves all sorts of mutual obligations and corresponding rights: If you have paid as agreed for some good, you have an ownership right and can dispose of the good as you wish, etc.

6 As indicated above, Searle's fourth conceptual tool, the 'background', could be introduced at this point. Searle uses it to account for action patterns that follow rules without there being an intention to follow rules. The 'background' takes over because the ability to perform an activity is learned, but may nonetheless have become an automatic, routine response in a standard situation.

7 Both of which need to be explained, not assumed as by Habermas (1980: 80f).

8 'The word, like the monetary unit, stands for a vast range of items with which it has no essential connection, reducing multiplicity and tangibility to a single abstraction, as part of a symbolic system which through rule-governed circulation promotes cohesion of action. Language and money have been compared since antiquity' (Seaford 2004: 8n).

9 The closest money comes to language is as money of account or measure of value. The presence and use of tangible money objects is not required when accounts are written or contracts are negotiated.

10 Wittgenstein's *Philosophical Investigations* are quoted according to his own numbering.

11 Note that the proposition – to be discussed below – that the primary function of money is that of a means of account, not that of a means of exchange, is closely related to the idea of money as a language in neglecting the use of money as a tool of appropriation.

12 See the term 'moneyness' in many texts on money (not to be confused with the 'moneyness' of options in financial markets).

13 As Walter Bagehot observed: 'Men of business in England do not ... like the currency question. They are perplexed to define accurately what money is; *how* to count they know, but *what* to count they do not know.' (quoted in Kindleberger 1989: 63) Nineteenth-century men of business in England are certainly not alone in this ignorance.

14 What we take as given appears to be 'natural' even if it is a social construction: 'The key aspect of many economic activities that differentiates them from the viewpoint of information processing and coding from say political or societal activities or from abstract games is that a natural metric exists on many of the strategies' (Shubik 1975: 560).

15 Bentham was more blunt in connecting money to pain and pleasure in a relation of measurement: 'Money is the instrument of measuring the quantity of pain or pleasure ... Let no man therefore be either surprised or scandalized if he find me in the course of this work valuing everything in money. 'Tis in this way only can we get aliquot parts to measure by. If we must not say of a pain or a pleasure that it is worth so much money, it is in vain, in point of quantity, to say anything at all about it ... ' (Bentham 1952, vol. 1: 117f.).

16 Codere does not consider one subsequent development that we have to take into account later on. It can be described as a switch from money as a means of accounting to accounting replacing the actual use of physical money objects in transactions.

When we talk about contemporary money, one of the interesting issues is the substitution of information technology based credit mechanisms (credit cards, etc.) for the use of traditional money objects such as cash.

17 This does not exclude the possibility of indirect measurement. In measuring physical objects, we can use indirect methods based on empirical laws that relate changes in one property of the objects measured in a determinate way to changes in another property. For example: Traditional thermometers measure temperature via the length of a column of quicksilver in a glass tube. We have to know how the volume of a given mass of quicksilver reacts to changes in temperature to perform this indirect measurement of temperature through length.

18 Obviously, the term 'equivalence' involves a reference to 'equal values', but in contrast to the reference to 'value' in many economic texts, equivalence relations are precisely defined in mathematics. See Krause (1979) for an economic application of the precise concept.

19 Oddly enough, however, while reversability may hold for the money–commodity relation in accounting (estimates of wealth in which all sorts of assets are aggregated according to their prices) as a mental operation, it does not hold for money–commodity exchanges. 'As the most liquid of all assets, money can be used in exchange for other assets more readily than other assets can be used in exchange for money. This is but another way of saying that it is easier to buy with money than to sell for money' (Dillard 1987: 1632).

20 The post-World-War-II Bretton Woods system combined fixed exchange rates among member country currencies with a fixed link of the US dollar to gold, so that, in theory, dollar holdings could be traded in for the corresponding amounts of gold by central banks of member countries. In practice, the system repeated a story already known from nation-state level banking systems: The gold (or other) reserves never were sufficient to fulfill the promise of convertibility. If doubts about the stability of a fiat currency became serious and too many people preferred gold instead, convertibility was suspended.

21 Note the difference to Menger's problem (Menger [1892] 1970: 3), where the puzzle is that rational agents accept useless metal disks or paper bills in exchange for useful goods. Every player in a modern economy knows that exchange, consumption and production are different spheres of life. So why should everything – regardless of the context in which it is encountered – always be judged according to the same subjectively defined standards of utility in consumption?

22 'Monetary units such as the dollar, franc, pound, mark, or yen, measure value separated from particular commodities' (Foley 1989: 248).

23 On commensuration, see Espeland and Stevens (1998).

24 The indeterminacy resulting from the ineradicable element of subjectivity in price formation may be the reason for the preoccupation with given prices in economic theory. Fictitious objectivity culminates in the idea of the 'parametric function of prices' (Lange, O. 1936/7: 59) in perfect competition. Prices, something that cannot but be made by us, are seen as something given to us. We are to adapt to prices as if they were set by Mother Nature.

25 Coase develops his famous argument on external effects in an 'analysis confined ... to comparisons of the value of production, as measured by the market' (1960: 43). In other words, he considers money prices to be the result of measurement performed by the market.

26 How to form prices – without regress to costs – seems to be a case of 'Something that we know when no one asks us, but no longer know when we are supposed to give an account of it' (Wittgenstein, PI 89).

27 Richard Seaford identifies this precondition for the first widespread use of coins in ancient Greece: 'For the institution of coined money to work, belief in its (socially constructed) unchanging identity over time is required (whether or not it turns out to be mistaken)' (Seaford 2004: 257f.).

28 Given such thin ice, economists pushing ideas like that of 'perfect markets' seem to answer needs for anxiety reduction in face of uncertainty. They have a therapeutic function – until the shock of market breakdown comes.

29 With the term, Philip Mirowski described a real problem in a way that poses a big challenge for theory: 'The overriding social problem of all market oriented societies is to find some means to maintain the working fiction of a monetary invariant through time' (Mirowski 1991: 581). In other words: there is no monetary invariant; it cannot be but a fiction, but the fiction is supposed to work.

30 Until 1872, the inscription on Prussian Talers ('XXX ein Pfund fein') stated that thirty of them have the weight of one pound of fine silver.

31 'But, with regard to money, everything is determined by human beings themselves' (Wicksell 1898, vol. 2: 3).

32 Estimates of future prices will be speculative, of course. Any reliable calculation has to be built on observed effective prices. The more volatile these are, the less possibilities exist for designing robust market strategies.

33 See the argument on double contingency in Section 3.1.

34 Of course, all sorts of specifications are required in terms of quality, space, time to make such a statement valid.

35 Instead of $1/2n(n-1)$ barter ratios, there will be n prices (or n-1, if one of the commodities is used as the numéraire).

36 Note that this discussion does not refer to credit. Credit should be understood as a way of loosening the budget constraint imposed by the need to present cash, as we will see in Section 3.5.

37 With more than two traders, additional problems of trust emerge, but the limits to cashless and unrecorded buying and selling can be made clear in the two-trader case already.

38 Max Weber (1970a: 305) described the role of membership in Protestant sects in the United States as a foundation for economic networks along those lines. Reputation is related to history and monitoring.

39 In a pure credit system à la Wicksell (1898), such settlements between any two traders may be accomplished by using the promise to pay of a third party. To illustrate, this is how a London bill-broker described a crisis situation as a witness in a nineteenth-century British parliamentary committee: 'If ... there should be no currency to settle the transactions at the clearing house, the only next alternative ... is to meet together, and to make our payments in first-class bills' (quoted in Marx 1992: 605).

40 Perfect monitoring is the active side of perfect memory. Some agency collects information, stores it and makes it available to those interested.

41 That markets require only limited knowledge was Hayek's one big and valid point in the so-called planning debate in the 1930s. Because Oskar Lange (1936/7), defending the possibility of socialist planning, demonstrated the functional equivalence of a price monitoring and price setting central planning board reacting to excess demands and a Walrasian market with a price monitoring and price setting auctioneer reacting to excess demands, Hayek had to reject Walrasian general equilibrium analysis (Hayek 1976).

42 As compared to barter, money use involves the splitting up of transactions into selling and buying. Therefore, as Hahn (1973: 230) put it, 'a minimum requirement of a representation of a monetary economy is that there should be transactions at varying dates. An economy which has transactions at every date I shall call a *sequence economy.*'

43 I do not want to argue about the 'purity' of the information. If we think of the world and its parts as composed of matter/energy and information, monetary systems seem to follow the general evolutionary social trend of replacing systems that use more matter/energy and less information by systems using less matter/energy and more information (Parsons 1966).

44 For a comprehensive account see E.M. Lange (1980).

45 It is familiar at least among non-economists who tend to stay away from technical details: 'money is the medium for executing the market's central function: coordinating economic activity. The very concept of a *self*-regulating market requires monetary feedback, and the market's network of transactions depends upon the information that money prices provide. The coordinating function of the market would not work without it' (Lane 1991: 79).

46 In part, commodity production will also take place on demand, without a need for the producer to anticipate what unknown buyers want.

47 Whatever an individual produces for the market not only has to be sold, but – as part of a sustainable process – it has to be sold at a price enabling the producer to repeat production.

48 Hayek (1976: 85) firmly believed that price signals, despite their limited informational content, can direct market participants in the right direction according to the law of supply and demand. However, in a dynamic setting, falling prices may not induce people to buy but to wait.

49 'Money is the most abstract and "impersonal" element that exists in human life' (Weber 1970: 331).

50 Richard Seaford (2004: 16) calls this the SCIATI-principle: Social Construction Is All There Is.

51 The case of credit creation by a bank opening an account for a borrower may look different, but see Section 3.5.

52 *Electron*, a gold–silver mix, was mined in ancient Asia Minor. It took a little while before gold and silver coins came into use.

53 Money started to fly quite a while ago: 'In the early ninth century, the Tang government created depositories at its capital of Chang'an where merchants could deposit bronze coin in return for promissory notes (known as *feiqian*, or "flying cash") that could be redeemed in provincial capitals. "Flying cash" was especially popular among tea merchants' Glahn (2005: 67).

54 Again: 'Money is a social relation of credit and debt denominated in a money of account' (Ingham 2004: 12).

3 Elementary theory

1 Insofar as you always have a choice, even if the alternative is between being shot or jumping off the cliff.

2 The concept of contingency, as I use it here, is best understood as covering the middle range of a scale with what is impossible at one end and what is necessary at the other end.

3 With a currency supposedly backed by land!

4 I use the term according to Knight's distinction between (calculable) risk and (incalculable) uncertainty. See Gigerenzer (2004: 351).

5 Of course, this is an incomplete quote; Keynes's complete question was: 'Why should anyone outside a lunatic asylum wish to use money as a store of wealth? (Keynes [1931] 1973, vol. 14: 115f.)?

6 For the true believer in the calculability of the economic world, such a recognition of uncertainty seems to be the original sin of monetary theory: 'There is a mystical school of monetary thought which holds that the existence of money has something to do with uncertainty (as distinct from risk) and the impossibility of rational calculation' (Gale 1982: 182). But it is the other way around: The refusal to admit that there are boundaries of rationality turns the assumption of rationality into a matter of mystical belief.

7 Nonetheless, Defoe has Robinson take money from the shipwreck to the island, just in case …

> I discover'd a Locker with Drawers in it, in one of which I found two or three Razors, and one Pair of large Sizzers, with some ten or a Dozen of good Knives and Forks; in another I found about Thirty six Pounds value in Money, some *European* Coin, some *Brazil*, some Pieces of Eight, some Gold, some Silver. I smil'd to my self at the Sight of this Money, O Drug Said I aloud, what art thou good for, Thou art not worth to me, no not the taking off of the Ground, one of those Knives is worth all this Heap, I have no Manner of use for thee, e'en remain where thou art, and go to the Bottom as a Creature whose Life is not worth saving. However, upon Second Thoughts, I took it away
>
> (Defoe 1719 ch. 5)

8 See Russell Hardin's *Indeterminacy and Society* (2003) for the general argument that the social sciences should start from acknowledging ubiquitous indeterminacy and see determinate solutions to action coordination problems as exceptions rather than as the rule that would allow us to ignore indeterminacy.

9 The Austrian tradition remained closer to the original explanatory trajectory 'from the subjective to the social' determination of economic quantities – however, with significant differences between such authors like Hayek and Mises on one, Wieser and Morgenstern (see below) on the other side. For a still enlightening account of the differences between the Austrian and the Walrasian approach from an Austrian perspective, see Mayer (1932).

10 Myrdal (1932) offers an interesting early account of that development.

11 See the significance of assuming the perspective of the 'impartial spectator' in Adam Smith's account of sympathy (Smith [1759] 1976: 22f.).

12

> Among the things that came up very early was that we were in need of a number for the pay-off matrices. We had the choice of merely putting in a number, calling it money, and making money equal for both participants and unrestrictedly transferable. I was not very happy about this, knowing the importance of the utility concept, and I insisted that we do more. At first, we were intending merely to postulate a numerical utility …
>
> (Morgenstern 1976: 809)

13 In the practice of 'silent trade', the fear of being exposed to the trading opponents' use of force seems to have outweighed the risk that they might simply take the goods and run without giving something in exchange.

14

> The very concept of, say, a zero-sum game makes sense only if my payoff and yours can be combined to yield a total of zero. This requires both a zero point for each of our scales and also interpersonal comparability.
>
> (Hardin 2003: 141f.)

15 They must have been ambiguous (see note 90 above). Despite anticipating criticism for not sticking to subjective utility, they assumed 'that the aim of all participants in the economic system, consumers as well as entrepreneurs, is money, or equivalently a single monetary commodity. This is supposed to be unrestrictedly divisible and substitutable, freely transferable and identical, even in the quantitative sense, with whatever 'satisfaction' or 'utility' is desired by each participant' (Neumann and Morgenstern 1953: 8, cf. 556n).

16 Interestingly, it seems that Parsons did not make the most of the fact that the utilitarian tradition he criticized as being unable to solve Hobbesian 'problem of order' (Parsons 1937: 91) implicitly relied on normative foundations of exchange at least in the rudimentary form of traders abstaining from the use of force. Thus, norms are not added as a factor in exchange analysis by sociologists to 'embed' the 'norm-free' space assumed by economists, as the traditional picture of the division

of labor between economics and sociology would have it. To put it plainly: Without expecting each other to be constrained by norms, players will not exchange.

17 We will return to that issue in discussing the compatibility of maximizing utility and money holdings.

18 Especially in modern financial markets, things may be too complicated to be reduced to the alternative: Pay or do not pay. There are quite a few players who 'sell the sizzle before they buy the steak' (Shubik 1999).

19 'The use of force is unquestionably very strongly opposed to the spirit of economic acquisition in the usual sense' (Weber 1964: 160; cf. Hirschman 1977; Jacobs 1992).

20 Neither public nor household production are for exchange.

21 This is a theoretical construction that does not have an empirical counterpart. It is similar to what is called 'simple commodity production' in the Marxist tradition, but frequently mistaken there as descriptive of a real, historical economic formation. I use this construction to be able to abstract, for the time being, from the complications introduced by capitalist production and the role of money as an instrument of social control in the wage–labor relation.

22 Alternatively, one might say that the economy became identifiable as a functionally differentiated social subsystem only once production for exchange became dominant.

23 'A *market* is a mechanism that processes *messages* (…) and produces *trades* … A *trade* is a mapping of *market input* by *i* into a *market output* to *i* …' (Shubik 1999, 1: 128).

24 When Abraham buys real estate from Ephron (see Chapter 1, Fn 19 above), they settle on a price in view of an observing public.

25 There is scarce any price fix'd for hops in England till they know how they sell at Sturbridge' (Defoe 1724, quoted in Shubik 1999, vol. 1: 278).

26 Although public and household production are not for exchange, these activities have nonetheless been 'coded' more and more in terms of money, so that the decision modes typical of production for monetary returns have spread into the public and the private household sectors.

27 Keynes was part of the mainstream in *this* respect – certainly not in others: 'All production is for the purpose of ultimately satisfying a consumer.' (Keynes 1936: 46) 'Consumption, to repeat the obvious, is the sole end and object of all economic activity' (Keynes 1936: 104).

28 They 'speak' even to the solipsist immersed in pure utility orientation. As we will see, such obsessive egocentrism can be irrational in social settings.

29 This will imply both temporal and social expansion, but the third person need not be present or known to *ego*.

30 Feldman constructs an interesting model of bilateral trading 'in which no prices are known, and in which traders, having no information or subjective probabilities about trading opportunities, only make trades when they can make themselves better (or no worse) off by so doing. They are truly groping in the dark. Yet … their myopic trading will lead to a pairwise optimal allocation' (Feldman 1973: 465). Introducing 'a good for which everyone has a positive marginal utility and of which everyone has a positive quantity … opens up trading possibilities that would otherwise remain closed', resulting even in 'a Pareto optimal allocation' (Feldman 1973: 468f.). For a discussion, see Cartelier (2000).

31 The ease with which they seem to overcome this problem appears to attract monetary theorists to (neo-)chartalist views of money (Knapp [1905] 1923; Aglietta and Cartelier 1998; Wray 2000; Ingham 2004). The state is the player that is taken to have the power to impose a unit of account and means of payment on all the other less weighty players trading in the territory. While one may have doubts about that kind of power, the more serious problem is: Where did the state, that is the prince or his bureaucrats, find the inspiration and the motives to introduce such innovations? Instead of invoking central authority as a *deus ex machina*, it is more plausible to

assume that, for example, the kings of Lydia who are held to be the inventors of coinage (cf. Seaford 2004: 125ff. for a more differentiated attribution), observed some proto-monetary use of precious metals before they could have the idea of paying mercenaries with electron coins. The soldiers accepting such pay must have expected to be able to buy things they wanted with the coins – and not just send them back to the king as payment of taxes, as neo-chartalists seem to imply when they argue that 'taxes drive money' (Wray 1998).

32 This is what Alfred Döblin in his novel *Babylonische Wandrung* (1982) has an ancient Babylonian god do that returns to earth in modern times and is confronted with the use money. The god finds no magic in the money objects, so his conclusion is that money users must be crazy: Instead of brains, they have holes in their heads.

33 If this is plausible it has some relevance for the frequently discussed issue of which function of money is primary. In contrast to Aglietta, Ingham, Wray and others – invoking Keynes (1930: 3) – who argue that the unit of account function is primary, I think that it can only be relevant once the qualitative obstacles to exchange are overcome. Evaluating resources in terms of a money of account can be a completely idiosyncratic individual exercise. To have a minimum of intersubjective validity, such evaluations have to be informed by effective market transactions.

34 Aglietta (2002), Ingham (2002), Wray (2004), in a less sweeping form Goodhart 1998. As Schumpeter (1954: 64) observed, one can easily find 'many an argument that presents itself in the garb of purely imaginary history.'

35 There is agreement that coins were not used before the sixth century BC (Seaford 2004, 2011; Schaps 2004). If one has a concept of money that gives some importance to the *form* of money objects, like Knapp, for example, the numerous references in Mesopotamian contracts and laws to payment obligations in terms of shekels of silver do not mean that ancient economies were monetary economies (Renger 1989; Peacock 2006; Renger 2011). Knapp ([1905] 1923: 23, 31) would say that shekels were 'pensatory' means of payment – you had to weigh –, but not money, the term 'money' being reserved for 'chartal' means of payment, meaning that they have a recognizable form imposed by the state.

36 See Lester (1939) for some real monetary experiments.

37 'In the crudest barter, when two commodities are exchanged for one another, each is first equated with a symbol which expresses their exchange value, e.g., among certain Negroes on the West African coast,=x bars .. . The commodities are first transformed into bars in the head and in speech before they are exchanged for one another' (Marx 1973: 142).

38 This argument can be extended to include the observation of third agents in their transactions. Agent B can respond to demands of A by maintaining that C and D or E and F traded on different terms more favorable for B.

39 Aglietta puts it quite bluntly: 'the social invention of money stems first and foremost from the sovereign authority' (Aglietta 2002: 37).

40 'We accept (S has power (S does A))' is Searle's second formula, expressing the deontic power derived from status (Searle 2004: 18).

41 Monetary idealism, as I am tempted to call it, rejects the argument that the universal equivalent must originally have been a commodity, some good that is actually traded. Such idealism leaves open the question of how a functioning equivalent – or general unit of account – could have been socially constructed even if an all-knowing and all-imposing authority is involved. Is it sufficient for the king to declare: (1) I hereby install '1 fuzz' to be the unit of account; (2) I herewith order all taxes to be paid in fuzzes; (3) in order to supply a sufficient amount of fuzzes to my people, I henceforth will use fuzzes to buy everything I need from them? In other words: How much of the definition of the monetary unit can the king leave to the imagination of his people? And how, other than referring to a physical object to which the functions of money are to be attached, can he constrain this imagination?

42 Marx is quoting Goethe's *Faust*: 'In the beginning, there was the act ...', which was, in turn, a polemical variation on the Genesis.

43 The problem is analogous to the 'problem of order' in Hobbes as seen by Parsons (1937: 91), insofar as individual players would serve their own interests by agreeing on a common medium for expressing prices, but there is no generally accepted mechanism for selecting one.

44 In a pattern described by Laplace's 'law' of succession (see Gigerenzer 2005: 286f.), according to which the degree of conviction that an event one has observed n times will take place again is $(n+1)/(n+2)$.

45 But experience may not be a sufficient guide in these matters. Remember Taleb's turkey. It learns for a thousand days that food is coming in every morning in ample quantities. But then the next day is Thanksgiving (Taleb 2004: 40f.).

46 When Shubik argues that 'a full commodity money eliminates the need for trust in trade' (Shubik vol. 2: 318), he seems to presuppose either that the commodity used as money is equally attractive for all or to consider trust – in the acceptability of money – as a substitute for knowledge of the preferences of others.

47 In a model building perspective, Hahn (1973: 230) argued that if 'transaction dates are *inessential* (as) the set of equilibria attainable by an economy is independent of these dates ... the description of the economy is not altered by concentrating all transactions at the first date. Accordingly in such an economy money is *inessential*'. No time, no money ...

48 Note the difficulty here that while the acceptance of money objects depends solely on their expected use in further transactions, people nonetheless not only hoard money objects, but the acquisition of more money even becomes a goal in itself.

49 Does this contradict the maxM proposition? The emphasis is on 'unwillingly'. As all the arguments against Say's law insisted, agents can interrupt the sequences of acquiring money to use it to buy goods. They may prefer to hold money at any given time. In Keynes's terms, liquidity preference may dominate other motives of money use.

50 'Money cannot be produced by any private individual' (Williamson and Wright 1994: 107).

51 For some analytic purposes, it would be appropriate to also include *spatial* expansion at this point (Gilbert 2005).

52 'Money in its significant attributes is, above all, a subtle device for linking the present to the future' (Keynes 1936: 294). The observation is certainly correct. The link must be there. But how is it constructed?

53 They would have to think in terms of expectations of expectations: 'There is an oddly circular characteristic in the value of fiat money – sellers are willing to accept it because other sellers are willing to accept it.' This should be a problem, but it seems to be too messy, as Arrow goes on: 'However that may be, and several hundred years of speculation and empirical study have not removed the perplexity, we can take the acceptability of money for granted' (Arrow 1981: 148).

54 Weber defines the medium of exchange explicitly as an object that is 'typically accepted primarily by virtue of the fact that the recipients estimate that they will, within the relevant time horizon, be able to utilize it in another exchange' (Weber 1964: 173 (ch. 2, § 6).

55 Notwithstanding the fact that severe crises occur regularly, they seem to be seen as mere footnotes in a long success story once the generation that was hurt has passed away.

56 Unless something turns out to be wrong with the commodities traded or with the money used, for example, if it is forged.

57 They normally do not come back as individual objects to individual players.

58 And the ensuing choice of saving in the form of holding cash or of investing in some interest bearing assets (Clower 1969a; Davidson 2005).

59 For Marx ([1867] 1975), the 'separation of purchase and sale' installed by money

use constituted the 'possibility of crisis'. For parallels to Keynes, see Kenway (1980).

60 A credit system will obviously soften that constraint, as we will see below.

61 'Whatever circumstances … act with assignable influence … on the mind in the interchange of commodities, may be considered as causes of value' (Bailey 1825: 182f.).

62 In general, such systems have a reputation of being much more resilient than rigid, determinate systems because they can adapt more easily to unforeseen changes.

63 Vs. Shubik 1999, I: 162ff.

64 Note, however, that this freedom may also hold for sellers selecting buyers. Nobody 'owes' commodities to a money-holder.

> Money is power, but never power in its own immediate reproduction. Whatever is acquired for it, it has to leave the hand of its holder to acquire something. It does not attribute a right to anybody. In face of money, everybody is free and unbound.
> (Tönnies [1887] 1922: 49, transl. HG; see Simmel 1907: 166)

65 Although Hayek was led astray in many directions by his ultraliberal convictions, he was right to insist on that point (Hayek 1976) against Walrasian general equilibrium theory.

66 This argument is theoretically interesting, especially because it is a perfect example of unintended consequences of actions in the form of self-destroying prophecies. Apparently it is hard to prove formally, but see Ellerman (2000).

67 For '~' to be an equivalence relation on a set of elements X, the following properties must hold:

> Reflexivity: $a \sim a$
> Symmetry: if $a \sim b$, then $b \sim a$
> Transitivity: if $a \sim b$ and $b \sim c$, then $a \sim c$.

Krause (1979) clarifies the implications of these formal properties for equivalence postulates in economic theories. See also Beckenbach (1987).

68 Or anything approaching perfect information. See Schmitz (2002) for an instructive comparison of information or foresight assumptions in recent neoclassical monetary theories.

69 'An economy whose activity extends over T elementary time-intervals, or dates, will be studied. It is assumed that the uncertainty of the environment during that period originates in the choice that Nature makes among a finite number of alternatives' (Debreu 1959: 98). Clearly and precisely, uncertainty generated socially is excluded.

70 Economists should have listened when Donald Rumsfeld distinguished between 'known unknowns' and 'unknown unknowns'.

71 See Chapter 1, Fn 1 above for the March–Simon concept of uncertainty absorption.

72 Talcott Parsons therefore misleadingly suggested that economists were assuming a 'randomness of ends' (Parsons 1937: 59f.). Not specifying 'the relations of ends to each other' (ibid.) is not the same thing as assuming their randomness.

73 The utility of a money object, if there is such a thing, derives from its use as money and is as such not comparable or commensurate with the utility of goods or services. One can argue that money is a placeholder for the goods one can buy with it, but that implies that all the heterogeneous goods within reach of an agent can be ordered according to preference *and* price before a decision 'pay/don't pay' can be made. This is why exchange ratios are assumed as given in search-theoretical models of money (e.g., Kiyotaki and Wright 1989: 931; Iwai 1996: 14).

74 Does this observation induce the observing agents themselves to maxM? It would be intriguing to show that. Fehr and Tyran (2007) have demonstrated such a lock-in effect experimentally. However, their subjects are rewarded for conformity, so the Fehr–Tyran result that players maximize monetary returns even when alternative

Pareto optimizing moves in terms of utility are possible is not simply an effect of money use.

75 One former Goldman banker describes Wall Street culture as

> completely money-obsessed. I was like a donkey driven forward by the biggest, juiciest carrot I could imagine. Money is the way you define your success. There's always room – need – for more. If you are not getting a bigger house or a bigger boat, you're falling behind. It's an addiction.
>
> (Arlidge 2009)

76 Evidently, there are adverse events or contexts in which having money to spend does not help at all.

77 This barrenness of money is the background for Keynes's question already quoted above (Keynes [1931a] 1973, vol. 14: 115f.) why anybody outside of a lunatic asylum would hold money as a store of wealth.

78 Other reasons might be fears concerning the instability of the monetary system, foreign exchange rates or inflation damaging the domestic purchasing power of a given currency. It may be crucial to react quickly to such changes.

79 'All you need is cash.' This cover title of *The Economist* in November 2008 can be read as an ironic comment from the real world on most economists' first article of faith, namely, that consumption is the sole end of production.

80 Their use may cause a shift in worries, however: In June 1667, the Dutch fleet was threatening London, so on June 13, Samuel Pepys sent his father and wife to take most of his considerable gold coin holdings to the country to hide. To his great dissatisfaction and worry, they buried the gold in the garden in plain daylight (19 June). In October, they tried to retrieve the gold, had considerable difficulties and a small part was lost. Pepys concluded the episode noting 'some kind of content to remember how painful it is sometimes to keep money, as well as to get it' (Diaries of Samuel Pepys, 11 October 1667). Worries about the future can be transformed into worries about how to safeguard your money.

81 Money partially replaces memory, not: 'Money is memory' (Kocherlakota 1998).

82 And occasional attempts to escape from such discipline, for example, when consumers spend windfall gains with disregard for their normal budgets.

83 But applying it repeatedly and stringently may lead to behavior changes – undermining the strategy. Example: Using priced-to-market accounting rules and fixed benchmarks for leveraging has procyclical aggregate effects (Adrian and Shin 2007) and can lead to 'irrational exuberance' in a boom and exaggerated lending restrictions in the bust.

84 In his *Medici Money*, Parks (2006) gives a fascinating account of how early Florentine bankers calmed their conscience by donating art to the church after they had found dubious ways to circumvent the prohibition of taking interest for loans.

85 Often described as a requirement of 'equivalence'.

86 Zelizer (1989, 1997) has shown that money has more meanings than the standard set of instrumental functions listed in traditional theories, depending on social context.

87 The first building erected by the United States government after the declaration of independence was the mint in Philadelphia.

88 A device used in 1717 by John Law for the paper money issued by his Banque Générale.

89 This happened in China. 'In 1394, after the value of the *baochao* had fallen to less than 20 percent of its face value, the Ming took the extraordinary step of banning the use of even its own coin in exchange' (Glahn 2005: 67f.).

90 The refusal to distinguish between money and credit instruments, discussed below in the case of Schumpeter, may have this practical background.

91 'Final payment is made whenever a seller of a good, or service, or another asset, receives something of equal value from the purchaser, which leaves the seller with

no further claim on the buyer' (Goodhart 1989: 26). Of course, this leaves open the meaning of 'equal value'.

92 Another example of creating a self-imposed need to rewrite the history of money by advocating the 'all money is credit' proposition is offered by Heinsohn and Steiger (2000). They argue that money is a title to property created in a credit contract. The credit is given against collateral, the lender demands some security in case the promise to pay back is not kept. The property offered as collateral can then no longer be fully used, especially, it cannot be sold. Interest is taken to be a compensation for this loss of freedom.

> When money – as an anonymized title to property – is created in a credit contract, the interest causing loss is the loss of an immaterial yield which we have called the *property premium* (...). In the money-creating and money-forwarding credit contract, property has to be encumbered. Through this collateralization, the freedom of property is temporarily blocked, that is, the property premium is given up.
>
> (Heinsohn and Steiger 2000: 67)

There seems to be a fundamental confusion: B is the banker and A wants a credit from B. A promises to pay back what B lends plus interest. B wants protection against the risk that A will not keep the promise. A offers security in the form of collateral. This means that A not only loses the freedom of disposing over the collateral, but that A also has to pay interest. To connect the two issues in the way of Heinsohn and Steiger is absurd: 'The loss which has to be compensated by interest' (ibid.) is the loss of the creditor, i.e., the owner of money. He cannot use his money. The freedom to dispose over the collateral is lost by the debtor, the person who has to *pay* interest on top of paying back the money borrowed.

93 According to Ingham, the debt relationship moves on from buyer to seller, along with the money: 'In the most basic sense, the possessor of money is owed goods ... Money cannot be said to exist without the simultaneous existence of a debt that it can discharge' (Ingham 2004: 12). Either this excludes some forms of money from 'moneyness' (whatever that is) or one has to over-generalize and thus water down the notion of 'debt' along the lines of Aglietta (1997: 416) who talks of '*une dette réciproque entre chaque individu et la société*'. Who *owes* goods to a possessor of money? Nobody: 'no one can compel another person to sell him anything in exchange for Money or Credit' (Macleod 1882/3: 45). I may be moved to sell you something if you offer enough money. But there simply is no debt-relation involved in normal buying and selling on spot markets. That one *has* to accept a given kind of money as a means of payment to extinguish a pre-existing debt, if it is legal tender, does not force anybody to *sell* goods to a holder of that money.

94 'The competitive market functions best under mass anonymous transactions (...), yet the credit markets function best with the availability of an analyzed dossier on each individual' (Shubik 2001: 5).

95 Because of the risks of theft and loss when transporting currency over long distances, the advantages of using promissory notes that can be cleared against each other seem to have impressed long distance traders first.

96 Contracts are called relational if they are entered with expectations of benefits from repetition.

97

> Lending creates equal amounts of positive (asset) and negative (liability) money. When economic textbooks describe how 'banks create money' or 'debt creates money', they do not count the negative liabilities as money, and thus their money is not conserved. In our operational definition of money, we include all financial instruments with fixed denomination, such as currency IOUs and bonds, but not

material wealth or stocks, and we count both assets and liabilities. With this definition, money is conserved.

(Dragulescu and Yakovenko 2000: 4)

98   First of all custom turns a certain, relatively worthless object, a piece of leather, a scrap of paper, etc., into a token of the material of which money consists, but it can maintain this position only if *its function as a symbol is guaranteed by the general intention of commodity owners*, in other words, if it acquires a legal conventional existence and hence a legal rate of exchange. Paper money issued by the state and given a legal rate is an advanced form of the token of value, and the only kind of paper money which directly arises from metallic currency or from simple commodity circulation itself.

(Marx [1859] 1970: 116)

99   But false theories of risk and probability may create false certainty; see Taleb (2008) vs. Merton, R.C. (1998), who lists among his assumptions: 'a technical requirement of bounded variation', and investors who 'are assumed to prefer more to less. All investors are assumed to agree on the function $\sigma 2$'. 'Bounded variation' and agreement on standard deviation $\sigma 2$ seem innocuous, but this is how rare but extreme events are assumed away.

100 As most large transactions are performed using credit, the cash economy will normally play only a minor part in contemporary economies.

101 As Wallace (2001: 853) notes for model building, one can 'rule out credit of any kind via the assumption that people are anonymous, are not monitored at all'.

102 Note the modeling costs of assuming the absence of money illusion. To guarantee the neutrality of money, you have to postulate that all prices are market clearing, all agents behave optimally in light of their objectives and expectations, and expectations are rational (see Lucas 1972).

103 The mechanism is pro-cyclical. The same process works in the downward direction: If asset prices fall, weaker balance sheets induce asset sales, thus depressing asset prices further.

104 An illustration for the role of faith in credit can be found in a New York Times report on Christian banking (Shorto 2004). It featured banker and customers generating confidence in what they were about to do by praying together for the success of credit-financed projects. In retrospect, the story turned out to be extremely fitting for underlining the role of faith in credit relations: In October 2009, the initially very successful Christian Riverview Bank in Minnesota was found unsound and closed by the state (http://minnesotaindependent.com/48014/the-bank-that-god-built-shuttered-by-state). This was not just a story from the periphery of the financial system. Recently, Goldman-Sachs chairman Lloyd Blankfein presented himself as 'just a banker "doing God's work"' (Arlidge 2009).

105

In an economy where all trades are for gold, no trust is needed in the goods exchange. The money market, however, requires that a set of individuals (lenders) temporarily exchange their gold for individual IOU notes or promises to pay. Trust may be ameliorated by laws imposing unpleasant consequences on those who default, but even so, the act of lending requires faith by the lenders in the laws, the borrowers, or both.

(Shubik 1999: 1, 259)

106 Of course, nowadays one can buy insurance and hope that the insurer will be bailed out by the government if things go wrong.

Conclusion

1 Richard Seaford (2004: 7, 18) has underlined the 'fiduciary' component present even in the use of the first Greek coins. Their purchasing power as coins exceeded the price of their (fluctuating) metal content, at least as long as they circulated in the communities of origin. The inscription on Maltese coins debased in 1565 was: *non aes sed fides* (not ore but faith) (Simmel 1907: 164).

2 Iwai (2011) says it bluntly: 'to hold 'money' – the lifeblood of capitalism – is nothing but the purest form of speculation'.

3 See Appendix A1 on the econophysics of money.

4 See Appendix A2 on money and the state.

5 The Adam Smith of the *Theory of Moral Sentiments* with his account of the emergence of norms could have provided a pattern for the required analysis (Smith 1976a: 22ff., cf. Ganssmann 1996: 203f.).

6 In an individual, personal perspective this is not true because almost all players of the money game seem to realize sooner or later that there are limits to their power of acquiring more and more money. Frustration sets in. But socially, the point is that there is always a sufficient number of new maxM players entering the game so that it continues as if the sky were the limit.

7 This is why Iwai (2011) argues that a crisis of money use does not result from deflation, but rather from hyperinflation: Everybody has to get rid of money as fast as possible. But even hyperinflation has not generated the terminal crisis of money. A monetary reform, though costly and redistributive, is all that is required for the return to business as usual.

Appendix

1 Cans of mackerel replaced packs of cigarettes in US prisons as currency after smoking was banished. Nobody seems to like the mackerels for eating (Scheck 2008).

Bibliography

Adrian, T. and Shin, H.S. (2007), 'Liquidity and leverage', available www.princeton. edu/~hsshin/www/LiquidityLeverage.pdf (accessed 23 March 2008).

Aglietta, M. (1997), *Régulation et crises du capitalisme*, Postface, 2nd edn, Paris: Odile Jacob, 409–477.

Aglietta, M. (2002), 'Whence and whither money?' in: Miller, R., Michalski, W. and Stevens, B. (eds), *The Future of Money*, Paris: OECD, 31–72.

Aglietta, M. and Cartelier, J. (1998), 'Ordre monétaire des économies de marché', in: Aglietta, M. and Orléan, A. (1998) (eds), *La Monnaie souveraine*, Paris: Odile Jacob, 129–157.

Aglietta, M. and Orléan, A. (1998) (eds), *La Monnaie souveraine*, Paris: Odile Jacob.

Alchian, A. (1977), 'Why money?' *Journal of Money, Credit and Banking*, vol. 58, 133–140.

Arlidge, J. (2009), 'I'm doing "God's work". Meet Mr. Goldman Sachs', *Sunday Times*, Nov. 8 2009, available www.timesonline.co.uk/tol/news/world/us_and_americas/article6907681.ece (accessed 12 March 2010).

Arrow, K.J. (1974), 'Limited knowledge and economic analysis', *American Economic Review*, 64, 1–10.

Arrow, K.J. (1981), 'Real and nominal magnitudes in economics', in: Bell, D. and Kristol, I. (1981) (eds), *The Crisis in Economic Theory*, New York: Basic Books, 139–150.

Aydinonat, N.E. (2008), *The Invisible Hand in Economics*, Abingdon: Routledge.

Bailey, S. (1825), *A Critical Dissertation on the Nature, Measure, Causes of Value*, London: Hunter.

Beckenbach, F. (1987), *Zwischen Gleichgewicht und Krise: Zur Konstitution einer Geldökonomie*, Frankfurt a. M.: Haag & Herchen.

Beckert, J. (1996), 'What is sociological about economic sociology? Uncertainty and the embeddedness of economic action', *Theory and Society*, vol. 25, 803–840.

Beckert, J., Diaz-Bone, R. and Ganssmann, H. (2007) (eds), *Märkte als soziale Strukturen*, Frankfurt a.M.: Campus.

Benetti, C. and Cartelier, J. (1980), *Marchands, salariat et capitalistes*, Paris: Maspero.

Benetti, C. and Cartelier, J. (1987), 'Monnaie, valeur et propriété privée', *Revue Economique*, vol. 38, no. 6, 1157–1170.

Bentham, J. (1952), 'The philosophy of economic science', in: Stark, W. (ed.), *Jeremy Bentham's Economic Writings*, vol. 1. London: Allen and Unwin for Royal Economic Society, 79–119.

Bernanke, B. (2004), 'The Great Moderation', available www.federalreserve.gov/ BOARDDOCS/SPEECHES/2004/20040220/default.htm (accessed 6 November 2009).

Bibow, J., Lewis, P. and Runde, J. (2001), 'Uncertainty, conventional behavior, and economic sociology', Levy Economics Institute of Bard College, Working Paper No. 339.

Bohannan, P. (1959), 'The impact of money on an African subsistence economy', *Journal of Economic History*, 19, 491–503.

Bourdieu, P. (1979) *La distinction. Critique sociale du jugement*, Paris: Éditions de Minuit.

Braudel, F. (1981), *The Structures of Everyday Life. Civilization and capitalism 15th–18th century*, trans. Reynolds, S., New York: Harper Row.

Bresciani-Turroni, C. (1931), *The Economics of Inflation. A study of currency depreciation in post-war Germany*, 1914–1923, 3rd Engl. edn, 1968, London: George Allen and Unwin.

Brunner, K. and Meltzer, A.H. (1971), 'The uses of money: money in the theory of an exchange economy', *American Economic Review*, vol. 61, no. 5, 784–805.

Bryan, D. and Rafferty, M. (2007), 'Financial derivatives and the theory of money', *Economy and Society*, vol. 36, no. 1, 134–158.

Buchan, J. (1997), *Frozen Desire. The meaning of money*, New York: Farrar, Strauss, Giroux.

Buchanan, M. (2002), *Nexus. Small Worlds and the Groundbreaking Theory of Networks*, New York: Norton.

Campbell, M. (2002), 'The credit system', in: Campbell, M. and Reuten, G. (2002) (eds), *The Culmination of Capital: Essays on Volume III of Marx's 'Capital'*, 212–227.

Carruthers, B.G. (2005), 'The sociology of money and credit', in: Smelser, N.J. and Swedberg, R. (eds), *The Handbook of Economic Sociology*, 2nd edn, Princeton: Princeton University Press, 355–378.

Carruthers, B.G. (2011), 'Money, liquidity and price', in: Ganssmann, H. (ed.), *New Approaches to Monetary Theory: Interdisciplinary perspectives*, Abingdon: Routledge, 144–157.

Carruthers, B.G. and Babb, S. (1996), 'The color of money and the nature of value: Greenbacks and gold in postbellum America', *The American Journal of Sociology*, vol. 101, no. 6., 1556–1591.

Carruthers, B.G. and Stinchcombe, A. (1999), 'The social structure of liquidity: Flexibility, markets, and states', *Theory and Society*, vol. 28, 353–382.

Cartelier, J. (1991), 'Marx's theory of value, exchange and surplus value: a suggested reformulation', *Cambridge Journal of Economics*, vol. 15, 257–269.

Cartelier, J. (1993), 'Récursivité et monnaie: un autre point de vue sur "Keynes and the Classics"', *Revue d'économie politique*, vol. 103, no. 4, 528–549.

Cartelier, J. (1995), *L'économie de Keynes*, Bruxelles: De Boeck-Wesmael.

Cartelier, J. (1996), *La Monnaie*, Paris: Flammarion.

Cartelier, J. (2000), 'Market Dynamics in a Monetary Approach: Unsettled Issues and Limited Conjectures', CIMPA's Summer School, August 2000, Beijing.

Cartelier, J. (2001), 'La Monnaie. Du concept économique au rapport social', *Science de la Société*, no. 52, 111–135.

Cartelier, J. (2002), 'Monnaie ou don: réflexion sur le mythe économique de la monnaie', *Journal des Anthropologues*, vol. 90–91, 352–374.

Cartelier, J. (2006), 'Comptabilité et pensée économique: Introduction à une réflexion théorique', *Revue Economique*, vol. 57, no. 5, 1009–1032.

Cartelier, J. (2007), 'The hypostasis of money: an economic point of view', *Cambridge Journal of Economics*, vol. 31, 217–233.

Clower, R.W. (1969), 'Foundations of monetary theory', in: Clower, R.W. (ed.), *Monetary Theory*, Harmondsworth: Penguin, 202–211.

Clower, R.W. (1969a), 'The Keynesian counter-revolution', in: Clower, R.W. (ed.), *Monetary Theory*, Harmondsworth: Penguin, 270–297.

Clower, R.W. (1995), 'On the origin of money', *Economic Inquiry*, vol. 33, no. 4, 525–536.

Coase, R. (1960), 'The problem of social cost', *Journal of Law and Economics*, vol. 3, 1–44.

Codere, H. (1968), 'Money-exchange systems and a theory of money', *Man*, N.S., vol. 3, no. 4, 557–577.

Commons, J.R. (1924), *The Legal Foundations of Capitalism*, New York: Macmillan.

Crouch, C. (2008), 'What will follow the demise of privatised Keynesianism?' *The Political Quarterly*, vol. 79, no. 4, 476–487.

Dalziel, P. (2000), 'On the evolution of money and its implications for price stability', *Journal of Economic Surveys*, vol. 14, no. 4, 373–393.

Davidson, P. (2005), 'Strong uncertainty and how to cope with it to improve action and capacity', Paper presented at the EAEPE Conference Bremen, 11 November 2005.

Debreu, G. (1959; 7th pr. 1976), *Theory of Value*, New Haven: Yale University Press.

Defoe, D. (1719), *Robinson Crusoe*, available at www.deadmentellnotales.com/online-texts/robinson/crusoe1.shtml (accessed 12 November 2006).

Defoe, D. (1724), *Tour through the Whole Island of Great Britain*, vol. 1, letter 1, available at www.stirbitch.com/cantab/resources/stourbridge_fair_defoe.html (accessed 25 January 2007).

Deutschmann, C. (1999), *Die Verheißung des absoluten Reichtums*, Frankfurt a. M.: Campus.

Deutschmann, C. (2007), 'Unsicherheit und soziale Einbettung: Konzeptionelle Probleme der Wirtschaftssoziologie', in: Beckert, J., Diaz-Bone, R. and Ganssmann, H. (2007) (eds), *Märkte als soziale Strukturen*, Frankfurt a.M.: Campus, 79–93.

Deutschmann, C. (2009), ´Soziologische Erklärungen kapitalistischer Dynamik´, in: Beckert, J. and Deutschmann, C. (eds), *Wirtschaftssoziologie*, Sonderheft 49, *Kölner Zeitschrift für Soziologie und Sozialpsychologie*, Wiesbaden: Verlag für Sozialwissenschaften, 43–66.

Dillard, D. (1948), *The Economics of John Maynard Keynes: The theory of a monetary economy*, New York: Prentice Hall.

Dillard, D. (1987), 'Money as an institution of capitalism', *Journal of Economic Issues*, vol. 21, no. 4, 1623–1647.

Dillard, D. (1988), 'The barter illusion in classical and neoclassical economics', *Eastern Economic Journal*, 1988, vol. 14, 299–318.

Döblin, A. (1982), *Babylonische Wandrung*, München: DTV.

Dodd, N. (1994), *The Sociology of Money: Economics, reason and contemporary society*, Cambridge: Polity.

Dragulescu, A., Yakovenko, V.M. (2000), 'Statistical mechanics of money', Department of Physics, University of Maryland, available http://www2. physics.umd.edu/yakovenk/econophysics.html (accessed 19 March 2007).

Dyer, A.W. (1989), Making semiotic sense of money as a medium of exchange, *Journal of Economic Issues*, vol. 23, no. 2, 503–510.

Edgeworth, F.Y. (1881), *Mathematical Psychics*, London: Kegan Paul.

Edgeworth, F.Y. (1919), 'Review: Gold prices and the Witwaterstrand, by R.A. Lehfeldt', *The Economic Journal*, vol. 29, no. 115, 327–330.

Edwards, C. (1906), *The Oldest Laws in the World: Being an account of the Hammurabi code and the Sinaitic legislation*, London: Watts.

Ellerman, D. (2000), 'Towards an arbitrage interpretation of optimizing theory', available www.ellerman.org/Davids-Stuff/Maths/Math.htm (accessed 27 April 2007).

Eschbach, A. (2002), 'Das Geld als Zeichen: Georg Simmel, Kurt Singer und Karl Bühler', *Ars Semeiotica*, vol. 25, no. 3–4, 205–220.

Espeland, W.N. and Stevens, M.L. (1998), 'Commensuration as a social process', *Annual Review of Sociology* 24, 313–343.

Fehr, E. and Tyran, J.-R. (2007), 'Money illusion and coordination failure', *Games and Economic Behavior*, vol. 58, 246–268.

Feldman, A.M. (1973), 'Bilateral trading processes, pairwise optimality, and Pareto optimality', *Review of Economic Studies*, vol. 40, no. 4, 463–473.

Fine, B. and Lapavitsas, C. (2000), 'Markets and money in social theory: what role for economics?', *Economy and Society*, vol. 29, no. 3, 357–382.

Firth, R. (1963), *Elements of Social Organization*, Boston: MIT Press.

Foley, K.D. (1983), 'On Marx's theory of money', *Social Concept*, vol. 1 no. 1, 5–19.

Foley, D. (1989), 'Money in economic activity', in: Eatwell, J., *et al.* (eds.), *The New Palgrave: Money*, New York: Norton, 248–262.

Friedman, M. (1968), 'The Role of Monetary Policy', *American Economic Review*, vol. 58, 1–17.

Friedman, M. (1969), *The Optimal Quantity of Money and Other Essays*, Chicago: Aldine.

Gale, D. (1982), *Money in Equilibrium*, Cambridge: Cambridge University Press.

Ganssmann, H. (1988), 'Money – a symbolically generalized medium of communication?' *Economy and Society*, vol. 17, 285–316.

Ganssmann, H. (1995), 'Geld, Arbeit und Herrschaft', in: Schelkle, W. and Nitsch, M. (eds), *Rätsel Geld*, Marburg: Metropolis, 125–143.

Ganssmann, H. (1996), 'Equivalence and interaction in Simmel's Philosophy of Money', in: Baldner, J.M. and Gillard, L. (1996) (eds), *Simmel et les normes sociales*, Paris: Harmattan, 85–97.

Ganssmann, H. (1996a), *Geld und Arbeit*, Frankfurt a. M.: Campus.

Ganssmann, H. (1998), 'The emergence of credit money', in: Bellofiore, R. (ed.), *Marxian Economics, vol. 1: Essays on Volume III of Capital – Method, Value and Money*, Basingstoke: Macmillan, 145–156.

Ganssmann, H. (2002), 'Das Geldspiel', in: Deutschmann, C. (2002) (ed.), Die gesellschaftliche Macht des Geldes, *Leviathan*, Sonderheft 21, 21–46.

Ganssmann, H. (2004) 'Review: Geoffrey Ingham: The Nature of Money, Cambridge: Polity Press, 2004', *Economic Sociology* – European electronic newsletter, vol. 6, no. 1 (Oct. 2004) 29–32, available http://econsoc.mpifg.de/archive/esoct04.pdf (accessed 19 February 2011).

Ganssmann, H. (2006), 'Double contingency', in: Becker, J. and Zafirowski, M. (eds) *International Encyclopedia of Economic Sociology*, London: Routledge.

Ganssmann, H. (2010) 'Review: Bruce G. Carruthers and Laura Ariovich, Money and Credit: A sociological approach, Cambridge: Polity', *Economic Sociology – European Electronic Newsletter*, vol. 11, no. 3, 71–75, available http://econsoc.mpifg.de/archive/econ_soc_11–3.pdf (accessed 19 February 2011).

Ganssmann, H. (2010a) 'Money and memory: Implicit agents in search theories of money, papers on agent-based economics, nr 9, Universität Kassel', available at www.unikassel.de/hrz/db4/extern/cmsbeckenbach/cms/files/pdfs/papers/poabe_nr9.pdf (accessed 19 February 2011).

Ganssmann, H. (2011), 'Money, credit and the structures of social action', in: Ganssmann, H. (ed.), *New Approaches to Monetary Theory: Interdisciplinary perspectives*, Abingdon: Routledge, 124–143.

Giddens, A. (1990), *The Consequences of Modernity*, Stanford: Stanford University Press.

Gigerenzer, G. (2004), *Das Einmaleins der Skepsis: Über den richtigen Umgang mit Zahlen*, Berlin: BVT.

Gilbert, E. (2005), 'Common cents: situating money in time and place', *Economy and Society*, vol. 34, no. 3, 357–388.

Glahn, R.V. (2005), 'Origins of paper money in China', in: Goetzmann, W.N. and Rouwenhorst, K.G. (eds), *The Origins of Value: The financial innovations that created modern capital markets*, Oxford: Oxford University Press, 65–89.

Godfrey, S. (1982), 'The dandy as ironic figure', *SubStance*, vol. 11, no. 3, issue 36, 21–33.

Goodhart, C.A.E. (1989), *Money, Information and Uncertainty*, 2nd edn, Basingstoke: Macmillan.

Goodhart, C.A.E. (1998), 'The two concepts of money: implications for the analysis of optimal currency areas', *European Journal of Political Economy*, vol. 14, 407–432.

Goodhart, C.A.E. (2005), 'Review of: *Credit and State Theories of Money: The Contributions of A. Mitchell Innes*. L. Randall Wray (ed.). Cheltenham, UK: Edward Elgar, 2004', *History of Political Economy*, vol. 37, issue 4, 759–761.

Goodwin, R. (1967), 'A growth cycle', in: Feinstein, C.H. (1967) (ed.), *Socialism, Capitalism and Economic Growth*, Cambridge: Cambridge University Press, 54–58.

Goodwin, R.M. (1970), *Elementary Economics from the Higher Standpoint*, Cambridge, Cambridge University Press.

Goodwin, R.M. (1989), 'The M–K–S System: the functioning and evolution of capitalism', Essay 6 in: R.M. Goodwin, *Essays in Nonlinear Economic Dynamics*, Bern: Peter Lang, repr. in: Flaschel, P. (2009), *The Macrodynamics of Capitalism: Elements for a Synthesis of Marx, Keynes and Schumpeter*, 2nd edn, Berlin: Springer, 376–382.

Grenier, J.-Y., *et al.* (1993), *A propos de "Philosophie de l'Argent" de Georg Simmel*, Paris: L'Harmattan.

Habermas, J. (1980), 'Handlung und System: Bemerkungen zu Parsons' Medientheorie', in: Schluchter, W. (1980) (ed.), *Verhalten, Handeln, System*, Frankfurt: Suhrkamp, 68–105.

Hahn, F. (1965), 'On some problems of proving the existence of an equilibrium in a monetary economy', in: Clower, R.W. (ed.), *Monetary Theory*, Harmondsworth: Penguin, 191–201.

Hahn, F. (1973), 'On the foundations of monetary theory', in: Parkin, M. (ed.), *Essays in modern economics*, New York: Barnes & Noble, 230–242.

Hahn, F. (1977), 'Keynesian economics and general equilibrium theory: reflections on some current debates', in: Harcourt, G.C. (ed.), *The Microeconomic Foundation of Macroeconomics*, London: Macmillan, 25–40.

Hahn, F. (1982), *Money and Inflation*, London: Blackwell.

Hahn, L.A. (1930), *Volkswirtschaftliche Theorie des Bankkredits*, Tübingen: Mohr.

Hall, Peter A. and Soskice, David (2001) (eds), *Varieties of Capitalism: the Institutional Foundations of Comparative Advantage*. Oxford: Oxford University Press.

Hardin, R. (2003), *Indeterminacy and Society*, Princeton: Princeton University Press.

Hart, K. (1986), 'Heads or tails? Two sides of the coin', *Man*, vol. 21, no. 4, 637–656.

Haslinger, F. (1979), 'Money and barter in general equilibrium: a review', *Zeitschr. f. Nationalökonomie*, vol. 39, no. 3–4, 385–400.

Hayek, F.V. (1976), *Individualism and Economic Order*, London: Routledge & Kegan Paul.

Hayek, F.V. (1976a), *Choice in currency: A way to stop inflation*, London: Institute of Economic Affairs, available at www.iea.org.uk/sites/default/files/publications/files/upldbook409.pdf (accessed 19 February 2011).

Heinsohn, G. and Steiger, O. (2000), 'The property theory of interest and money', in: Smithin, J. (2000) (ed.), *What is Money?*, London: Routledge, 67–100.

Hellwig, M.F. (1993), 'The challenge of monetary theory', *European Economic Review* 37, 215–242.

Hicks, J. (1967), *Critical Essays in Monetary Theory*, Oxford: Clarendon.

Hicks, J. (1989), *A Market Theory of Money*, Oxford: Clarendon.

Hirschman, A. (1977), *The Passions and the Interests*, Princeton: Princeton University Press.

Horwitz, S. (1992), 'Monetary exchange as an extra-linguistic social communication process', *Review of Social Economy*, vol. 50, no. 2, 193–214.

Howitt, P. (1989), 'Money illusion', in: Eatwell, J., *et al.* (eds), *The New Palgrave: Money*, New York: Norton, 244–247.

Hume, D. ([1739] 1992), *A Treatise on Human Nature*, Amherst: Prometheus.

Hume, D. ([1752] 1970), 'Of money', in: Rotwein, E. (ed.), *David Hume – Writings on Economics*, Madison: University of Wisconsin Press, 33–46.

Hutter, M. (1996), 'Signum non olet: Grundzüge einer Zeichentheorie des Geldes', in: Schelkle, W. and Nitsch, M. (eds), *Rätsel Geld*, Marburg, 325–352.

Ingham, G. (1999), 'Money is a social relation', in: Fleetwood, S. (ed.), *Critical Realism in Economics*, London: Routledge.

Ingham, G. (2000), '"Babylonian madness"': on the historical and sociological origins of money', in: Smithin, J. (2000) (ed.), *What is Money?* London: Routledge, 16–41.

Ingham, G. (2001), 'Fundamentals of a theory of money: untangling Fine, Lapavitsas and Zelizer', *Economy and Society*, vol. 30, no. 3, 304–323.

Ingham, G. (2002), 'New monetary spaces', in: Miller, R., Michalski, W. and Stevens, B. (eds), *The Future of Money*, Paris: OECD, 123–146.

Ingham, G. (2004), *The Nature of Money*, Cambridge: Polity.

Ingham, G. (2005) (ed.), *Concepts of Money*, Cheltenham: Edward Elgar.

Ingham, G. (2006), 'Further reflections on the ontology of money: responses to Lapavitsas and Dodd', *Economy and Society*, vol. 35, no. 2, 259–278.

Ingham, G. (2007), 'The specifity of money', *Archives Européennes de Sociologie*, vol XLVIII, no. 2, 265–272.

Innes, A.M. (1913), 'What is money?', *Banking Law Journal*, May: 377–408.

Iwai, K. (1996), 'The bootstrap theory of money: A search-rheoretic foundation of monetary economics', *Structural Change and Economic Dynamics*, vol. 7, no. 4, 451–477; plus 'Corrigendum', col. 9, no. 2, (1998), 269, available online http://iwai-k.com/BootstrapTheoryOfMoney.pdf

Iwai, K. (2001), 'Evolution of money', in: Pagano, U. and Nicita, A. (eds), *The Evolution of Economic Diversity*, London: Routledge, 396–431.

Iwai, K. (2011), 'The second end of Laissez-Faire: The bootstrapping nature of money and the inherent instability of capitalism', in: Ganssmann, H. (ed.), *New Approaches to Monetary Theory: Interdisciplinary perspectives*, London: Routledge, 237–266.

Jacobs, J. (1992), *Systems of Survival: A dialogue on the moral foundations of commerce and politics*, New York: Vintage.

Jevons, W.S. (1876), *Money and the Mechanism of Exchange*, New York: Appleton.

Jones, R.A. (1976), 'The origin and development of media of exchange', *Journal of Political Economy*, vol. 84, no. 4, 757–775.

Kalecki, M. (1943), Political aspects of full employment', *Political Quarterly*, vol. 14, 322–331.

Kalecki, M. (1954), *The Theory of Economic Dynamics*, London: George Allen & Unwin.

Kant, I. (1920), *Metaphysik der Sitten*, in: Sämtliche Werke, Bd. 5, Leipzig: Insel.

Kaube, J., Schelkle, W. (1993), 'Das Diabolische des Geldes', in: Stadermann, H.J. and Steiger, O. (eds), *Der Stand und die nächste Zukunft der Geldforschung*, Berlin, 43–56.

Keen, S. (1995), 'Finance and economic breakdown: modeling Minsky's "financial instability hypothesis" ', *Journal of Post Keynesian Economics*, vol. 17, no. 4, 607–635.

Kempski, J.V. (1954), 'Handlung, Maxime und Situation', in: Kempski, J.V. (1992), *Recht und Politik*, Schrifen 2, Frankfurt a. M.: Suhrkamp, 405–422.

Kenway, P. (1980), 'Marx, Keynes and the possibility of crisis', *Cambridge Journal of Economics*, vol. 4, 23–36.

Keynes, J.M. (1930), *A Treatise on Money*, vol. 1, London: Macmillan.

Keynes, J.M. (1931), 'The consequences to the banks of the collapse of money values', in: Moggridge, D. (1972) (ed.), *The Collected Writings of John Maynard Keynes*, vol. xiii, London: Macmillan, 150–158.

Keynes, J.M. (1931a), 'A monetary theory of production', repr. in: Moggridge, D. (1973) (ed.), *The Collected Writings of John Maynard Keynes*, vol. xiii, London: Macmillan, 408–411.

Keynes, J.M. (1936), *The General Theory of Employment, Interest and Money*, repr. 1967, London: Macmillan.

Keynes, J.M. (1937), 'The general theory of employment', *Quarterly Journal of Economics*, February, repr. in: Moggridge, D. (1973) (ed.), *The Collected Writings of John Maynard Keynes*, vol. xiv, London: Macmillan, 109–123.

Kindleberger, C. (1989), *Manias, Panics, and Crashes*, rev. edn, New York: Basic Books.

Kirshner, J. (2000), 'The study of money', *World Politics*, vol. 52, 407–436.

Kiyotaki, N. and Wright, R. (1989), 'On money as a medium of exchange', *Journal of Political Economy*, vol. 97, 927–954.

Kiyotaki, N. and Wright, R. (1993), 'A search-theoretic approach to monetary economics', *American Economic Review*, vol. 83, 63–77.

Knapp, G.F. ([1905] 1923), *Staatliche Theorie des Geldes*, 4th edn, München: Duncker & Humblot.

Knapp, G.F. and Gutmann, F. (1927), 'Staatliche Geldtheorie', in: Elster, L., *et al.* (ed.), *Handwörterbuch der Staatswissenschaften*, Bd. 4, 4. Aufl., Jena, 752–762.

Knight, F.H. (1921), *Risk, Uncertainty and Profits*, Boston: Houghton Mifflin.

Knight, F.H. (1951), *The Ethics of Competition*, New York: Kelley.

Knight, F.H. (1933), 'Profit', in: *Encyclopedia of the Social Sciences*, 10th printing 1953, vol. 11–12, 480–486.

Knorr Cetina, K. and Preda, A. (2005) (eds), *The Sociology of Financial Markets*, New York: Oxford University Press.

Kocherlakota, N.R. (1998), 'Money is memory', *Journal of Economic Theory*, vol. 81, 232–251.

Koepsell, D. and Moss, L.S. (2003), *John Searle's Ideas about Social Reality: Extensions, criticisms and reconstructions*, Malden: Blackwell.

Krause, U. (1979), *Geld und abstrakte Arbeit*, Frankfurt a. M.: Campus.

Laidler, D. (1988), 'Taking money seriously', *Canadian Journal of Economics*, vol. 21, no. 4, 687–713.

Lane, R. (1991), *The Market Experience*, Cambridge: Cambridge University Press.

Lange, E.M. (1980), *Das Prinzip Arbeit*, Frankfurt a. M.: Ullstein.

Lange, E.M. (1992), 'Übereinstimmung bei Wittgenstein', in: Angehrn, E., *et al.* (Hrsg.), *Dialektischer Negativismus – Michael Theunissen zum 60. Geburtstag*, Frankfurt a. M. (Suhrkamp), 82–102.

Lange, O. (1936/7), 'On the economic theory of socialism', *Review of Economic Studies*, vol. iv, 53–71, 123–142.

Latsis, S. (1972), 'Situational determinism in economics', *British Journal for the Philosophy of Science*, vol. 23, 207–245.

Lavoie, D. (1983), 'Some strengths in Marx's disequilibrium theory of money', *Cambridge Journal of Economics*, 55–68.

Lawson, T. (1985), 'Uncertainty and economic analysis', *Economic Journal*, vol. 95, no. 380, 909–927.

Leijonhufvud, A. (1968), *On Keynesian Economics and the Economics of Keynes*, New York: Oxford University Press.

Lerner, A.P. (1947), 'Money as a creature of the state', *American Economic Review*, vol. 37, no. 2, 312–317.

Lester, R.A. (1939), *Monetary Experiments*, Princeton: Princeton University Press.

Lewis, D.K. (1969), *Convention*, Cambridge, Mass.: Harvard University Press.

Lowe, A. (1935), *Economics and Sociology: A plea for co-operation in the social sciences*, London: Allen & Unwin.

Lowe, A. (1965), *On Economic Knowledge*, New York: Harper & Row.

Lucas, R.E. (1972), 'Expectations and the neutrality of money', *Journal of Economic Theory*, vol. 4, no. 2, 103–124.

Lucas, R.E. (1995), 'Monetary Neutrality', Nobel Prize Lecture; available at http://nobelprize.org/nobel_prizes/economics/laureates/1995/lucas-lecture.html (accessed 1 April 2007).

Luhmann, N. (1972), 'Knappheit, Geld und die bürgerliche Gesellschaft', *Jahrbuch f. Sozialwissenschaft*, vol. 23/2, 186–210.

Luhmann, N. (1975), 'Einführende Bemerkungen zu einer Theorie symbolisch generalisierter Kommunikationsmedien', in: Luhmann, N. (1975), *Soziologische Aufklärung*, Bd. 2, Opladen, S. 170–192.

Luhmann, N. (1983), 'Das sind Preise', *Soziale Welt*, H.2, S.153–170.

Luhmann, N. (1984), *Soziale Systeme*, Frankfurt a. M.: Suhrkamp (Engl. transl: Social Systems, Stanford, Stanford University Press, 1995).

Luhmann, N. (1984a), 'Die Wirtschaft der Gesellschaft als autopoetisches System', *Zeitschrift für Soziologie*, Jg.13, H.4, 308–327.

Luhmann, N., (1988; 3rd edn 1994), *Die Wirtschaft der Gesellschaft*, Frankfurt a. M.: Suhrkamp.

Luhmann, N. (1995), *Social Systems*, Stanford, Stanford University Press (German original: (1984), *Soziale Systeme*, Frankfurt a.M.: Suhrkamp).

Macleod, H.D. (1892–3), *The Theory and Practice of Banking*, 5th edn London; New York: Longmans, Green, vol. 1 of 2.

Malinvaud, E. (1972), *Lectures on Microeconomic Theory*, Amsterdam: North-Holland.

Mannheim, K. (1951), *Freedom, Power and Democratic Planning*, London: Routledge.

March, J.G. and Simon, H.A. (1958), *Organizations*, New York: John Wiley.

Marschak, J. (1950), 'The rationale of money demand and of money illusion', *Econometrica*, vol. 18, no. 3, 71–100.

Marshall, A. ([1890] 1966), *Principles of Economics*, 8th ed., London: Macmillan.

Marx, K. (1973), *Grundrisse*, transl. M. Nicolaus, New York: Vintage.

Marx, K. ([1859] 1970), *Contribution to the Critique of Political Economy*, New York: New World.

Marx, K. ([1867] 1975), *Capital*, vol. 1, New York: International.

Marx, K. (1986), *Exzerpte und Notizen, März bis Juni 1851*, MEGA, IV. Abt., Bd 8, Berlin: Dietz.

Marx, K. (1992), *Ökonomische Manuskripte 1863–67*, Teil 2, Karl Marx, Friedrich Engels Gesamtausgabe (MEGA), II. Abt., Bd. 4.2, Berlin: Dietz.

Mauss, M. ([1922] 1990), *The Gift: forms and functions of exchange in archaic societies*, London: Routledge.

Mayer, H. (1932), 'Der Erkenntniswert der funktionellen Preistheorien', in: *Die Wirtschaftstheorie der Gegenwart*, vol. II, Wien, 147–239b.

Meijers, W.M. (2003), 'Can collective action be individualized?' in: Koepsell, D. and Moss, L.S. *John Searle's Ideas about Social Reality: Extensions, criticisms and reconstructions*, Malden: Blackwell, 167–183.

Meikle, S. (2000), 'Aristotle on money', in: Smithin, J. (2000) (ed.), *What is Money?* London: Routledge, 157–173.

Melitz, J. (1970), 'The Polanyi school of anthropology on money: An economist's view', *American Anthropologist*, vol. 72, 1020–1040.

Menger, C. ([1892] 1970), 'Geld', repr. in: Menger, C. (1970), Gesammelte Werke Bd. IV, Tübingen: Mohr, 1–116.

Merton, R.C. (1998), 'Applications of option-pricing theory: Twenty-five years later', *American Economic Review*, vol. 88, no. 3, 323–249.

Mill, J.S. (1900), *Principles of Political Economy*, 2 vls., London: Colonial Press.

Miller, R., Michalski, W. and Stevens, B. (2002) (eds), *The Future of Money*, Paris: OECD.

Minsky, H.P. (1992), 'The financial instability hypothesis', Working Paper No. 74, The Jerome Levy Economics Institute of Bard College.

Minsky, H.P. (1996), 'Uncertainty and the institutional structure of capitalist economies', Working Paper No. 155, The Jerome Levy Economics Institute of Bard College.

Mirowski, P. (1990), 'Learning the meaning of a dollar: Conservation principles and the social theory of value in economic thought', *Social Research*, Fall, 689–717.

Mirowski, P. (1991), 'Postmodernism and the social theory of value', *Journal of Post Keynesian Economics*, vol. 13, no. 4, 565–581.

Mirowski, P. (1991a), 'The when, the how and the why of mathematical expression in the history of economic analysis', *Journal of Economic Perspectives*, vol. 5, no. 1, 145–157.

Mises, L. (1929), 'Soziologie und Geschichte', *Archiv f. Sozialwiss. und Sozialpol.*, vol. 61, 465–512.

Mises, L. (1931) 'Vom Weg der subjektivistischen Wertlehre', in: Mises, L. and Spiethoff, A. (eds) *Probleme der Wertlehre*, Teil I, *Schriften des Vereins für Sozialpolitik*, 183, Munich and Leipzig: Duncker & Humblot, 73–93.

Mitchell, W. (1950), *The Backward Art of Spending Money*, New York: Kelley.

Morgenstern, Oskar (1935), 'Vollkommene Voraussicht und wirtschaftliches Gleichgewicht (Perfect foresight and economic equilibrium)', *Zeitschrift für Nationalökonomie*, vol. 6, no. 3, 337–357.

Morgenstern, O. (1976), 'The collaboration between Oskar Morgenstern and John von Neumann on the theory of games', *Journal of Economic Literature*, vol. 14, no. 3, 805–816.

Myrdal, G. (1932), *Das politische Element in der nationalökonomischen Doktrinbildung*, Berlin: Junker & Dünnhaupt.

Neumann, J.v. and Morgenstern, O. (1953), *Theory of Games and Economic Behavior*, Princeton: Princeton University Press.

Niehans, J. (1978), *The Theory of Money*, Baltimore: Johns Hopkins University Press.

Oresme, N. ([1356] 1999), *De Mutatione Monetarium*, in German: Traktat über Geldabwertungen, Berlin: Kadmos.

Ostroy, J.M. (1989), 'Money and general equilibrium theory', in: Eatwell, J., *et al.* (eds), *The New Palgrave: General Equilibrium*, London: Macmillan, 187–193.

Pareto, V. (1909), *Manuel d'Économie politique*, Genève: Droz, 1966.

Parks, T. (2006), *Medici Money*, London: Profile Books.

Parsons, T. (1937), *The Structure of Social Action*, New York: McGraw-Hill.

Parsons, T. (1963), 'On the concept of political power', in: Parsons (1967), *Sociological Theory and Modern Society*, New York: Free Press, 297–354.

Parsons, T. ([1951] 1964), *The Social System*, New York: Free Press.

Parsons, T. (1966), *Societies*, Englewood Cliffs: Prentice-Hall.

Parsons, T. (1968), 'Social interaction', in: Sills, David L. (ed.), *International Encyclopedia of the Social Sciences*, New York: Macmillan, vol. 7, 429–441.

Parsons, T. (1978), 'Soziale Struktur und die symbolischen Tauschmedien', in: P.M. Blau (ed.), *Theorien sozialer Strukturen*, 93–115.

Parsons, T. (1979), 'The symbolic environment of modern economies, *Social Research*, vol. 46, no. 3, S. 436–453.

Parsons, T. and Shils, E. (eds) ([1951] 1965), *Toward a General Theory of Action*, New York: Harper.

Peacock, M.S. (2006), 'Review article: The origins of money in Ancient Greece: the political economy of coinage and exchange', *Cambridge Journal of Economics*, vol. 30, 637–650.

Peter, H. (1950), *Einführung in die politische Ökonomie*, Stuttgart: Kohlhammer.

Pettit, P. (2001), 'Collective intentions', in: Owens, R. and Ngaire, N. (2001) (eds), *Intention in Law and Philosophy*, Aldershot: Ashate, 241–254.

Pfanzagl, J. (1971), *Theory of Measurement*, Würzburg: Physica.

Polanyi, K. (1957), *The Great Transformation*, Boston: Beacon.

Polanyi, K. (1968), 'The economy as an instituted process', in: Dalton, G. (ed.), *Primitive, Archaic and Modern Economies. Essays of Karl Polanyi*, Garden City: Doubleday, 139–174.

Polanyi, K. (1968a), 'The semantics of money-uses', in: in: Dalton, G. (ed.), *Primitive, Archaic and Modern Economies. Essays of Karl Polanyi*, Garden City: Doubleday,, 175–203.

Postan, M.M. (1944), 'The rise of a money economy', *The Economic History Review*, vol. 14, no. 2., 123–134.

Reden, S. von (1997), 'Money, law and exchange: Coinage in the Greek polis', *Journal of Hellenic Studies*, vol. 117, 154–176.

Renger, J. (1995), Subsistenzproduktion und redistributive Palastwirtschaft: Wo bleibt die Nische für das Geld? in: Schelkle, W. and Nitsch, M. (eds), *Rätsel Geld*, Marburg: Metropolis, 271–324.

Renger, J. (2011), 'The role and the place of money and credit in the economy of Ancient Mesopotamia', in: Ganssmann, H. (ed.), *New Approaches to Monetary Theory: Interdisciplinary Perspectives*, Abingdon: Routledge, 15–36.

Ricardo, D. ([1823] 1986), *On the Principles of Political Economy and Taxation*, Cambridge: Cambridge University Press.

Richter, R. (2002), 'Why Price Stability?' Available at www.uni-saarland.de/fak1/fr12/richter/institut/WhyPrice.pdf (accessed 27 January 2011).

Riese, H. (1995), 'Geld – das letzte Rätsel der Nationalökonomie', in: Schelkle, W. and Nitsch, M. (eds), *Rätsel Geld*, Marburg: Metropolis, 45–62.

Rocheteau, G., and Wright, R. (2005) 'Money in search equilibrium, in competitive equilibrium, and in competitive search equilibrium', *Econometrica* 73 (January): 175–202.

Ruben, P. (1979), *Philosophie und Mathematik*, Leipzig: Teubner.

Salais, R., Chatel, E. and Rivaud-Danset, D. (1998), *Institutions et conventions: La réflexivité de l'action économique*, Paris: Éditions de l'EHESS.

Samuelson, P.A. (1958), 'An exact consumption-loan model of interest with or without the social contrivance of money', *Journal of Political Economy*, vol. 66, no. 6, 467–482.

Samuelson, P.A. (1969), 'Classical and neo-classical monetary theory', in: Clower, R.W. (ed.) (1969), *Monetary Theory*, Harmondsworth: Penguin, 170–190.

Schaps, D. (2004), *The Invention of Coinage and the Monetization of Ancient Greece*, Ann Arbor: University of Michigan Press.

Scheck, J. (2008), 'Mackerel economics in prison', *Wall Street Journal*, 2 October, available http://online.wsj.com/article/SB122290720439096481.html?mod=yhoofront (accessed 18 December 2009).

Schelkle, W. (1995), 'Motive der ökonomischen Geldkritik', in: Schelkle, W. and Nitsch, M. (eds), *Rätsel Geld*, Marburg: Metropolis, 11–44.

Schmitz, S.W. (2002), 'Carl Menger's "Money" and the current neoclassical models of money', in: Latzer, M. and Schmitz, S.W. (eds), *Carl Menger and the Evolution of Payments Systems: From barter to electronic money*, Cheltenham: Edward Elgar, 159–183.

Schopenhauer, A. ([1851] 2004), *The Essays of Arthur Schopenhauer*, transl. Bailey Saunders, T., Project Gutenberg (2004), EBook #1074, available at www.gutenberg.org/catalog/world/readfile?fk_files=1477836&pageno=23.

Schumpeter, J.A. (1917), 'Das Sozialprodukt und die Rechenpfennige', *Archiv für Sozialwissenschaft und Sozialpolitik*, vol. 44, 1917/8, 627–715.

Schumpeter, J.A. (1939), *Business Cycles*, 2 vols, New York: McGraw-Hill.

Schumpeter, J.A. (1943), *Capitalism, Socialism and Democracy*, London: George Allen & Unwin.

Schumpeter, J.A. ([1926] 1952), *Theorie der wirtschaftlichen Entwicklung*, Berlin: Duncker & Humblot.

Schumpeter, J.A. (1952), *Aufsätze zur ökonomischen Theorie*, Tübingen: Mohr.

Schumpeter, J.A. (1954), *History of Economic Analysis*, New York: Oxford University Press.

Schumpeter, J.A. (1991), 'Money and currency', *Social Research*, vol. 58, no. 3, 499–543.

Seaford, R. (2004), *Money and the Early Greek Mind: Homer, Philosophy, Tragedy*, Cambridge: Cambridge University Press.

Seaford, R. (2011), 'The Greek invention of money', in: Ganssmann, H. (2011) (ed.), *New Approaches to Monetary Theory*, London: Routledge, 37–45.

Searle, J. (1991), 'Intentionalistic explanations in the social sciences', *Philosophy of the Social Sciences*, vol. 21, no. 3, 332–344.

Searle, J. (1995), *The Construction of Social Reality*, New York: Free Press.

Searle, J. (2002), 'Collective intentions and actions' (1990), repr. in: Searle, J. (2002), *Consciousness and Language*, Cambridge, Cambridge University Press, 90–105.

Searle, J. (2003), 'Reply to Barry Smith', in: Koepsell, D. and Moss, L.S. (eds), *John Searle's Ideas about Social Reality*, Malden: Blackwell, 299–309.

Searle, J. (2004), 'Social Ontology: Some Basic Principles', available at http://socrates.berkeley.edu/~jsearle/articles.html (accessed 21 February 2011).

Searle, J. (2005), 'What is an institution?', available at http://socrates.berkeley.edu/~jsearle/articles.html (accessed 21 February 2011).

Senior, N.W. (1854) *Political Economy*, 3rd ed., London: Richard Griffin.

Senior, W.N. (1910), 'Drei Vorlesungen über den Wert des Geldes', in: Diehl, K. and Mombert, P. (eds), Ausgewählte Lesestücke zum Studium der politischen Ökonomie, Bd.1, *Zur Lehre vom Geld*, Karlsruhe, 135–180.

Shackle, G.L.S. (1974), *Keynesian Kaleidics*, Edinburgh: Edinburgh University Press.

Shackle, G.L.S. (1990) 'Coping with uncertainty in economics: G.L.S. Shackle interviewed by Peter Earl', *Review of Political Economy*, vol. 2, no. 1, 105–114.

Shapley, L.S. and Shubik, M. (1963), *Concepts and Theories of Pure Competition, Rand Memorandum*, Pittsburgh: Rand.

Shi, S. (1995), 'Money and prices: A model of search and bargaining', *Journal of Economic Theory*, vol. 67 (December), 467–498.

Shi, S. (2006), 'Viewpoint: A microfoundation of monetary economics', *Canadian Journal of Economics*, vol. 39, no. 3, 643–688.

Shorto, R. (2004), 'Faith at work', *New York Times Magazine*, October 21, 2004.

Shubik, M. (1975), 'The general equilibrium model is incomplete and not adequate for the reconciliation of macro and micro theory', *Kyklos* vol. 28, 545–573.

Shubik, M. (1999), *The Theory of Money and Financial Institutions*, 2 vols, Cambridge, Mass.: MIT Press.

Shubik, M. (2001), 'Money and the monetization of credit', Cowles Foundation discussion paper No. 1343, available at http://cowles.econ.yale.edu/P/cd/dy2001.htm (accessed 21 February 2011).

Simmel, G. ([1907] 2004), *Philosophie des Geldes*, 2nd edn, Leipzig: Duncker & Humblot; Engl. edit. (2004), Philosophy of Money, trans. Bottomore, T. and Frisby, D., London: Routledge.

Simon, H. (1955), 'A behavioral model of rational choice', *Quarterly Journal of Economics*, vol. LXIX, 99–118.

Singer, K. (1920), *Das Geld als Zeichen*, Jena: Fischer.

Smith, A. ([1759] 1976), *The Theory of Moral Sentiments*, Oxford: Oxford University Press.

Smith, A. ([1776] 1976a), *An Inquiry into the Nature and Causes of the Wealth of Nations*, 2 vols, Oxford: Oxford University Press.

Smithin, J. (2000) (ed.), *What is Money?* London: Routledge.

Solow, R.M. (2005), 'How did economics get that way and what way did it get?' *Daedalus*, Fall 2005, 87–100.

Spahn, P. (2002), 'Geld als Institution einer Marktökonomie', in: Schmid, M. and Maurer, A. (eds), *Ökonomischer und soziologischer Institutionalismus*, Marburg: Metropolis, 307–329.

Spence, A.M. (2001), 'Signaling in retrospect and the informational structure of markets', Nobel Prize Lecture, Stockholm.

Spitz, R.A. (1957), *No and Yes: On the beginning of human communication*, New York: International University Press.

Spotton Visano, B. (2002), 'Financial manias and panics: a socioeconomic perspective', *American Journal of Economics and Sociology*, vol. 61, no. 4, 801–827.

Sraffa, P. (1960), *Production of Commodities by Means of Commodities: Prelude to a critique of economic theory*, Cambridge: Cambridge University Press.

Swift, J. ([1726] 1973), *Gulliver's Travels*, Harmondsworth: Penguin.

Taleb, N.N. (2008), *The Black Swan. The Impact of the Highly Improbable*, London: Penguin.

Tawney, R.H. ([1926] 1954), *Religion and the Rise of Capitalism*, New York: Mentor Books.

Thalos, M. (1999), 'Degrees of freedom in the social world: Towards a systems analysis of decision', *Journal of Political Philosophy*, vol. 7, no. 4, 453–477.

Thornton, H. ([1802] 1939), *An Enquiry into the Nature and Effects of the Paper Credit of Great Britain*, New York: Rinehart.

Tilly, C. and Tilly, C. (1998), *Work Under Capitalism*, Boulder: Westview.

Tobin, J. (1992), 'Money', in: Eatwell, J. *et al.* (eds), *The New Palgrave Dictionary of Money and Finance*, Basingstoke: Palgrave Macmillan, 770–779.

Tönnies, F. ([1887] 1922), *Gemeinschaft und Gesellschaft. Grundbegriffe der reinen Soziologie*, 5th edn, Berlin: Curtius. (English edition: Toennies, F. (1963), *Community and Society*, trans. Charles P. Looomis, New York: Harper & Row).

Turner, S.P. (1999), 'Review: Searle's social reality', *History and Theory*, vol. 38, no. 2, 211–231.

Vanderstraeten, Raf (2002), 'Parsons, Luhmann, and the theorem of double contingency', *Journal of Classical Sociology*, vol. 2, 77–92.

Wagner, V.F. (1937), *Geschichte der Kredittheorien*, Wien: Springer.

Wallace, N. (1998) 'A dictum for monetary theory', *Federal Reserve Bank of Minneapolis Quarterly Review*, vol. 22, 20–26.

Wallace, N. (2001), 'Whither monetary economics?' (Lawrence R. Klein Lecture 2000), *International Economic Review*, vol. 42, no. 4, 847–869.

Walras, L. (1954), *Elements of Pure Economics*, transl. W. Jaffé, Homewood: Richard D. Irwin.

Watzlawick, P., Bavelas, J.B. and Jackson, D.D. (1967), *Pragmatics of Human Communication*, New York: Norton.

Weber, M. (1924), *Wirtschaftsgeschichte*, München: Duncker & Humblot.

Weber, M. (([1920] 1947), *Gesammelte Aufsätze zur Religionssoziologie I*, Tübingen: Mohr.

Weber, M. ([1922] 1964), *Wirtschaft und Gesellschaft*, 4th edn, Tübingen (Mohr), English editions: (1964), *The Theory of Social and Economic Organization*, Parsons, T. (ed.), New York, Free Press; (1978), *Economy and Society: An Outline of Interpretive Sociology*, Roth, G. and Wittich, C. (eds.) Berkeley: University of California Press.

Weber, M. ([1905] 1970), 'Religious rejections of the world and their directions', in: Gerth, H. and Mills, C.W., *From Max Weber: Essays in Sociology*, New York: Oxford University Press, 323–359.

Weber, M. ([1905] 1970a), 'The protestant sects and the spirit of capitalism', in: Gerth, H., Mills and C.W., *From Max Weber: Essays in Sociology*, New York: Oxford University Press, 302–322.

Weber, M. ([1908] 1981), 'Some categories of interpretative sociology', transl. Graber, E., *The Sociological Quarterly*, vol. 22, no. 2, 151–180.

Wennerlind, C. (2001), 'Money talks, but what is it saying? Semiotics of money and social control', *Journal of Economic Issues*, vol. 35, no. 3, 557–574.

White, H.C. (1981), 'Where do markets come from?', *American Journal of Sociology*, vol. 87, 517–547.

White, Harrison C. (2002), *Markets from Networks: Socioeconomic models of production*, Princeton, N.J.: Princeton University Press.

Wicksell, K. (1898), *Geldzins und Güterpreise*, Jena: Fischer.

Wicksell, K. (1906), *Lectures on Political Economy*, vol. 2 (transl. Claassen, E.) (1935), London: Routledge and Kegan Paul.

Williamson, O. (1985) *The Economic Institutions of Capitalism*, New York: Free Press.

Williamson, S. and Wright, R. (1994), 'Barter and monetary exchange under private information', *American Economic Review*, vol. 84, no. 1, 104–123.

Wittfogel, K. (1957), *Oriental Despotism*, New Haven: Yale University Press.

Wittgenstein, L. (1984), 'Philosophische Untersuchungen', in: *Werkausgabe*, Bd.1, Frankfurt a.M.: Suhrkamp, 225–485 (English edition: (1953) *Philosophical Investigations*, trans. Anscombe, G.E.M, Oxford: Blackwell).

Wittgenstein, L. (1984a), 'Ludwig Wittgenstein und der Wiener Kreis', in: *Werkausgabe*, Bd. 3, Frankfurt a. M: Suhrkamp.

Woodford, M. (2007), 'How important is money in the conduct of monetary policy?' Discussion Paper No.: 0607–0616, Department of Economics, Columbia University, New York, July.

Wray, L.R. (1998), 'Money and taxes: the chartalist approach', in: Ingham, G. (2005) (ed.), *Concepts of Money*, Cheltenham: Edward Elgar, 473–495.

Wray, L.R. (2000), 'Modern money', in: Smithin, J. (ed.), *What is Money?* London: Routledge, 42–66.

Wray, L.R. (2004) (ed.), *Credit and State Theories of Money: The contributions of A. Mitchell Innes*, Cheltenham: Edward Elgar.

Yakovenko, V. (2011), 'Statistical mechanics approach to the probability distribution of money', in: Ganssmann, H. (ed.), *New Approaches to Monetary Theory: Interdisciplinary perspectives*, Abingdon: Routledge, 104–123.

Zelizer, V. (1989), 'The social meaning of money: "Special monies"', *American Journal of Sociology*, vol. 95, no. 2, 342–377.

Zelizer, V. (1997), *The Social Meaning of Money*, Princeton: Princeton University Press.

Index

abstraction and money 18, 31, 146n8, 149n49
accounting 147n19
Adrian, T. 131, 155n83, 159
Aglietta, M. 18, 61, 145n19, 151n31, 152n33, n34, n39, 156n93, 159
Alchian, A.A. 16, 159
alienation 55, 57
appropriation 3, 32–4, 55, 61, 77, 114, 121, 146n11
arbitrage 98–102, 108, 127
Arlidge, J. 155n75, 157n104, 159
Arrow, K.J. 43, 135, 144n6, 153n53, 159
auctioneer 5, 42, 66, 148n41
Aydinonat, E. 159

Babb, S. 160
Bailey, S. 154n61, 159
bankruptcy 12, 131
banks 10–12, 34, 57, 107, 109, 111, 115, 123–6, 129–30, 156n97
barter 4, 15–16, 30, 48, 53–4, 65–6, 76, 79–82, 84, 86, 88–91, 98, 104–5, 118, 145n19, 148n35, n42, 152n37
Beckenbach, F. 99, 154n67, 159
Beckert, J. xvi, 96, 143n4, 159, 161
Bell, D. 159
Bellofiore, R. xvi, 162
Benetti, C. 159
Bentham, J. 35, 104, 144n13, 146n15, 159
Bernanke, B. 111, 160
Bibow, J. 160
bill of exchange 122, 125
Blau, P.M. 168
Bohannan, P. 30, 160
bootstrap 20, 78, 92
Bourdieu, P. 106, 160
Braudel, F. 160
Bresciani-Turroni, C. 160

Bretton Woods 39, 147n20
Brunner, K. 14, 16, 160
Bryan, D. 160
bubbles and busts i, xiv, 17, 127, 137
Buchan, J. 160
budget constraint 47–51, 53–4, 111, 126–7, 148n36

Campbell, M. 160
capital 9–13, 125, 129–31, 139
capital, financial 11–12
capitalism 7–13, 55, 74, 76, 87, 110, 141, 143n4, 158n2
capitalist economy i, xiv, 3, 7–13, 56
Carruthers, B. 31, 35, 131, 160
Cartelier, J. xvi, 83, 123, 140, 151n30, n31, 159
cash 3, 21, 34, 46–51, 87, 107, 115–17, 119, 121, 123–4, 126–8, 130, 137, 147n16, 148n36, 153n58, 155n79, 157n100
catallactic atom 4, 63–4, 66, 76, 91, 94, 119
central bank 34, 38, 40, 46, 107, 111, 115–17, 123, 125–6, 128, 144n7, 147n20
chartalism 81, 113, 115, 136, 141–2, 145n19, 151n31
Chatel, E. 169
circular flow 6, 10, 129
Clower, R.W. 1, 86–7, 113, 153n58, 161
Codere, H. 18, 36–8, 161
coinage 114, 151n31
coins 2, 18, 32, 34, 39, 43, 46, 59–60, 80, 93, 107, 110–11, 114–15, 117, 124, 126, 133, 147n27, 149n52, 152n31, n35, 157n1
collateral 120–1, 123, 125–6, 128, 131–2, 156n92

collective intentionality 23–4, 93, 136, 142, 145n1, 146n2
commensurability 40, 80
commitment 21, 92, 106, 121
commodity 8–9, 20, 35, 39–43, 45, 48–9, 53, 55–60, 74–5, 82–5, 88, 90, 94–7, 104–5, 115, 126, 140, 145n17, 147n19, 149n46
commodity money 39, 115, 142, 144n16, 150n15, 151n21, 152n41, 153n46, 157n98
Commons, J.R. xiv, 161
competition 5, 9, 42, 66–7, 70, 97–8, 102, 108, 147n24
consumer 13, 34, 87, 90, 94, 101, 131, 143n3, 151n27, 155n82
consumer goods 118–19
contingency 1, 4, 17, 62–3, 67, 70–3, 75, 86, 143n2, 149n2
contingency, double 63–4, 66–73, 76, 94, 104
contingent commodities 15, 103
contracts 9, 103–4, 106, 113, 115–16, 132, 146n9, 152n35, 156n96
control, social 7, 9, 49, 75, 125, 151n21
convention 31, 90, 157n98
coordination 1–5, 30, 32, 55, 57–60, 71, 73–4, 76, 78–9, 86, 89, 129, 137, 150n8
credit 8, 16, 38–9, 49, 110–29, 131–3, 148n36, 156n92, n94, 157n100, n101, n104
credit card 21, 34, 46, 48, 122, 147n16
credit creation 10, 124, 129, 149n51
credit crunch 107, 123, 128
credit money 61, 113–21, 124, 126, 128, 142, 149n54
credit relation 5, 50, 59–61, 73, 95, 109–23, 126, 128–9, 132
credit system 11, 124, 127, 148n39, 154n60
credit theory of money 112–13, 117–20, 156n92
crisis xv, 3, 56, 110–11, 115, 117, 123, 129, 131–2, 134, 137, 148n39, 158n7
crisis, possibility of 2–3, 129, 153n59
crisis, financial 62, 144
Crouch, C. 131, 161

Dalton, G. 168
Dalziel, P. 47, 161
Davidson, P. 106, 153n58, 161
Debreu, G. 14, 19, 135, 154n69, 161
debt 59, 98, 110, 113–17, 119, 123, 126–32, 139, 156n93, n97

debt, public 11, 62, 115
decentralized economy 11, 48, 52–5, 79, 95, 99–100, 102, 108
default 50, 75, 157n105
deflation 131, 158n7
Defoe, D. 149n7, 151n25, 161
demand deposit 107
derivatives 128
Deutschmann, C. xvi, 144, 161–2
Diaz-Bone, R. 159, 161
Dillard, D. 118, 147n19, 161
discount 125
Döblin, A. 152n32, 161
Dodd, N. xiii, 161–2
DoL-PiP economy 4, 17, 60, 73–6, 82, 95
dollar 27–9, 44, 46, 75, 98, 147n20, n22
double coincidence of wants 16, 53, 66, 76–7, 80, 84, 86–7, 91
Dragulescu, A. 156n97, 161
Dyer, A.W. 33, 161

econophysics 139–41, 158n3, 161
Edgeworth, F.Y. 4, 63–6, 76, 81, 105, 161
Edwards, C. 162
efficiency 95
Egypt 71, 81
Ellerman, D. 154n66, 162
entrepreneur 8, 11, 124, 129, 150n15
equilibrium xiv, 2, 14–17, 42, 53, 65–7, 83–4, 90, 95–7, 99, 101, 103–4, 108, 135–6, 145n20, 148n41, 154n65
equivalence 19, 38, 41, 45, 48, 81, 99, 101, 108–9, 147n18, 154n67, 155n85
Eschbach, A. 162
Espeland, W.N. 147n23, 162
essentiality of money 5, 52
exchange 2, 4, 9, 13–16, 19, 30–1, 33, 38, 40–1, 44, 47–8, 53, 58–9, 63–8, 71–7, 80–6, 88, 90–2, 98, 104–5, 112, 136, 147n21, 150n16, 152n37, 153n54
exchange rates or ratios 98, 101, 145n17, 147n20, 154n73, 157n98, n105
exchange value 88, 145n17, 152n37
expectations 12, 17, 26–7, 67–8, 72, 83–4, 90–2, 94, 104–6, 109, 127, 129–30, 133, 137, 145n20, 153n53
expectation, rational 15, 130, 132, 157n102
exploitation 55, 59

Fehr, E. 154n74, 162
Feldman, A.M. 95, 151n30, 162
fetishism 56–60

fiat money 18, 90, 117, 126, 133, 147n20, 153n53

final payment 113, 116, 118–19, 126, 128, 155n91

finance capital 11–12

financial markets 6, 11–12, 98, 111, 132, 151n18

financial system 110–11, 117, 134, 157n104

Fine, B. 162, 164

firms 9–10, 12, 129

Firth, R. 144n15, 162

Foley, D. 57, 147, 162

Friedman, M 15, 41, 80, 162

function assignment 23–9, 40, 83, 88–90, 93, 130, 146n4

Gale, D. 85, 149n6, 162

game theory 2, 64, 66–8, 70–2

Ganssmann, H. 58, 145, 158–64, 168–9, 172

Giddens, A. 46, 50, 163

gifts and exchange 74, 112

Gigerenzer, G. 149n4, 153n44, 163

Gilbert, E. 153n51, 163

Glahn, R. v. 149n53, 155n89, 163

Godfrey, S. xvi, 163

gold xv, 4, 18, 39–40, 44–5, 57, 60, 83, 109, 116, 123, 125, 147n20, 149, 155n80, 157n105

gold standard 18, 39, 109

Goodhart, C.A.E. 86, 113, 119, 122, 141, 152n34, 155n91, 163

Goodwin, R.M. 26, 143n4, 163

goods 32

government 14, 62, 114–15, 117, 126, 131, 149n53, 155n87, 157n106

Great Moderation 111

Grenier, J.Y. 163

Gutmann, F. 165

Habermas, J. 21, 33, 159n7, 163

Hahn, F. 148n42, 153n47, 163

Hahn, L.A. 163

Hardin, R. 16, 65, 81, 105, 150n8, n14, 163

Hart, K. 163

Haslinger , F. 163

Hayek, F. v. 144n9, 148n41, 149n48, 150n9, 154n65, 164

Heinsohn, G. 156n92, 164

Hellwig, M. 164

Hicks, J. 6, 16, 102, 164

Hirschman, A. 151n19, 164

hoarding 62, 105–6, 153n48

Hobbesian problem of order 150n16, 153n43

Horwitz, S. 164

Howitt, P. 164

Hübner, K. xvi

Hume, D. 43, 144n8, 164

Hutter, M. 164

hyperinflation 62, 158n7

inequality 139–41

inflation 44, 46, 62, 144n7, 155n78, 158n7

information 4, 12, 15–17, 20, 30, 37, 42, 44–7, 49–53, 55, 60, 67, 69, 82, 94, 96, 103–4, 109, 122, 128, 132, 135–6, 140–1, 145n20, 146n14, 148n40, n43, 149n45, n48, 154n68

Ingham, G. 58–60, 87, 114–16, 142, 145n19, 149n54, 151n31, 152n33, 156n93, 162, 164, 172

Innes, A.M. 38, 113–16, 121, 123, 172

instability 69–70, 155n78

institutions xiii, xiv, 1–2, 6, 11–13, 17, 20, 23–9, 38, 46–7, 49–50, 55–6, 61–2, 72, 80, 83–4, 87, 91, 95, 117, 132, 136, 140, 143n4, 144n5, 147n27

insurance 75, 106, 111, 143n3, 157n106

interaction i, xiv, xv, 1–6, 13, 16–17, 20, 30, 37, 58, 62–77, 90, 104, 108, 111, 122, 129, 136–7, 140, 145n19, n20

interest 11–12, 44, 98, 106–7, 111, 124–6, 130, 153n58, 155n84, 156n92

interests, conflicting 4–5, 16, 19, 37, 41–2, 51–2, 54, 81, 88, 104–5, 112

investment 10–12, 129–30, 132

irrationality xiv, xv, 92–3, 151n28, 155n83

Iwai, K. 12, 20, 78, 87, 154n73, 158n2, n7

Jacobs, J. 151n19, 164

Jevons, W.S. 16, 164

Jones, R.A. 164

Kalecki, M. 12, 107, 165

Kaube, J. 165

Keen, S. 143n4, 165

Kempski, J. v. 165

Kenway, P. 153n59, 165

Keynes, J.M. 2, 12, 21, 63, 76, 107, 128, 130, 133, 143n4, 144n13, 149n5, 151n27, 152n33, 153n49, n52, n59, 155n77, 165

Kindleberger, C. 110, 146n13, 165

Kirshner, J. 165

Kiyotaki, N. 140, 145n20, 154n73, 165

Knapp, G.F. 145n19, 151n31, 152n35, 165
Knight, F.H. 58–9, 143n3, 149n4, 165
Knorr Cetina, K. 6, 165
Kocherlakota, N.R. 46–7, 52, 54, 140,
    145n20, 155n81, 165
Koepsell, D. 165
Krause, U. 147n18, 154n67
Kristol, I. 159

labor 3–4, 7–10, 32, 35, 55–8, 73–4, 86–7,
    94–5, 139, 144n5, 151n21
labor market 9, 12
Laidler, D. 165
Lane, R. 149n45, 166
Lange, E.M. xvi, 148n44, 166
Lange, O 48, 70, 147n24, 148n41, 166
language 3, 18, 20–1, 23–34, 41, 51, 61,
    72, 92–3, 146n8, n9, n11
Lapavitsas, C. 162, 164
Latsis, S. 42, 70, 166
Latzer, M. 169
Lavoie, D. 166
Lawson, T. 166
Leijonhufvud, A. 166
lender 60, 77, 111, 113–14, 118–19,
    123–9, 131–2, 156n92, 157n105
Lerner, A.P. 126, 142, 166
Lester, R.A. 152n36, 166
leverage 130–1
Lewis, D.K. 83, 89, 166
Lewis, P. 160
liquidity 11, 106, 126–7
liquidity preference 153n49
loan 10, 111, 124, 126–7, 130–2
Lowe, A. xiii, 2, 5, 166
Lucas, R.E. 157n102, 166
Luhmann, N. 19, 33, 64, 69–70, 72, 96, 166
Lydia 59, 151n31

Macleod, H.D. 156n93, 166
Malinvaud, E. 66, 103, 166
manager 12, 131
Mannheim, K. 7, 166
March J.G. 143n1, 154n71, 166
markets 3, 5–6, 9–10, 12–17, 19–20, 31,
    35–9, 42, 44–5, 48, 53–7, 59–60, 62–3,
    67, 74–7, 81–2, 85–8, 90, 94–102, 105,
    108, 123, 128–32, 140, 142, 142n5,
    145n17, n19, 147n25, 148n28, n32, n41,
    149n45, n47–8, 151n23, 152n33,
    156n93–4, 157n102
markets, financial 6, 11–12, 98, 111, 132,
    146n12, 151n18
Marschak, J. xv, 166

Marshall, A. 35–6, 166
Marx, K. 1–2, 8–10, 55–60, 82–3, 107,
    143n4, 144n14, 148n39, 152n37, n42,
    153n59, 157n98, 167
Maurer, B. 170
Mauss, M. 112, 167
Mayer, H. 150n9, 167
maxM 10, 76, 105, 108, 133, 135, 150n15,
    154n74, 155n75, 158n6
measurement 3, 35–6, 38–45, 61–2,
    146n15, 147n17, n25
Meijers, W.M. 145n1, 167
Meikle, S. 167
Melitz, J. 167
Meltzer, A. 14, 16, 160
Menger, C. 80, 84–5, 87, 147n21, 167
Mengerians 141–2
Merton, R.C. 157n99
Mesopotamia 152n35
methodological individualism 79, 135–6,
    142, 146n2
Michalski, W. 167
Mill, J.S. 2, 14, 167
Miller, R. 167
Minsky, H.P. 130–2, 167
Mirowski, P. 3, 35, 101–2, 108, 140,
    148n29, 167
Mises, L. v. 13–14, 136, 150n9, 167
Mitchell, W. 143n1, 167
monetary invariant 3, 43, 45, 102, 108,
    110, 140, 147n27, 148n29
monetary system
money, acceptability of 79, 83, 87–92,
    105, 113–14, 125, 127, 133, 153n46,
    153n53
money and capital 9
money and credit 61, 111–19, 124–6, 128,
    155n90, 156n92
money and domination 106–7
money and irrationality 92–3, 152n32
money and language 18, 20–1, 23–9, 30,
    146n8, n9, n11
money and measurement (money metric)
    34–3, 38–46, 146n15, 147n25
money and social control 151n21
money and speculation 158n2
money and the state (authority) 80–1, 87,
    114, 141–2, 145n19, 152n39, n41,
    153n50
money and time 90–1, 107, 130, 148n42,
    153n47, n52
money and uncertainty xiv, 2–3, 7, 17, 63,
    102, 103–10, 126–33, 137–8, 143n1,
    149n6

money and work 7, 87
money as commodity 152n41, 153n46, 157n105
money as language 20–1, 30–4, 146n9, n11
money as medium of communication 3, 19–21, 72, 145n18
money as memory 46, 51–3, 155n81
money as power 154n64
money as public good 32
money as social fact 2, 23, 29, 133, 137, 142
money as social relation 57–61, 149n54
money as symbol 7, 18–20, 27–9, 36–7, 123, 136, 144n15, 157n98
money as store of value (wealth) 149n5, 155n77, n80
money as tool of appropriation 40, 146n11
money as universal equivalent 83
money as veil 13–17, 105, 118, 130
money, creation of 11, 29, 124
money illusion i, xiv, xv, 7, 14–15, 43, 105, 130, , 135, 157n102
money, origin of 79–83, 136
money objects 1–2, 18–20, 27–8, 32, 36, 46–51, 54, 60, 89–91, 94, 136, 146n3, n16, 152n32, n35
money, purchasing power of 40, 43–6, 53, 102, 107
money, neutrality of xiv, 14–17, 118, 157n102
money, means of exchange 19, 80–1, 89
money, means of payment 112, 118, 156n93
money, measure of value 39, 41, 102, 145n17, 146n9
money, unit of account 41, 80–1, 101, 143n3, 146n9, n11, 149n54, 152n33, n41
money supply 6
moneyness 146n12, 156n93
moral hazard 124, 128, 131
Morgenstern, O. 66–7, 71–2, 150n9, n12, n15, 167–8
Moss, L.S. 165
Myrdal, G. 150n10, 167

Nash equilibrium 83–4
neo-chartalism 113, 115, 136, 141–2, 152n31
neoclassical theory i, xiii–xv, 1, 66, 69–70, 89, 105, 118, 144n6, 154n68
Neumann, J. v. 67, 71–2, 150n15, 168
Niehans, J. 16, 47–8, 168

Nitsch, W. 162, 168
numeraire 148n35

Oresme, N. 44, 46, 168
Orléan, A. 159
Ostroy, J.M. 168

Pareto, V. 15, 64–6, 71, 104, 139, 151n30, 154n74, 168
Parks, T. 155n84, 168
Parkin, M. 163
Parsons, T. 18–19, 63–4, 68–70, 72, 78, 148n43, 150n16, 153n43, 154n72, 168
Peacock, M.S. 168
Peter, H. 168
Pettit, P. 39, 80, 168
perfect foresight 15, 66–7, 135
perfect information 103–4, 154n68
perfect monitoring 50–4, 148n40
Pfanzagl, J. 38, 168
Polanyi, K. 1, 13, 74, 112, 144n5, 168
Ponzi 130–1
Postan, M.M. 168
power 11, 78, 80–1, 142, 151n31, 152n40
price 15, 21, 33–4, 39, 43–4, 56
price formation 31, 37, 40–2, 52–4, 61, 94–103, 108, 147n24
price, effective 9, 17, 41, 45, 62, 75, 144n12
privatized Keynesianism 131
profit 8–11, 130
promise to pay 25, 49, 111, 113, 115, 120–3, 125–6, 134, 148n39
property, private 28, 55–6, 61, 66, 71–4

quantity theory of money 5–6, 43
Quesnay, F. 10

reciprocity 74, 112–13
Reden, S. v. 168
redistribution 74, 79, 81, 140
reification 55, 57
relational contract 121, 156n96
Renger, J. 79, 81, 168, 152n35
Reuten, G. 160
Ricardo, D. 81, 168
Richter, R. 169
Riese, H. 124, 169
risk 2, 4, 11, 77–8, 85–6, 91, 102, 107, 111, 115, 123–5, 128, 133–4, 137, 150n13, 156n92, n95
risk and uncertainty 111, 121, 123, 127, 129, 131, 143n3, 149n4, n6, 157n99
Rivaud-Danset, D. 169

Rocheteau, G. 169
Ruben, P. 38, 169
rules 20, 23, 26–9, 40, 42, 48, 66, 68, 70, 77, 84, 140, 145n20, n1, 146n6
Runde, J. 160

Salais, R. 96, 169
Samuelson, P.A. 16, 21, 169
saving 10–11, 94, 106–7, 129, 153n58
Schaps, D. 152n35
Scheck, J. 158n1, 169
Schelkle, W. 169
Schmitz, S.W. 144n10, 154n68, 169
Schopenhauer, A. 133, 169
Schumpeter, J.A. 11, 12, 39, 98–101, 111–12, 117–19, 123, 128–9, 133, 136, 143n4, 145n17, 152n34, 155n90, 169
Seaford, R. 4, 142, 146n8, 147n27, 149n50, 151n31, 152n35, 157n1, 169
search theory of money 4, 50, 140, 154n73
Searle, J. 23–9, 40, 46–7, 57, 72, 78–9, 83, 87–9, 93, 136, 142, 145n1, 146n2, n6, 152n40, 169–70
Senior, N.W. 170
Shackle, G.L.S. 103, 119, 135, 170
Shapley, L. 42, 170
shekel 79, 145n19, 152n35
Shi, S. 170
Shils, E. 68, 168
Shin, H.S. 131, 155n83, 159
Shubik, M. 42, 49, 77, 121, 146n14, 151n18, n23, 153n46, 154n63, 156n94, 157n105, 170
Sills, D.L. 168
Simmel, G. xiv, 1, 10, 33, 37, 58, 137, 154n64, 158n1, 170
Simon, H. 132, 143n1, 154n71, 166, 170
Singer, K. 170
Smelser, N.160
Smith, Adam 30, 81, 88, 150n11, 158n5, 170
Smithin, J. xvi, 170
sociology, economic 2–3, 16, 143n4
Solow, R.M. 170
Spahn, P. 170
speculation xiv, 11–12, 16–17, 98, 110–11, 123, 127, 130–1, 133–4, 137, 148n32, 158n2
Spence, A.M. 170
Spitz, R. 63, 170
Spotton Visano, B. xvi, 170
Sraffa, P. 10, 170
state 11–14, 39, 48, 74, 87, 107, 114–15,

125–6, 128, 134, 136, 139, 141–2, 145n19, 151n31, 152n35, 157n98
Steiger, O. 156n92, 164, 165
Stevens, B. 159
Stevens, M.L. 147n23, 162
Stinchcombe, A. 31, 35, 160
subprime mortgages 45, 131
Swedberg, R. 167
Swift, J. 33, 171

Taleb, N.N. 134, 153n45, 157n99, 171
taxes and money 87, 114, 152n31, n41
Thalos, M. 71, 171
Thornton, H. 171
Tilly, C. 9, 171
Tobin, J. 16, 32, 171
Tönnies, F. 112, 144n16, 154n64, 171
transaction costs 14, 16, 32, 39, 98, 106
trust 15, 50–2, 72, 108, 113, 121–3, 133, 148n37, 153n46, 157n105
Turner, S.P. 23, 171
Tyran, J.R. 154n74, 162

uncertainty i, xiv, xv, 1–7, 16–18, 45, 63, 67, 70–1, 73, 75, 79, 85–6, 92–3, 102–11, 121–3, 126–35, 137–8, 143n3, n4; n1, 144n13, 148n28, 149n4, n6, 154n69
utility xiv, 8, 15, 18, 65–6, 71–2, 76, 84–92, 95, 98–9, 104–5, 119, 132, 135, 147n21, 150n12, n15, n17, 151n28, n30, 154n74
utility of money 18, 96, 154n73

value 3–4, 18–20, 28, 38–9, 54, 68, 83, 88, 123, 144n16, 145n17, 147n18, 154n61, 155n91
Vanderstraeten, R. 171

Wagner, V.F. 171
Wallace, N. 52–4, 145n20, 157n101, 171
Walras, L., Walrasian 5, 42, 66, 99, 148n41, 150n9, 154n65, 171
Watzlawick, P. 69, 171
wealth 8, 10, 12, 31, 44, 48, 56, 76, 90, 105, 130, 137, 139, 147n19, 156n97
Weber, M. i, xiv, 1, 5, 8–10, 13, 16, 37, 49, 58, 75, 82, 108, 122, 135, 144n12, 148n38, 149n49, 151n19, 153n54, 171
Wennerlind, C. 171
White, H.C. xvi, 96, 98, 171
Wicksell, K. 81, 126, 148n31, n39, 171
Williamson, O. 97, 172
Williamson, S. 153n49, 172

Wittfogel, K. 79, 172
Wittgenstein, L. 3, 19–20, 32, 43, 146n10, 147n26, 172
Woodford, M. 17, 144n7, 172
work 127, 141, 157n104
Wray, L.R. 61, 87, 113, 151n31, 152n33, n34, 172

Wright, R. 140, 145n20, 153n50, 154n73, 165, 169, 172

Yakovenko, V. 139, 156n97, 161, 172

Zelizer, V. 6, 155n86, 172